Rooms with a View

Rooms with a View

Feminist Diary Fiction, 1952–1999

Giancarlo Lombardi

Madison • Teaneck
Fairleigh Dickinson University Press
London: Associated University Presses

Associated University Presses
440 Forsgate Drive
Cranbury, NJ 08512

Associated University Presses
16 Barter Street
London WC1A 2AH, England

Associated University Presses
P.O. Box 338, Port Credit
Mississauga, Ontario
Canada L5G 4L8

The paper used in this publication meets the requirements of the American National Standard for Permanence of Paper for Printed Library Materials Z39.48–1984.

Library of Congress Cataloging-in-Publication Data

Lombardi, Giancarlo, 1965–
Rooms with a view : feminist diary fiction, 1952–1999 / Giancarlo Lombardi.
p. cm.
Includes bibliographical references and index.
ISBN 0-8386-3853-8 (alk. paper)
1. Autobiographical fiction—History and criticism. 2. Diary fiction—History and criticism. 3. Feminist fiction—History and criticism. I. Title.

PN3448.A8 L66 2002
809.3′0082—dc21

2001033642

PRINTED IN THE UNITED STATES OF AMERICA

Alla maggiore e alla minore,
Anna Baltera
e
Federica Coluzzi

Contents

Acknowledgments

WHEN THE MANUSCRIPT OF THIS BOOK FINALLY CAME TO ITS LONG-awaited conclusion, I felt the sudden urge to send e-mails to all my friends and to all those other people whose input had been instrumental in its creation. Before long, however, I realized the impossibility of such a task: too many persons had, in different roles, been involved in this project, and, had I decided to contact them all, I would have been forced to spend an entire night at my laptop. This list of acknowledgments, then, should be read as a substitute for all those letters I never sent, it should be considered as a last attempt to give thanks where it is due. As a "man in feminism", a male scholar involved in feminist studies, I feel particularly compelled to thank all the women who have instructed me and encouraged me along the way. At Cornell University, Marilyn Migiel was the first person who believed in me; most of what I know, I learned from her. For all that, and for being what a true mentor and friend should be, I thank her. Beverly Ballaro has been an acute reader of my work, and another most cherished friend; I feel blessed by her presence in my life, a presence that I am sure will remain constant through the years. At Smith College, Anna Botta began to follow this manuscript from its very early stage, providing insight, advice, and encouragement when it was most sorely needed. Words cannot express how grateful I feel for her precious friendship. Giovanna Bellesia always demonstrated unwavering confidence in my knowledge of this field: I thank her for believing in me, and for allowing me to test my scholarship in her Italian women writers' class. At The College of Staten Island, Kate Crehan has welcomed me with open arms in the Women's Studies program, soon becoming a good friend and a rigorous critic of my work. Ruth Calderon, Claudia Corradini, Jane Marcus-Delgado, Laura Pirott-Quintero, Mara Salvati, Ella Shohat, Kathryn Talarico, and Cindy Wong have offered invaluable support and encouragement. Rosa Schirripa has proven to me that women can overcome just about any adversity. A few more friends still need to be acknowledged: Katherine Baer, Maria Enrica Balestra, Maria Adelaide Basile, Jessica Barbagallo, Elisabetta Cacialli, Alessandra Campana, Isa

Chierchia, Ioana Chitoran, Alessandra Di Maio, Irene Eibeinstein Alvisi, Daniela Fargione, Maria Galli Stampino, Cosetta Gaudenzi, Maria Paola Guarducci, Els Huybens, Angela Lepori, Stefania Lucamante, Roberta Maldarelli, Paola Nieddu, Donatella Saroli, Serena Scaiola, Barbara Spinelli, Suzanne Stewart, Marie Michelle Strah, Pina Swenson, Fiorella Troiani, Silvia Troiani, and Maria Valentini, longtime "partners in crime" who have accompanied me in the academic adventure from both sides of the Ocean. Last, but not least, my infinite gratitude goes to the women in my family: my grandmothers and my niece, my aunts, my sister, and my mother. With the blessing of my father, the only man to be included in this neverending list, they have made me the man I am now, a man who is proud of standing up for the feminist cause.

An earlier, and much shorter version of chapter 1 originally appeared as "The Gift of an Italian 'Feu la Cendre': A Derridean Reading of *Quanderno proibito*" in *Writing Beyond Fascism: Cutlural Resistance in the Life and Works of Alba de Céspedes* edited by Carole C. Gallucci and Ellen Nerenberg, Madison, Fairleigh Dickinson University Press, 2000.
Part of chapter 2 was originally published as "*A memoria:* Charting a Cultural Map for Women's Transition from *Storia* to *Preistoria*" in *The Pleasure of Writing: Critical Essays on Dacia Maraini* by Rodica Diaconescu-Blumenfeld and Ada Testaferri, West Lafayette, Purdue University Press, 2000.
An abridged part of the conclusion appeared as "Thou Shalt Not Break the Mold: Patriarchal Discourse in *Va'dove ti porta il cuore*" in *Romance Languages Annual* 9, 1997.
Selections from Alba de Céspedes's *Quaderno proibito* appear with the permission of Arnoldo Mondadori Editore.
Selections from Dacia Maraini's *Donna in guerra* and its English translation, *Woman at War,* appear with the permission of RCS Libri and Italica Press.

Stefano, grazie della bellissima illustrazione.

Rooms with a View

Introduction: From One Room to Another

"A WOMAN MUST HAVE MONEY AND A ROOM OF HER OWN IF SHE IS TO write fiction" (1929, 6). With such a lapidary sentence, Virginia Woolf expressed in 1929 the basic needs of a woman writer. The evoked presence of the public and the domestic spheres is central to this statement. Money insures a woman's safe interaction with the outside world, granting her a superior status that allows her to pursue the domain of the letters without financial pressures. On the other hand, the "room of her own" defines a different sort of independence, that which should derive from the loosening of those ties that bind her to domestic duties. In that room, a woman is neither mother nor wife; in that room, she does not derive her own sense of identity from her relation to the people around her; in that room she relates only to the characters she creates on the pages of her writings; in that room, she is just a writer. Paradoxically, it is from the enclosure of that room that a woman takes her most distant flights, those in which she ventures on the wings of her own imagination. Reacting against patriarchal society, which wants her enslaved to her body, a body which cannot and should not think, a woman frees herself, in that "room of her own," from a wall of constraints which was built around her for far too many centuries. She escapes from the enforced seclusion in the domestic space, that house which too often resembles a prison, by choosing to inhabit another enclosed area, a room in which, however, she has freely elected to live.

In *Nonostante Platone*, feminist philosopher Adriana Cavarero describes Penelope as the mythic representative of a form of female independence which shapes itself exactly through the voluntary withdrawal into a Woolfian *room of one's own:* "Penelope, though staying in the royal palace, by endlessly weaving and unweaving delimits her own place where she is nobody's wife. Neither the wife of one of her suitors, nor of Ulysses, who is elsewhere, having been gone for twenty years" (1990, 14, my translation). Penelope's weaving-room is a place which shelters her from men, a place where she weaves her own story, a place where her endless weaving grants her a different temporal dimension which cannot be entered, and understood, by men. By spinning during the day the same threads that she unspins at night, Penelope "fabricates" a fictional texture that allows her to escape from the male symbolic order. And her "plot" shall not be unmasked because her suitors cannot access the weaving-room, the room in which she has secretly construed her ultimate mockery of the patriarchal system.

High is the price that women often pay, however, when they decide to claim a space of their own. In a phallogocentric society[1] which has long founded its welfare on female disempowerment, those women who attempt to escape its constricting *diktat* sometimes come to realize that there is no possibility of reconciling their desire for independence with the order established by their husbands and fathers. As they retreat into their own rooms, these women sometimes withdraw into the silent worlds of madness and death. The protagonist of "The Yellow Wallpaper," written by Charlotte Perkins Gilman in 1892, experiences a slow descent into madness as she turns the room in which her husband has forced her to recuperate from postpartum depression into a prison she willingly chooses to inhabit. In this room, she initiates her rebellion by deciding to keep a journal of her captivity, even though she was forbidden to write, because that activity would supposedly hinder her recovery. Devoting extreme attention to the reasons that lie behind her initial rejection of her new surroundings, she ascribes her feelings of uneasiness to the yellow wallpaper that covers the bedroom walls. This wallpaper, stripped off in certain places, attracts and repels her because of its complicated pattern:

> It is dull enough to confuse the eye in following, pronounced enough to constantly irritate and provoke study, and when you follow the lame uncertain curves for a little distance they suddenly commit suicide—plunge off at outrageous angles, destroy themselves in unheard of contradictions. (4)

As she plunges deeper into the dark recesses of depression, the wallpaper comes alive and its patterns reveal the hidden presence of prison bars similar to those that protect the windows of her suffocating room. A new impetus possesses her: she willingly decides to remain in that room so as to free the woman she sees imprisoned behind the fences perceived on the paper that covers the four walls. As she frantically peels away the yellow wallpaper, she suddenly identifies with that woman. That woman's freedom is indeed her own freedom, a freedom she achieves through her descent into madness.

In "To Room Nineteen," written by Doris Lessing in 1958, another woman chooses seclusion in order to escape an antagonistic environment. Not a writer, but a housewife, Lessing's middle-aged protagonist suddenly comes to grips with the necessity to be alone in order to regain independence from her family. When her suburban house suddenly becomes a prison, in which her children increasingly crowd her, she decides to rent an anonymous room at a cheap London hotel. In this room she spends long hours sitting on a chair, enjoying her autonomy:

> What did she *do* in the room? Why, nothing at all. From the chair, when it had rested her, she went to the window, stretching her arms, smiling, treasuring her anonymity, to look out. She was no longer Susan Rawlings, mother of four, wife of Matthew, employer of Mrs. Parkes and of Sophie Traub, with these and those relations with friends, school-teachers, tradesmen. She no longer was mistress of the big white house and garden, owning clothes suitable for this and that activity or occasion. She was Mrs. Jones, and she was alone, and she had no past and no future.(419)

However, once her past catches up with her, Susan comes to the realization that, like Mrs. Jones, she cannot have a future: when her husband discovers her secret whereabouts, she feels as if her family had once again crossed the sacred threshold of her own intimate, private world. Only one means of escape is then possible: withdrawn for one last time into her hotel room, Susan commits suicide without writing a note to her relatives. No explanation, in fact, could be possibly offered for that gesture, no words borrowed from a patriarchal language could possibly make sense of her last attempt to achieve ultimate freedom from the constraining world of family relations.

Women's literature has often painted a universe of female protagonists in seclusion. And if some of these protagonists, following Woolf's example, claim their desire for autonomy, many others lie in a helpless state of captivity, dispossessed of agency, deprived of basic civil rights. Feminist diary fiction conjures up the image of women sitting behind desks, often near a window and/or a mirror.[2] In the privacy of their own rooms, whose walls secretly shelter them from the intrusive male gaze, the female protagonists of these literary works seek to capture, in their journals, their own perception of reality. The mirror and the window are there to remind them that, in their writings, two different discourses will be interwoven. Mirrors of their souls, their diaries will bear witness to their internal struggles while reflecting, at the same time, (on) the external world, whose sociopolitical turmoil will be observed, however, from afar. Constantly excluded from history, women have been forced to act as mere spectators to events which have nevertheless shaped their subjugated condition: the window thus remains their assigned place, and it is a window which often contains prison bars, if only at a symbolic level.[3]

The ideal coexistence of the internal and external world, that of the emotions and that of politics, lies at the core of most feminist fictional diaries. My analysis of fictional journals by Alba de Céspedes, Dacia Maraini, Susanna Tamaro, Doris Lessing, Margaret Atwood, and Simone de Beauvoir indeed aims at exploring the multifaceted presence of this very coexistence. In order to demonstrate such presence, I will perform a critical reading aimed at teasing out significant textual passages that most clearly reveal a struggle occurring on two different levels, within the psyche of the diarist and between the diarist and the phallogocentric society that opposes her access to writing. And in tracing the individual struggles encountered by each single diarist, I will also present, as a result of the juxtaposition of so many different texts, a wider portrayal of women's struggles across five decades and four different national cultures

The recent history of a handful of Western countries indeed stands as a most relevant background to the thoughts and actions described in the fictional journals I set out to analyze in my project. And to the history and politics of countries that have resurfaced from the devastation and the trauma of World War II, another history, and other politics must be juxtaposed: women's history and feminist politics. When World War II ended, many European countries embarked on a long journey of recovery, a journey which eventually led them to the economic boom of the sixties, soon followed by the widespread rebellion of 1968, and by a decade that witnessed significant advancement in civil rights. A different path had taken North America to similar achievements: World War II had not left any significant scar other than the painful memory of Pearl Harbor, yet other wars were to affect the entire population in more dramatic fashion. From the very end of the sixties, the entire North American population had witnessed the televised tragedy of the Vietnam War, a tragedy that ushered America into the seventies, fostering unparalleled civil unrest. The battle for civil rights begun during the "roaring sixties" continued well into the seventies, the decade that will always be remembered for witnessing one of the greatest Republican defeats, the Watergate. Remarkable progress was indeed achieved by the civil rights movement in that decade. It was in the eighties, forever remembered as the Reagan-Bush era, that a dramatic inversion of pace marked the occurring of a true backlash. That same reactionary climate was also deeply felt in Great Britain, where Margaret Thatcher had virtually found in Ronald Reagan an ideological soul mate. A different path took Italy towards the return to power of reactionary forces, an event that occurred much later, in the mid-nineties. The 1994 political elections marked the advent of the New Right, helmed by Silvio Berlusconi, the reactionary media mogul who became prime minister only a few months after entering politics and forming his own political party. Until then, Italy had enjoyed a relatively steady progress in the civil rights movement, notwithstanding the regime of corruption established by Christian Democrats and socialists alike. In France, the fifties were essentially marked by the Algerian wars, and by de Gaulle's creation of the Fifth Republic, which he headed until 1969. The reactionary climate established by de Gaulle was shaken to its roots by the events of May 1968, which led to de Gaulle's resignation and to the return to power of the left. At the very end of the seventies, in 1978, the left was indeed defeated, and the country suddenly shifted right. While socialist leader François Mitterand was President of the Republic during most of the following decade, reactionary forces were indeed deeply present in the country, and remained strong during the nineties.

A different history and different politics inform the background against which feminist diary fiction is set: women's history and feminist politics, which were both strictly intertwined, however, with the historical events recorded in the previous paragraph. When World War II ended, four out of five American women tried to retain their jobs, yet they had to give up the privileged position they had suddenly gained. Women in France, Great Britain, and Italy faced a similar impasse. In 1949, Simone de Beauvoir had leveled her first attack against the patriarchal establishment through the pages of *Le deuxième sexe*, where she maintained that the image of women had been constructed by men as "other," different and inferior. Beauvoir's long essay was a precursor in its genre. Women's literature of the fifties was indeed still coming to terms with a new reality, mostly signified by women's forced return to the *foyer*. In Italy, the voices of several influential women writers had suddenly emerged. Elsa Morante published *Menzogna e sortilegio* in 1948, and *L'isola d'Arturo* in 1957. Natalia Ginzburg wrote *E' stato così* in 1947, *Tutti i nostri ieri* in 1952, and *Valentino* in 1957. Gianna Manzini penned one of her most famous novels, *La sparviera*, in 1956. However, none of these books captured the dramatic condition of women all over Italy as well as Alba de Céspedes's *Quaderno proibito* (1952). The author of two very successful novels, *Nessuno torna indietro* (1938) and *Dalla parte di lei* (1944), de Céspedes had already reached international fame because of her acute portrayal of Italian society and of the constrained role in which women had been forced. The first chapter of my work indeed focuses on *Quaderno proibito*, and sets out to discuss the interiorization of those patriarchal norms that most effectively reduced women to silence. Its protagonist, Valeria, experiences writing as a sinful activity, one that she must hide from the rest of her family. What is most subversive about keeping a journal, for this woman, is the effect it has on her family life. As she sets out to pour her frustrations onto paper, Valeria comes to acknowledge the necessity to exit the economy of the *foyer.* Writing distracts her from her role as care-provider, while actually awakening, in her, a sudden need for solitude. A room of her own is what this woman desperately comes to yearn for, but without success. Victim of her own love for a family that exploits her, Valeria follows the destiny of many Italian women of her own generation, reprising her constricting roles of wife, mother, and grandmother.

The sixties were virtually opened on a political and sociological note by the publication of Betty Friedan's *Feminine Mystique* (1963), a study in which the American sociologist identified a common malaise experienced by women of her own generation, a malaise that she appropriately called "the problem that has no name." Shaken by a sense of futility, emptiness, and guilt, the women interviewed by Friedan became the representatives of entire generations of women all over the world who were experiencing similar feelings. It was in the name of these women that feminism reprised its battle, joining in the revolution of customs that occurred in the western world in 1968. The National Organization of Women, formed by Friedan in 1966, became America's leading feminist political organization, launching in epic battles that it eventually won. The same years that witnessed "the problem that has no name" were then stage to the early victories of the feminist movement, which was soon to be renamed Women's Lib. In literature, existentialism lent further force to the many inspired voices that set out to describe the female malaise. In Italy, Dacia Maraini's early novels clearly betrayed the deep influence of the existentialist movement: *La vacanza* (1962), *L'età del malessere* (1962), and *A memoria* (1967) presented a similar disturbing representation of women who failed to conform to societal norms. Along similar lines, Alba de Céspedes produced a most effective critique of the dysfunctional aspects of the *Italia del boom* in *Il rimorso* (1963), a most peculiar rewriting of the French masterpiece *Les liaisons dangereuses.* Not all Italian women writers chose to delve into "the problem that has no name": Ginzburg's *Lessico famigliare* (1963) and Morante's *Il mondo salvato dai ragazzini* (1968) depicted a universe in which gender issues were hardly discussed. Simone de Beauvoir and Marguerite Duras will indeed be remembered among the most valuable literary contributors to the feminist debate, mostly because of their sophisticated portrayal of unforgettably complex female characters. Duras's *Le ravissement de Lol V. Stein* (1964) and Beauvoir's *La femme rompue* (1968) are two of their most exemplary works of the decade. Around the same time, Beauvoir also published the first three volumes of her massive autobiography: *Mémoires d'une jeune fille rangée* (1958), *La force de l'age* (1960), and *La force des choses* (1963). In Great Britain, Doris Lessing authored a novel that would eventually be considered as a landmark in feminist writing, *The Golden Notebook* (1962), which was preceded and followed by the five novels that celebrated the "Children of Violence": *Martha Quest* (1952), *A Proper Marriage* (1952), *Landlocked* (1958), *A Ripple from the Storm* (1958), and *The Four-Gated City* (1969). Around the same time, Margaret Drabble also produced a most unforgettable tale of motherhood, *The Millstone* (1965), while Jean Rhys returned to a very familiar narrative, telling the story of *Jane Eyre*'s "madwoman in the attic" in *Wide Sargasso Sea* (1966). In the United States, another disturbing and haunting voice joined into the chorus, that of Sylvia Plath, who penned another disturbing story of female alienation in *The Bell Jar* the year she died, in 1963. Only six years later, at the very end of the decade, Margaret Atwood began her career as the most successful Canadian woman writer with *The Edible Woman* (1969), a novel which tackles the controversial issue of female anorexia. The second chapter of my study of fictional diaries analyzes the sixties through three of the works previously mentioned, in the attempt to demonstrate how this decade witnessed slightly different stages of feminist struggle in Western Europe. Three different fictional diaries, written in three different countries, show three different realities, realities that could be appropriately defined as "site-specific." The British "free women" portrayed by Doris Lessing in *The Golden Notebook* experience their new status through a profound identity crisis. The nervous breakdown of Lessing's diarist, Anna Wulf, stems from the extreme difficulty of adjusting to a new world, one which has witnessed the collapse of boundaries. Entrenched in her London apartment, Anna lives through the cathartic dismantlement of her previous *modus vivendi* and emerges, at the end of the novel, a "free woman." A different freedom is experienced by Maria, the protagonist of the Italian *A memoria*, written by Dacia Maraini five years later. Victim of dysmnesia, Maria lacks social memory, that component which should enable her to function according to societal norms. She moves recklessly around the streets of Rome, defying all rules and taboos by being sexually promiscuous with several young men while her husband is dying in a hospital bed. In a conservative country like Italy, where feminism would fight its first significant battles only in the seventies, such subversive behavior could only lead to the untimely demise of its protagonist. Her husband dead, Maria suddenly loses her aggressive edge and withdraws into her empty apartment, where death strikes her as she attempts to write one last entry on her journal. Monique, whose diary is contained in Simone de Beauvoir's "La femme rompue," is a married woman who fears her own independence. Abandoned by an unfaithful husband around whom she had built her entire life, Monique records in her journal her desperate attempt to hold onto a lost family life which once constituted her only reason of being. Another cathartic descent, this time into depression, marks the trajectory followed by the protagonist of this novella. As she finally makes peace with the departure of her husband, Monique ends her diary on her first attempt to reconstruct her life, a life that will not be spent in the always populated living room that she once shared with her beloved, but in the empty rooms of an apartment which is, now, exclusively hers. The juxtaposition of these three tales clearly highlights the different pace taken by the evolution of the female condition in England, France, and Italy: not surprisingly, it is this last country, which most experienced patriarchal domination, that most evidently lagged behind in its full recognition of women's rights.

The publication of Kate Millett's *Sexual Politics* and Monique Wittig's *Les guerrilléres* in 1969 marks the true beginning of the seventies, years of war, years of political unrest. In particular, Millett's subversive investigation into the Western canon, and her unveiling of the inherent misogyny of most male writers, whose representation of women inevitably reduced them to virgins or prostitutes, frigid or licentious, paved the way to a decade that witnessed unprecedented struggles and victories. In Italy, divorce became legal in 1971, family rights were significantly revised in 1975, and abortion was legalized in 1978. In France, the divorce law was significantly reformed in 1975, while prostitutes led a nationwide protest demanding for their civil rights, and organizing sit-ins in city halls and cathedrals in 1976; three years later, in 1979, the Parliament passed a law which permitted termination of pregnancy. In Great Britain abortion had been legalized in 1967, and for many years Italian and Irish women had flocked to its hospitals to obtain what was strictly denied them in their home country. Significant achievements were indeed obtained in the U.K. when, in 1975, legislation on civil rights was formally passed. A similar legislation was recognized in Canada, where abortion had been legalized since 1969. However, the most historical battle for abortion rights was staged in the United States, where the

Supreme Court granted women such debated right in 1973, through the famous Roe vs. Wade case. During the previous year, in 1972, the United States Constitution had been significantly changed by the Equal Rights Amendment. Throughout all this turmoil, Kate Millett's was not the only voice that called women to arms: in 1970, Robin Morgan edited a collection of Women's Lib writings appropriately entitled *Sisterhood is Powerful*, and in England Germaine Greer published another seminal text, *The Female Eunuch.* In France, Claudine Herrmann followed in Millett's tradition by discussing the way in which patriarchal language and the literary tradition forcefully oppress women in *Les voleuses de langue* (1976). Around the same time, the two major theorists of *écriture féminine*, Hélène Cixous and Luce Irigaray, produced some of their most representative work. The former coauthored with Catherine Clément *La jeune née* in 1975, while the latter wrote her critique of Western philosophy, *Speculum de l'autre femme*, in 1974, and published her acclaimed collection of essays entitled *Ce sexe qui n'est pas un* three years later, in 1977. Italy witnessed its own very original flourishing of feminist theorization through the collective writings of feminist organizations such as *Demau*, *Rivolta Femminile*, the Roman feminist movement, and the group revolving around the feminist bookstore in Milan. One theorist in particular, Carla Lonzi, manifested her original and subversive position in the critique of patriarchy produced in *Sputiamo su Hegel* (1970), a seminal work within the Italian feminist tradition. In the United States and in Britain, two fundamental essays investigated women's psyche, Phyllis Chesler's *Women and Madness* (1972) and Juliet Mitchell's *Psychoanalysis and Feminism* (1974), both of which inaugurated a tradition of feminist rewritings of a field which had only known one significant female contribution, that of Melanie Klein. On a different note, motherhood and the mother/daughter relationship were explored in three groundbreaking studies: Adrienne Rich's *Of Woman Born* (1976), Nancy Friday's *My Mother/My Self (*1977), and Nancy Chodorow's *The Reproduction of Mothering* (1978). The literary production of the seventies included some works that are now considered part of the feminist literary canon. In Canada, Margaret Atwood published *Surfacing* (1972), a novel which combined a harsh critique of sexual politics with an equally strong attack on American imperialism. The United States witnessed the success of two most inspiring African-American women writers: Toni Morrison published three of her most incisive novels, *The Bluest Eye* (1971), *Sula* (1973), and *Song of Solomon* (1977) while Alice Walker re-evoked the Civil Rights battles in *Meridian* (1976). At the same time, female readers all over the country also discovered the talents of militant writers such as Erica Jong, Rita Mae Brown, Marilyn French, and Marge Piercy. All these authors' influential writings were soon disseminated all over the Western world. In Great Britain, Doris Lessing began her investigation on women and aging with *Briefing for a Descent into Hell* (1971), *The Summer Before the Dark* (1973), and *Memoirs of a Survivor* (1974) whereas Margaret Drabble produced a haunting self-reflexive story about writing in *The Waterfall* (1977). That same year, Angela Carter produced a most acute satire of the feminist movement in *The Passion of New Eve.* France saw the triumph of Marguerite Duras's *India Song* (1974) and Marie Cardinal's *Les mots pur le dire* (1975), as well as the creation of the publishing house *des femmes*, which came to play a fundamental role in the movement. Dacia Maraini's *Donna in guerra* (1975) is likely to be considered the most important feminist work of fiction to be produced in Italy in the seventies, the decade which also witnessed the publication of Elsa Morante's masterpiece, *La storia* (1974). Maraini's *Memorie di una ladra* (1972) as well as Oriana Fallaci's *Lettera a un bambino mai nato* (1975) and Amanda Guiducci's *Due donne da buttare* (1976) do deserve to be mentioned in this context, yet it is undisputable that *Donna in guerra* belongs to a league of its own. It is for this reason that the chapter I dedicate to the seventies exclusively focuses on this novel, which is the only work of feminist diary fiction of that decade that deserves to be included in a comparative study. The woman at war mentioned in the title of the novel is Vannina, the young diarist who chronicles her suffered transition from a segregated condition to a full rebirth into a new, emancipated state. Once again, what appears most striking in the depiction of such a process of awakening is the use of those open and closed spaces that act as background to the actions narrated by the protagonist. Her narrative moves from the suffocating summer house where she initially lives with her abusive husband to the netherworldly cave where she socializes with her women friends. It describes the streets of Naples where she investigates the exploited condition of female workers, as well as the stuffy classrooms where she eventually shares with her students her new social awareness. And such an initiatory path finally leads her to the dramatic realization that, in order to become a free woman, she needs to wage war against the patriarchal regime. The last lines of her diary find her, like Beauvoir's Monique, at the threshold of an apartment where she will live on her own. Unlike the French diarist, however, Vannina will consider her newly achieved independence as a symbol of her victory, and not as a painful reminder of her solitude.

The eighties will go down in history as the decade ruled by the reactionary politics of Ronald Reagan and Margaret Thatcher. *Dallas*, *Dynasty*, and *Thirtysomething* acted as powerful agents of cultural imperialism all over the world, championing reactionary values that subtly undermined the women's present condition. Movies such as *Fatal Attraction*, *Baby Boom*, and *Working Girl* showed the entire world that women had paid a high price for advancing their station in life. And just as the American New Right found in its tele-evangelists its ruthless accusers of women's newly achieved status, Thatcher and Reagan effectively set out to turn back the clock on civil rights battles. The years of the backlash, so powerfully analyzed by Susan Faludi in *Backlash: The Undeclared War Against American Women* (1991), were also the years that witnessed a rich debate among feminist theorists all over the world. Non-western feminists such as Gayatry Spivak, Rey Chow, and Trin Minh-ha began their investigation on the condition of those women whose voice had never been heard and had often been misrepresented, the women from Third World countries. Jane Gallop, Alice Jardine, and Toril Moi brought their unique contribution to the study of the complex relationship between psychoanalysis and feminism. Gallop's *Feminism and Psychoanalysis: The Daughter's Seduction* (1982), Jardine's *Gynesis: Configurations of Women and Modernity* (1985), and Moi's *Sexual/Textual Politics* (1985) all shared a common interest in the theoretical applications of feminism and psychoanalysis to literary studies. While their work was undoubtedly precious in its originality, it sanctioned the indirect closeting of the feminist struggle back into the academic world. The appearance of Betty Friedan's *Second Stage* (1981) and Germaine Greer's *Sex and Destiny* (1984) was found most disturbing by many women, since both radical feminists seemed to champion, in their new writings, much more conservative values. Not much ground was lost in Italy, however, where *Diotima*, a group of feminist philosophers formed in 1983, published *Il pensiero della differenza sessuale* in 1987. In France, Julia Kristeva produced a most complex and intriguing psychoanalytic reading of the Oedipus complex and the maternal body in *Pouvoirs de l'horreur* (1980) and later turned to a powerful interpretation of depression and melancholia in *Soleil noir* (1987). Three French women writers produced a group of haunting narratives that were rife with autobiographical overtones: Annie Ernaux wrote *La femme gelée* in 1981, Marie Cardinal's *Le passé empiété* appeared in 1983, while Marguerite Duras published her widely acclaimed *L'amant* in 1984. In Italy, Francesca Sanvitale authored a text which was soon to become a classic, *Madre e figlia* (1980), while Gina Lagorio produced her most vivid and haunting female portrayal in *Tosca dei gatti* (1983). Five years later, in 1988, Rosetta Loy published *Le strade di polvere*, calling forth the ghosts of a nineteenth-century dynasty on the eve of the birth of the Italian state. Canada, Great Britain, and the United States witnessed an unparalleled blooming of women's writing. Margaret Atwood penned three of her most haunting narratives, *Bodily Harm* (1982), *The Handmaid's Tale* (1985), and *Cat's Eye* (1988) just as other Canadian women writers such as Alice Munro, Marie Claire Blaïs, and Gabrielle Roy achieved worldwide success. In Great Britain, the voices of veterans such as Doris Lessing and Margaret Drabble remained powerful and strong. Among other novels, Lessing published *The Diaries of Jane Somers* (1983–84), *The Good Terrorist* (1985), and *The Fifth Child* (1988). Drabble addressed the British social condition of the time in *The Middle Ground* (1980) and *The Radiant Way* (1987). In 1985, a new voice came to join the rich firmament of British women writers, Anita Brookner's, whose *Hotel du Lac* portrayed a sparse and suffering universe in a style that was suffused with a mix of Woolfian and Jamesian nuances. Joyce Carol Oates, Marge Piercy, and Gloria Naylor are probably three of the most inspired and inspiring American women writers writing in the eighties, a decade which was dominated, however, by the highly deserved success of Alice Walker's *The Color Purple* (1982). Having witnessed both the final affirmation of the women's movement and the unexpected backlash that such event prompted from the most reactionary political fringes, the eighties are analyzed, in my study, through a critical reading of two novels which present both sides of the coin quite effectively. The two fictional diaries analyzed, Doris Lessing's *The Diaries of Jane Somers* (1984) and Margaret Atwood's *The Handmaid's Tale* (1986), indeed complement each other by offering suggestive depictions of these crucial stages of the feminist struggle. Jane Somers is a self-made woman: she has achieved independence and success, but at the expense of her personal life. As she sets out to revisit her past, she comes to realize the immensity of what she has missed, and thus embarks on a desperate attempt to make up for lost time. As feelings she had never experienced suddenly come to the fore, she is also forced to confront the inevitability of the passage of time, and, consequently, of the slow approach of death. Her love story with a man equally encumbered by similar feelings comes to a halt, however, as their mutual responsibilities towards their own families and their professional lives draw them fatally apart. Jane's retreat, at the end of her diary, contains extremely dramatic overtones, because it anticipates her own demise. Tired of being prey to feelings she has not yet learned to master, she decides, in fact, to withdraw in her solitary apartment, in the dark rooms from whose windows she observes the many lights of the lively city of London. The journey that turns Jane Somers from a career woman into a broken woman acts as an ominous introduction to the even bleaker portrayal of the female condition presented in Atwood's novel. This dystopic tale of a futurist society where women have been utterly disempowered by a totalitarian regime founded by Christian Fundamentalists is directly inspired by the unexpected consensus gathered around American Right-wing politicians and teleevangelists. The story of Offred, a woman torn away from her family, and deprived of her most basic rights, even of her real name, is the story of an "everyvictim" of the backlash years. In her foray into science fiction Atwood seems to be telling the reader that, far-fetched at it might seem, Offred's predicament could in fact resemble the future of many a woman. Her novel certainly hides, behind the desperate words of its narrator, a call to arms, a powerful reminder, to the many women who believe their war has been won, that nothing is written in stone, and that a dramatic involution of female emancipation could indeed occur. Held captive in a suffocating room, Offred thus narrates her tale in order to ensure that history does not repeat itself. By risking her life to leave a trace of her tragic existence, she reminds her audience that all women should always, at all costs, refuse to fall victims to patriarchy.

"While there were plenty of feminist thinkers—new and old, famous and obscure—who stood firm in their political beliefs, they were invisible to the media's roving eye. The one new self-proclaimed 'feminist' theoretician that the press did pluck from obscurity was actually an embittered anti-feminist academic" (Faludi 317). The embittered anti-feminist described by Faludi in this passage from *Backlash* is Camille Paglia, the woman who launched, at the very beginning of the nineties, the most vehement attack against feminism. From the pages of *Sexual Personae* (1990), *Sex, Art, and American Culture* (1992), and *Vamps and Tramps* (1994) Paglia denounced the death of the feminist cause, calling "victim feminism" the most recent stage of the women's movement. Nominating herself the leading intellectual of the nineties, Paglia dedicated several essays to Madonna, whom she saw as a true feminist icon, and to a most controversial and disturbing reading of date rape. This new wave of reactionary thought breezed across Europe, reaching France and Italy. In Italy, Benito Mussolini's granddaughter was almost elected as mayor of Naples in 1994; the same year, the newly elected president of the house of representatives, Irene Pivetti, gave a speech in which she referred to herself using only masculine terms, calling herself a *cittadino* and a *cattolico*. Her stern anti-feminist views were further demonstrated through the many reactionary stances she took during her short period in office. The victory of the Center-Right at the 1994 elections in Italy marked the presence of a backlash that did not erase, however, the strong feminist presence in the country. The philosophers who had formed *Diotima* published several influential essays in this period: Luisa Muraro produced her own reading of the mother/daughter relationship in *L'ordine simbolico della madre* (1991) while Adriana Cavarero traced a female genealogy of classic philosophers in *Nonostante Platone* (1992). In Great Britain and North America, the newly born discipline of "women's studies" increasingly gave way to a new presence, that of "gender studies." In this context, the work of theorists such as Judith Butler and Eve Sedgwick is to be seen as fundamental. And while the production of prolific women writers such as Atwood, Lessing, Drabble, Maraini, and Duras gradually decreased and lost its political edge, a handful of fairly unknown writers became practitioners of diary fiction, authoring novels which, in some cases, proved to be extremely well-liked by readers all over the world. It is the case, in particular, of Susanno Tamaro's *Va' dove ti porta il cuore* (1994) and Helen Fielding's *Bridget Jones's Diary* (1996), two very different novels which became instant best-sellers mostly because of their extreme immediacy. And I firmly believe that Tamaro's *Va' dove ti porta il cuore* (1994), a bundle of unsent letters written by an old woman to her distant granddaughter, represents a fitting conclusion to this study because it delves into the lives of women belonging to three different generations, the same generations portrayed in all the other fictional diaries presented in the previous chapters. As the old grandmother narrates the story of her family to her younger relative, metaphors of space come again into play. Enthroned in the old villa which witnessed the most crucial events of many people's lives, a villa which is now populated only by ghostly memories, the old protagonist attempts, through her guilt-laden and guilt-inducing missives, to lure back into the somber and secluded *foyer* the only bird that dared to fly the nest, her granddaughter. A profound generation gap marks the pages of Tamaro's novel, stemming from the confrontation between two women whose lives have been deeply affected by different processes of socialization, different beliefs, different values. Confined in a prison she chose to inhabit, the narrator can hardly comprehend the strife undertaken by her younger relative, a strife symbolizing the extent to which women have gone in order to rebuild new lives, and new rooms of their own.

Unique in its feminist perspective, this study of fictional diaries follows in the footsteps of other interesting analyses of the same literary genre. However, it strongly resists being pigeonholed in a category of genre-criticism that has been too often associated with sterile structuralist endeavors. In many respects, its methodological approach rests within the area of gender criticism; I espouse a close textual analysis that is informed by a critique of the discourse of patriarchal ideology, rather than opting for the formalist approach that usually pervades most genre criticism. This should not be read as a dismissal of the material previously written on fictional diaries, but as a statement of the subject position from which my reading of these texts stems. While previous book-length analyses of diary fiction were usually aimed at depicting the multilayered structure and the multifaceted aspects of such a genre, this study of fictional journals aims at portraying the use that feminist writers have made of this category of fiction. I have chosen to analyze diaries because they seem to lend themselves better than any other works to a critical portrayal of the recent history of women's condition. And it is quite unfortunate that, until now, no formal study of feminist diary fiction has ever been produced. It is my sincere hope that other scholars will eventually choose to carry out similar studies because I firmly believe that much work is yet to be done within this particular field.

In order to familiarize the reader, however, with the (non-feminist) scholarship previously produced on fictional diaries, I conclude my introductory remarks by offering a succinct overview of this material. Valerie Raoul has written both the oldest and the most recent contributions to this field. In *The French Fictional Journal: Fictional Narcissism/Narcissistic Fiction* (1980) and *Distinctly Narcissistic: Diary Fiction in Quebec* (1993), she combines a structuralist perspective, aimed at the depiction of a model for an archetypal diary novel, with a psychoanalytic approach that informs her reading of these works in the light of their narcissistic overtones. Limiting her analysis to two national literatures, Raoul effectively juxtaposes the psychoanalytic discourse to the analysis of two specific cultural discourses, the French and the Quebecquois. In *Diary Fiction: Writing as Action* (1984) H. Porter Abbott performs a different analysis of fictional journals, one that essentially starts from a structuralist analysis of the genre, and then sets out to categorize the different types of fictional journals ever produced. Drawing specific distinctions between the works of eminent writers such as Goethe, Richardson, Sartre, and Lessing, the critic thus embarks on an exhaustive survey of the works produced in this slippery genre. His use of the term "diary fiction," in opposition to Raoul's previous adoption of the term "diary novel," brings about a veritable widening of the genre. Works of fiction which are not fully written in the diary form thus come to fall under this new heading, as well as those epistolary novels which are composed of unmailed and, therefore, unanswered letters. Subsuming short and long narrative works under a common term, the word "fiction" also allows, when applied to the diaristic genre, the inclusion of novellas such as Simone de Beauvoir's "La femme rompue," which I analyze in the second chapter of my study. In *The Diary Novel* (1985) Lorna Martens carries out a historical survey of the genre: again, the return to the term "novel" effectively restricts the number of works analyzed. Martens's most original contribution to the field rests essentially on the identification of "expressive" utterances as the common element to diary narrative. Her entire study thus revolves around the examination of the role played, in different diary novels, by such expressives, that she defines as "utterances that express a 'feeling or desire' or, most generally, the speaker's 'attitude'" (43). Trevor Field's *Form and Function in the Diary Novel* (1989) is a sound structuralist analysis of an enormous number of diary novels. In his work he draws no distinctions between canonical and non-canonical texts, and its merit essentially rests on the uncommon ability demonstrated by its author in addressing his analysis to works which had never been previously discussed. Last but not least is Andrew Hassam's *Writing and Reality: A Study of Modern British Diary Fiction*, published in 1993. Hassam's critical exegesis is essentially informed by the espousal of structuralist and neo-historicist approaches. Combining an attentive analysis of the formal aspects of the genre with a discussion of diary writing as representation of reality, Hassam embarks on a lengthy disquisition on the influence of ideological discourses in diaristic portrayals. In many respects, it is to Hassam's work that my analysis of diary fiction is most akin. A similar attention to discourses of dominant ideology, in fact, informs my critical study of those literary mirrors in which women diarists attempted to reflect their own complex image.

1

Time Given, Time Taken, Time Lost: De Céspedes's Bleak Tale of the Fifties

> 26 novembre 1950
> . . . Dal tabaccaio c'era molta gente. Nell'aspettare il mio turno vidi una pila di quaderni nella vetrina. Erano quaderni neri, lucidi, spessi, di quelli che si usano a scuola e sui quali—prima ancora d'incominciarli—scrivevo subito, in prima pagina, con trasporto, il mio nome: Valeria. "Mi dia anche un quaderno" dissi frugando nella borsa per trovare altro denaro. Ma, quando rialzai gli occhi, vidi che il tabaccaio aveva assunto un'espressione severa per dirmi: "Non si può, è proibito". Mi spiegò che l'agente stava di guardia sulla porta, ogni domenica affinché si vendessero tabacchi soltanto, null'altro. Ero rimasta sola nel negozio. "Ne ho bisogno" gli dissi "ne ho bisogno assolutamente". Parlavo sottovoce, concitata, ero pronta a insistere, a scongiurare. Allora egli si guardò attorno poi, lesto, prese un quaderno e me lo tese attraverso il bancone, dicendo: "Lo metta sotto il cappotto." (7–8)
>
> [There was a crowd at the tobacconist's. While I was waiting my turn, with the money ready, I saw a pile of notebooks in the window. They were those thick, shiny, black composition books I used to use at school—and before starting one I always wrote my name on the first page with a bit of a thrill: Valeria. "Would you please give me a composition book, too?" I said, rummaging in my purse for some more money; but when I looked up I saw the tobacconist looking stern. "I can't" he said "It's not allowed." He told me a policeman stood on guard at the door to see he sold only tobacco and nothing else on Sundays. We were alone in the shop. "But I need it" I said "I've absolutely got to have it." I was talking low and excitedly; I was going to insist and beg. He looked around and then quickly picked up a notebook and handed it to me across the counter. "Put it under your coat" he said. (1–2)].

Thus begins the diary of Valeria Cossati, protagonist of *Quaderno proibito*, a novel written by Alba de Céspedes in 1952. As a middle-aged, middle-class Roman housewife, an Italian *everywoman* of the fifties, Valeria is the apt representative of what Margaret Drabble called *the middle ground.* The desperate urgency with which she persuades the tobacconist to sell her a notebook and the resistance she encounters as she symbolically invokes *male consent to write* act as an appropriate introduction to a novel that delves into the impassionate analysis of a phallocratic establishment, with the intent to denounce the dramatic influence such an iniquitous system exerts on its female victims.

In the six months covered by the diary, Valeria records the daily events which punctuate the life of her family, unveiling, through a meticulous transcription of conversations and personal reflections, the underlying tension that turns a supposedly happy family into a viper's nest. Prompted by the sudden desire to eternalize the best moments of her family life, diary writing soon becomes a source of apprehension and awakening for Valeria. Forced to keep her journal secret from her nosy and selfish family, she realizes that, for the first time in her life, she must become a liar. All her life has been devoted to the care of the others. She is the reliable daughter in an old-fashioned family, with a self-effacing mother and a detached father, the irreproachable wife of a mediocre man, Michele, a frustrated bank clerk, the nurturing mother of two selfish children, ambitious Mirella and weak Riccardo. Early in her diary, she registers her intense pain at Mirella's growing involvement with a separated man, Sandro, who seems to foster her daughter's sudden revolt against those traditional values according to which she, and her mother before her, were brought up. Soon after this, Valeria finds herself questioning the same moral constructs when, faced with an unexpected attraction towards her boss, she starts considering the possibility of initiating a liaison through which she would surrender her fossilized role as care provider. All this is further encouraged by her husband's growing estrangement: initially lost in his reveries, Michele also seems to be led astray from the family after his encounter with Valeria's best friend, Clara, who, working in the film industry, suddenly offers to turn him into a rich screenwriter. What could possibly save the Cossatis from the final diaspora? Enter Riccardo, with his selfish needs and his immature outlook on life; once aspiring to move to Argentina after his law degree, the young man falls in love with passive aggressive Marina, an apparently chaste and naïve maiden who suddenly finds herself pregnant with his child. Once the deed is done, there is only one solution admissible in Catholic Italy: the two will have to marry and, lacking independent means of support, they will install their newly founded family in Valeria's house. No more romantic elopements for Valeria, no more artistic moonlighting for Michele: as good grandparents-to-be, they will give up their dreams and return to the *foyer*. Only Mirella will leave, fulfilling a dream of independence that, by then, her mother also shares. A new-old life is about to start for Valeria, an existence which holds no space for writing, no room for emancipation. She will follow her own mother's path and slowly reduce herself to a self-effacing silence foreseen by the burning of the diary, which closes the novel on a deeply ominous tone.

Constrained by patriarchal values which, like many other women of her time, she thoroughly internalized and never questioned, Valeria begins her journal interpreting the world around her in the light of those principles, but as her process of awakening unfolds, she achieves a different level of awareness. The diary opens, quite significantly, on Valeria's regrets regarding the purchase of the black notebook: "Ho fatto male a comperare questo quaderno, malissimo" (7) [I was wrong to buy this notebook, terribly wrong (1)]. The secrecy it fosters makes it appear a sinful activity, a subversive gesture that can only bring turmoil in the household. The disruptiveness of the diary stems from the fact that, in order to write in it, Valeria must put aside her familial duties and find time for herself: "a casa, non so perché, ho sempre voglia di chiedere scusa. Forse perché so di trascurare molte cose a causa di questo quaderno" (105) [At home, I don't know why, I'm always apologetic—maybe because I know I'm neglecting all sorts of things because of this diary (96)]. Brought up in Fascist Italy, where little girls were taught in school that "the Nation is served even by keeping the house swept, civic discipline commences with family discipline" (De Grazia 1992, 116), Valeria was raised by a mother who never allowed her, as a child, to remain idle: "Non permetteva mai che restassi inoperosa, non si dimenticava mai di me. Se per un momento non mi vedeva, entrava in camera mia e mi domandava che facessi. 'Una donna non deve stare mai senza far nulla'" (105) [She never let me be without some work or other, and she never forgot me. If I was out of sight for a moment she'd come into my room and ask what I was up to. "A woman must never be idle" she used to say (97)].

The notebook, therefore, acts as a symbolic separation from an engulfing family. In searching for a place where she can hide it, she realizes that there is no place in the house that she can claim as her own: she is not even allowed a safely locked drawer, such as the ones that both her children and her husband so jealously cherish. The fact that her husband keeps in his secret drawer the family money, while her children save theirs for their love letters, is a potent reminder of what Valeria has given up in her married life—economic and emotional independence. To the same effect, it is worth remembering that, in one of the first entries, Valeria mentions that the very possession of the notebook would be itself threatened by her family members because, if they were to realize that she owned it, "Riccardo se ne sarebbe impadronito per prendere appunti all'università o Mirella per il diario che tiene chiuso a chiave nel suo cassetto. . . . Michele . . . mi avrebbe consigliato gentilmente di cederlo a Riccardo" (9) [Riccardo would have made off with it at once for his lecture notes, or Mirella would have used it for the diary she keeps locked up in the drawer. . . . Michele . . . would have advised me, quite nicely, to give it up to Riccardo (3)]. If, until she bought her diary, Valeria had never realized her constricted position in the family, once she starts writing she awakens to her need and, little by little, she tries to reclaim the Woolfian room of her own: "Comunque, ho quarantatré anni e mi pare vergognoso ricorrere a simili puerili sotterfugi per scrivere in un quaderno perciò è assolutamente necessario che confessi a Michele e ai ragazzi l'esistenza di questo diario e affermi il mio diritto di chiudermi in una stanza a scrivere quando ne ho voglia" (12) [Anyway, I'm forty-three, and it seems shameful to resort to childish subterfuges just to write in a notebook. I really ought to confess that this diary exists and assert my right to shut myself up when I want to and write it (6)].

In another doomed enterprise, that of taking stock of her life, Valeria initiates a process of self-reappropriation through the symbolic inscription of her name on the first page of the notebook: ". . . erano quaderni neri, lucidi, spessi, di quelli che usano a scuola e sui quali—prima ancora d'incominciarli—scrivevo subito, in prima pagina, con trasporto, il mio nome: Valeria" (8) [They were those thick, shiny, black composition books I used to use at school—and before starting one I always wrote my name on the first page with a bit of a thrill: Valeria (2)]. Gone is the family name, which symbolically binds her to the *Law of the Father*, gone are the relational ties that, until then, had established her identity: Bebe for her parents, Mammà for her husband and children, Pisani for her old schoolmates. Valeria, repossessing her name, makes a statement about the frailty of the sense of autonomous independence felt by a woman in her time. Nancy Chodorow, in *The Reproduction of Mothering* (1978) states that "Feminine personality comes to be based less on repression of inner objects, and fixed and firm splits in the ego, and more on retention and continuity of external relationships. From the retention of pre-oedipal attachments to the mother, growing girls come to define themselves as continuous to others . . . "(169); according to E. Ann Kaplan, Chodorow's theories "describe the reproduction of white, bourgeois, mothering in the period from 1860 to 1960" (1992,

34). Valeria, when writing her diary, wants to defy such a relational state of being, trying to forget that she is "la moglie di Michele, la madre di Riccardo e Mirella" (11) [Michele's wife or as the children's mother (5)]. Once she has a pen in her hand, she just wants to be *a person.*

When she writes about her family, and about her undivided devotion to her children, Valeria adopts economic terms: "Pensavo di *possedere* il tempo che ho *investito* nei figli, come un *capitale* ma adesso essi se lo *rubano*, se lo portano via" (103, emphasis mine) [I used to think my capital was the time I had invested in my children but they're stealing it, taking it away from me (95)] and large part of Valeria's writing is furthermore devoted to the discussion of her family's financial problems. The limited means afforded by Michele's meager salary should all be directed, according to Valeria, towards a unique investment, her daughter's search for a good husband: "Avrei voluto promettere a Riccardo di comprargli uno smoking, a rate, come avevamo comparato il vestito da sera di Mirella; ma un vestito da uomo è sempre più caro, *e poi un uomo non deve trovare marito*" (18) [I should have liked to promise to buy Riccardo a dinner jacket—in installments, as we had bought Mirella's evening dress; but then, men's clothes are always more expensive, and a man doesn't need to find a husband (12)]. All the presents Mirella will receive from her mother will thus be aimed at making her more *marketable:* from the powder[1] that should symbolically help her create a profitable *mask*, to the red coat, which should turn her into an ideal *target* for the *male hunter:* ". . . ho concluso che no, era più urgente comperare qualcosa per Mirella, lui ha chiesto che cosa, e io ho risposto che non sapevo ancora precisamente, forse il cappotto rosso di cui tanto spesso aveva manifestato desiderio, le scarpe, e altre piccolezze che sono necessarie a una ragazza della sua età" (51–52) [I decided not to and said it was more important to buy something for Mirella. He asked me what it was, and I told him I didn't know exactly yet, maybe the red coat she had asked for so often, and other little things a girl of her age needs (44)].

In *Donner le temps*, Jacques Derrida relates economics to the institution of the family: "L'économie . . . la gestion de l'*oikos*, de la maison, de la famille ou du foyer, se limite aux biens nécessaires à la vie" (200) [Economy . . . the management of the *oikos*, of the home, the family, or the hearth, is limited to the goods necessary to life (158)]. In the Derridean perspective the *gift*, the discussion of which lies at the core of *Donner le temps*, is aneconomic by default: "Le don . . . ne doit pas circuler, il ne doit pas s'échanger . . . Si la figure du cercle est essentielle à l'économique, le don doit rester *anéconomique*"

(19) [The gift . . . must not circulate, it must not be exchanged. . . . If the figure of the circle is essential to economics, the gift must remain *aneconomic* (7)]. If family relations, therefore, appear in *Quaderno proibito* as rooted in economic values, Valeria's decision to keep a diary, and to find some time for herself, on the other hand, goes against the same economic principle, it implies a *perdita*, a loss, a waste of *good, productive time:* "Un'altra cosa mi trattiene dal confessare che scrivo: ed è il rimorso di perdere tanto tempo a scrivere" (22) [There's something else that stops me from confessing, and that's the guilty feeling I have at the thought of spending so much time on it (16)]. Valeria's diary is clearly defined as *aneconomic* when she compares it to her husband's creative writing which, being a screenplay, he considers as a lucrative source of income: "Gli ho domandato di che cosa il soggetto trattasse e lui ha risposto evasivamente, dicendo che le storie d'amore sono quelle che piacciono di più al pubblico. Per un momento avevo avuto la tentazione di parlargli del quaderno, ma l'insistenza con la quale egli sottolineava l'aspetto economico di quanto aveva fatto me lo impediva, giacché io non potevo invocare la stessa giustificazione" (100) [I asked him what the story was about and he answered evasively, saying that love stories are what the public wants. For a moment I was tempted to tell him about my diary, but when he harped on the economic aspect of what he had done it stopped me, because I couldn't justify it like that (92)]. While her husband's script assumes a value through its economic relevance, her diary, being devoid of monetary potential, is not even worth mentioning. Within the economic context of the family, it actually becomes a source of shame, because its disruptive potential endangers the structure of an institution that is rooted in self-sacrifice, sincerity, and cooperation.

Through the separation from her family enacted in the diary, Valeria symbolically recreates the Woolfian *room of her own* in the notebook itself, that she has given herself as a gift. Not only is the diary a gift, but it is, more significantly, a gift of time,[2] symbolically similar to the gold watch Mirella receives from her lover, who is responsible for disrupting Valeria's investment on her daughter's idealized future as a happily married homemaker. Indeed, both Mirella's watch and Valeria's diary grant their owners a new and independent conception of time, thus marking their exit from the *oikos*.

By allowing herself some time alone, by stealing some time away from that time-consuming activity of nurturing mother and wife, which has made her life a series of cyclical events strictly related to her role in a family, Valeria achieves a new temporal dimension. If the unrecorded past once appeared to her as a gray mass of uneventful days, the diary finally gives her a new perspective on the present. Daily written recollection brings to light a different reality: "Non avrei mai creduto che tutto quanto m'accade nel corso della giornata valesse la pena di essere notato. . . . Invece da quando, per caso, ho cominciato a tenere un diario, mi pare di scoprire che una parola, un accento, possono essere altrettanto importanti, o anche più, dei fatti che siamo abituati a considerare tali." (33) [I'd never have thought that everything that happens to me during the day would be worth putting down . . . But since I began keeping a diary, I seem to have discovered that a word, a tone of voice, can be as important as—or more important than—the facts that we generally think are important (26)]. This new awareness of the passage of time is accompanied by her rediscovery of desire: the diary, acting as a specular surface in which she mirrors herself, sets off a rejuvenating process which eventually leads her to start an affair with her boss. The *liaison* itself once again stresses Valeria's attempt to leave the *oikos*, the familiar economy that forces her into a specific role. Time linearized, time reacquired, time eternalized: these are some of the many implications stemming from the simple purchase of a diary, from a simple *present* that a woman gives herself with the hope of shaping her new future.

In a significant passage of her notebook, Valeria describes the content of the only drawer which is rightfully hers: the one belonging to her office desk, where she keeps "solo cose prive d'interesse, carte, forbici, colla, il pettine e la cipria" (85) [Only uninteresting things—papers, scissors, glue, a comb, and some powder (77)], objects which are extremely relevant. They represent the writing she has suddenly taken up and that is changing her life (paper), the sudden desire to cut loose with her past life of submission (scissors), the actual reconstruction of her own existence through a symbolic pasting of many events (glue), the rediscovery of her beauty (comb) and, last but not least, the need to keep this process hidden from the rest of the world (powder). What seems somehow missing from the drawer, along with the comb and the powder, is a mirror, and its absence is essentially due to the fact that Valeria, once she had children, obliterated her womanhood, sublimating her sexual needs through motherhood:[3] "In una lettera [Michele] diceva: 'Voglio ritrovarti, Valeria mia. A volte non mi riesce più di vederti: ti sei nascosta tra i figli.' Mentre leggevo queste parole, iersera, ho avuto un brivido di freddo . . . " (169) [In a letter (Michele) said. "I want to find you again, Valeria darling. Sometimes I can't see you any more: you're hidden by the children" When I read this yesterday evening, I shivered (161)]. However, the diary itself starts acting as a mirror, which aims not only at reflecting and restoring the image of a still good-looking mature woman, but also provokes the sudden emergence of a repressed self. What started out as a mere recording of events, becomes an impassioned mirroring of the soul, a painful act of discovery and recovery.

In *Diary Fiction*, H. Porter Abbott implicitly draws the connection between diaries and mirrors during his discussion of the typical setting of the diarist: ". . . where is the diarist? In the male version (the version most frequently imitated) he is seated at a desk. On the desk there is ink, pen, and a paper. The desk is in a room. The room contains at least two things: a window with a view and a mirror" (1984, 15). De Céspedes's female version is quite different. Valeria's desk is in her office, and no journal writing ever takes place there. Strangely enough, the windows she describes usually acquire a symbolic meaning not associated with diary writing. The impulse to leave the bedroom window open for the night occurs when both Valeria and her husband are about to be drawn out of domestic boredom by Guido and Clara: "Entrambi fingevamo disinvoltura, eppure io sapevo quali fossero i miei pensieri e anche lui conosceva i miei, ne ero certa. Avrei voluto parlargli, esser franca, ma qualcosa mi tratteneva, mi imbavagliava, quasi: la disperata certezza che non bastassero più le parole a superare il silenzio che s'era andato ammassando tra noi, giorno dopo giorno, ed è ormai un ostacolo invalicabile. . . . 'E' già caldo' ha detto, e la sua voce era appannata: 'Forse sarà bene lasciare la finestra aperta'" (139) [Both of us pretended to be at ease, but I knew what he was thinking, and he knew what I was thinking, I'm certain. I should have liked to talk to him frankly, but something held me back, almost gagged me—the desperate certainty that words wouldn't be able to overcome the silence that has been piling up between us, day after day, and that has now become an impossible barrier. . . . "It's warm these days," he said dully. "Maybe it would be a good idea to leave the window open" (130)]. As if to signify a means of escape from an oppressive condition, another open window is described in Valeria's office,[4] the actual place which comes to represent her hiding place. It is 20 March, and as a prelude to spring, the period of rebirth, it bespeaks the protagonist's full reawakening to desire: after only two days, she will have her first intimate conversation with Guido.

If both desk and window are absent from the writing scene, the mirror, instead, is constantly present, and is often invoked throughout the narration. The same Valeria who had been running away from mirrors for so many years, choosing to reflect her own image through the eyes of her beloved, finally acknowledges the importance of trusting her own judgment and thus rediscovers the pleasure of observing herself in the *looking glass*. Her estrangement from Michele, her longtime companion, comes to be signified through his inability to provide her with a correct specular reflection: "Egli continua a rivolgersi a me attraverso una immagine che non mi specchia più" (81) [He goes on talking to me through an image that no longer reflects me (my modified translation)]. In another passage, the diary and the mirror are significantly combined in an image of *specularity* which appropriately summarizes Valeria's new attitude towards her life: "Eppure adesso trovo il tempo per specchiarmi, per scrivere il diario; mi domando com'è che prima non lo trovassi. Mi sono guardata a lungo il viso, gli occhi, e la mia immagine mi comunicava un senso di allegria" (136) [Yet now I find time to look at myself, to write my diary, and I wonder why I didn't before. I looked at my face for a long time, at my eyes, and was pleased with what I saw (127)].

In *Herself Beheld*, Jenijoy La Belle identifies the act of mirroring, in a woman, as a self-empowering gesture: "the mirror does not make the woman a slave to the male world, but stimulates a woman's self-consciousness that inhibits her merging into the male"(1988, 72). However, she points out that such a rebellious move away from the patriarchal system is forcefully restricted by the pressure exerted by religious authorities onto females: "If, as I have tried to show, the mirror is a primal tool for forming a female presence, then there is an attempt . . . to prevent independent self-creation and a desire to have . . . [women] concentrate on the Immaculate Conception instead of on self-conception."(80)

In order to clarify the reference of such statements to the situation depicted in *Quaderno proibito*, it is worth remembering the overbearing presence of the Catholic Church in twentieth-century Italy, from which stem a paternalistic repression and a strictness of morals that still constitute two peculiar traits of the country. The pervasive influence of the Catholic Church has always been so deeply felt that no Italian can avoid taking a position vis-à-vis its morally conditioning force: whether they embrace the dogma or they define themselves against it, Italians cannot overlook the presence of such a powerful religious establishment. The political influence of the Vatican reached its apex during the first half of the twentieth century, when the Catholic Church joined forces, in 1929, with the Fascist regime. The patriarchal roots of Catholicism and Fascism facilitated the reinforcement of a phallocratic system of values to which all Italians were asked to conform. The life and morals of an entire population were thus influenced by such a panoptical establishment. The sudden fall of Mussolini, along with the monarchy that had supported him, clearly brought about significant changes. It coincided, and not by mere chance, with the growing emancipation of women, who were finally allowed to cast their first electoral vote. However, the overbearing influence of the Catholic establishment still remained, finding new political alliances which were willing to subscribe to its traditional values: "The new Republic, though admitting formal equality and significant gains such as the vote, maintained laws and conventions that had been codified under fascist rule and that treated women as subordinate" (De Grazia 1992, 278). Such a peculiar sociopolitical situation constitutes the background of De Céspedes's novel.

Product of her times, Valeria soon realizes the sinfulness of her quest for independence, giving in to the old belief that, if one looks in the mirror for too long, the devil will appear. The notebook, like the Derridean *pharmakon*, turns from medicine into poison.[5] Its *aneconomic* nature, which had signaled Valeria's attempt to escape the constrictive *oikos*, suddenly disappears turning the diary into the quintessential economic symbol, an account book: "Gli altri dormono, a quest'ora: il sonno cancella la giornata che hanno vissuto e il nuovo giorno si presenta loro libero dalle giornate precedenti che io invece conservo in queste pagine come in un *esoso libro di conti da cui nessun debito sia mai rimesso* " (243, emphasis mine) [The others are asleep by now. Sleep cancels the day they have lived and the new day arrives unencumbered by what has gone before it; but I keep everything in these pages, as if in an account book where no debt is ever forgiven (235)].

Feeling responsible for the crises which are now taking place in her household, she sees the diary as the germ of an irredeemable sin: "Tutto è incominciato allora . . . il giorno in cui ho ammesso di poter nascondere qualcosa a mio marito, sia pure un quaderno. Volevo essere sola, per scrivere; e chi vuole chiudersi nella propria solitudine, in famiglia, porta sempre con sé il germe del peccato" (216) [Everything started then . . . the day I admitted I could hide something from Michele, if only a diary. I wanted to be alone to write, and whoever wants to shut himself up with his own solitude, in a family, always bears in him the seeds of sin (207)]. In *Le journal intime,* Béatrice Didier identifies journal keeping as an activity that has replaced the Catholic institutions of confession and repentance (1976, 83). Writing a diary gives Valeria a different outlook on life: being raised in a Catholic environment, she was accustomed to submit her life to public scrutiny through the confessional practice. As Michel Foucault (1976) amply proved in his *History of Sexuality,* confession is a powerful reinscription of male hegemony, a form of social surveillance that exerts its power through repression and guilt. From this point of view, Valeria's decision to keep a diary parallels her unconscious attempt to remove herself from the influence of the church. The confessional ritual is mentioned only once in the novel, as something that the protagonist intends to do, probably out of guilt, but its actual performance is never reported in the journal: "Domani voglio andare a confessarmi, è tanto tempo che non ci vado più" (60) [On Sunday I want to go to confession—it's ages since I went (52)]. In writing her own life, Valeria reserves for herself the right to pass a judgment on her actions, thus resisting the paternalistic establishment.

The Catholic influence, however, is so pervasive that the religious panoptical presence has established its effects within her in the shape of a Freudian superego. Faced with her sinful desire to commit an adultery which has been fostered by the secrecy she embraced after buying her journal, she becomes aware of the dangerous potential that writing has. Taken by despair, she calls her black, shiny notebook a leech, a term similar to the one used by Romans to identify priests and bugs, *bacarozzi*, other black, shiny animals: "Dovrei riconoscere che lo sforzo fatto per dimenticare me stessa durante venti anni è stato inutile. Vi sono riuscita fino al momento in cui nascosto sotto il cappotto, ho portato a casa questo quaderno nero e lucido come una sanguisuga" (217) [And so I must acknowledge that the effort to forget myself that I've been making for twenty years has been useless. Till the moment when I brought home this notebook hidden under my coat, shiny and black as a leech, I succeeded. Everything started then (207)]. The language used by Valeria in many a passage borrows from the religious discourse in order to raise the pitch of its dramatic overtones. Silence and secrecy are sinful, and keeping a diary is often described as an interaction with Satan. ". . . quando scrivo in questo quaderno, sento di commettere un grave peccato, un sacrilegio: mi pare di discorrere col diavolo" (231) [When I write this diary, I feel I'm committing a grave sin, a sacrilege. I feel I'm talking to the devil (223)]. By the same token, this sense of shame is displaced into the desire to look at her reflection in the mirror: "Mi vergogno persino di questo quaderno, di me stessa, non oso più scrivere, come l'altra sera non osavo più guardarmi . . . allo specchio" (205) [I'm ashamed even of this diary, of myself; I don't dare to write any more, as the other day I didn't dare look at myself any longer . . . in the mirror (196)]. The rejection of the diary becomes, therefore, a symbolic rebellion against the mirror, an action frequently performed by women characters ". . . not in order to preserve the self but to lose it" (Labelle 1988, 149).

Prior to the destruction of the diary, however, Valeria begins a symbolic expurgation through her dismissal of Guido, her platonic lover. What seems most powerful about this character's presence in the novel is the profound similarity between him and Valeria: like her, he feels trapped by a demanding family from which he escapes by spending more time in his office.[6] The intense dissatisfaction that possesses him stems from a midlife crisis, the causes of which he describes with terms which echo those adopted by Valeria while speaking her discontent: "'Io ho lavorato tutta la vita, ho impiegato trent'anni a divenire quello che sono. E adesso?' Ha rivolto questa domanda nel vuoto con grande amarezza. Poi, quasi pentito di essersi lasciato andare, ha aggiunto ridendo che bisognerebbe stabilire un'età 'quarantacinque anni, mettiamo' oltre la quale si avesse diritto a essere soli al mondo, e a poter scegliere daccapo la propria vita. " (133) ["I've worked all my life, I've spent thirty years becoming what I am. And what for?" He flung this question out into the air with tremendous violence. Then, almost as if he repented having said so much, he said, laughing, that one should establish an age—"say forty-five"—beyond which one would have the right to be alone in the world and be able to choose one's life over again (124)]. Once their secret camaraderie has been established, Valeria starts feeling that Guido fulfills an important role in her life because "Lui è la sola persona alla quale io possa parlare" (103) [He's the only person I could talk to (95)] and her desire to talk to him, to answer back to the message she finds on her desk, "Parliamone" (103) [Talk to me" (95)], becomes parallel to her urge to write on the secret diary. Indeed, Guido, as an ideal alter-ego of Valeria, appears as her male *mirror image*, as a material projection of the journal itself. Not only was their relationship brought about by the diary[7] but the notebook itself acts as a continuous reminder of him: ". . . appena ho avuto in mano questo quaderno ho perduto la pace. In esso l'immagine di Guido affiora dappertutto, tra le righe" (255) [. . . as soon as I had the diary in my hand I lost all peace. Guido's image comes before me everywhere, between the lines (248)]. His name, which in Italian means *I drive*, stresses his function as guidance towards a new path, a path materially undertaken during their escapades, which always consist in long drives around the streets of Rome, those same streets that used to terrify and attract Valeria at the same time, and that she once compares to the blank lines of her diary: "Neppure ora, sola col quaderno, mi riesce di capire: questo quaderno, con le sue pagine bianche, mi attrae e allo stesso tempo mi sgomenta, come la strada" (59) [Even now, alone with my notebook, I can't understand: this notebook, with its blank pages, attracts me and scares me, like the streets of Rome (my translation)]. The trip to Venice, planned in order to break away from their entrapped existence, eventually falls through: Venice, which symbolically represents both beginnings and ends, since the dying city is also a place for elopements and honeymoons, takes on the image of *the road not taken*. By rejecting Guido, and the path to self-reappraisal that he comes to represent, Valeria follows her own Catholic superego which forces her not to indulge into a sinful quest for knowledge, a knowledge which seems to have fostered only a profound sense of perdition: "Forse vi sono persone che, conoscendosi, riescono a migliorarsi; io, invece, più mi conosco e più mi perdo" (231) [Maybe there are people who, by knowing themselves, manage to improve; but in my case the more I know myself the more I'm lost (223)].

In perfect compliance with the corollary *diktat* that wants Italian mothers to forget the possibility of a self-conception in favor of a transformation into the Immaculate Conception, Valeria remembers how her mother-in-law, a woman she despised, but who had devoted all her life to the family, had been eternalized in a framed portrait hung on a wall in their bedroom: "Rivedevo la grande fotografia di mia suocera che domina la nostra camera da letto: era una donna mediocre, ma Michele sempre me la porta a esempio" (119) [I seemed to see the large photograph of my mother-in-law that dominates our bedroom. She was an ordinary sort of woman, yet Michele always holds her up as an example (110)]. The aura of holiness surrounding this woman, her objectification as a revered image, is a pointed correlative of the myth of maternal sacrifice that pervaded the cultural discourse of the period. At the inception of the novel, Valeria herself sees martyrdom as the only positive recognition that a woman can expect within a family: ". . . in un certo senso questa schiavitù è divenuta anche la mia forza, l'aureola del mio martirio" (22) [In a way this enslavement of mine has become my strength, my martyr's crown (16)]. As time goes by, however, the framing power of male hegemony, exemplified by the canonization of the maternal figure, becomes a haunting omen for her: "Mi chiedevo se per Michele sono una donna viva o già, come sua madre, un ritratto sulla parete. Così sono per i miei figli, così mia madre è per me. Disperatamente desideravo sfuggire il maligno incantesimo di quel ritratto" (147) [I wonder if he still sees me as a living woman at all, or whether, like his mother, I'm already a picture on the wall. I'm sure I am to the children, and certainly my mother is to me. Desperately I longed to escape the gloomy spell of that picture (138)]. By the end of the novel, Valeria's decision to burn the diary makes her come full circle. As if the mobility of her symbolically broken mirror were arrested, she resigns herself to the act of framing which time will impose on her image: "Liscia sarà la grande pietra bianca sulla quale, alla fine, tornerò a chiamarmi Valeria. 'Era una santa', Riccardo dirà a Marina singhiozzando, come Michele disse a me. E lei non potrà smentirlo" (257) [Smooth will be the great white stone on which in the end I'll go back to being called Valeria. "She was a saint" Riccardo will say sobbing to Marina, as Michele said to me. And she won't be able to contradict him (249)].

When E. Ann Kaplan states, at the end of *Motherhood and Representation*, that "for women, one of the most subordinated *and* fetishized positions has been that of 'mother,'" (1992, 219) it almost seems that she is referring to the situation portrayed in *Quaderno proibito*. Indeed, Valeria's narrative essentially revolves around her relationship with her daughter and son, Mirella and Riccardo. In the six months covered by the diary, the narrator is faced with two major family crises. Mirella's affair with a much older man constitutes the focus of most of the first part of the journal, while the rest of the book centers on Riccardo's sudden marriage to Marina, his young and inept fiancée who is pregnant with his child. From the beginning of the novel, the reader is aware of Valeria's utter dependence on the constant presence of her children. In her husband, Michele, she identifies another child: ". . . in tal modo riuscivo a giustificare l'impeto di tenerezza suscitato in me dal fare di Michele che è rimasto candido, ingenuo, anche ora che ha quasi cinquant'anni. Quando mi chiama 'mammà' io gli rispondo con un piglio tra severo e tenero, lo stesso che usavo con Riccardo quando era bambino" (11) [It seemed to justify the tenderness I've always felt for Michele, who has remained an open and ingenuous person, even now, when he's nearly fifty. When he calls me "Mamma" I look at him half gently, half severely, just as I used to look at Riccardo when he was a baby (5)]. Childish as he may appear, Michele still retains his role as *pater familias*, and Valeria often feels compelled to remind her children of their father's undeserved status. In the Italian society of the fifties, a *good reputation* was the only measure of a woman's value and the greatest beneficiary of its awarding was not the woman who enjoyed it, but the paternal figure that had shaped it. Valeria's obsession with her daughter's behavior derives from such conviction. The fear that Mirella's relationship with an older man, coming from a broken marriage, could disgrace her entire family does not stem from personal concern: rather, it is actually motivated by its repercussion on her husband's reputation: "Io ho risposto che non era libera di fare tutto ciò che voleva impunemente, che doveva rispetto alla casa di suo padre, che non sarebbe riuscita ad ingannarmi" (84) [I told her she wasn't free to do just what she liked, that she ought to respect her father's house and wouldn't be able to deceive me (76)]. In this passage, Valeria is depicted as a guardian of phallocentrism, and her intrinsic weakness is shown: the product of a patriarchal system of values, she unconsciously represents her worst enemy. Desperate to gather information about her daughter's private life, she forces Mirella's locked drawer open in order to read her diary, performing that same censory gesture she has herself been fearing all along. Caught between a rebellious daughter and a phallocratic son, Valeria can also see, however, the dangers embodied in the constrictive traditional ideology. Confronted with her own son's chauvinistic attacks, she defends women strenuously, thus protecting her newly born desire for emancipation: "Oggi [Riccardo] mi ha detto che le donne approfittano del lavoro per fare il comodo proprio. Gli ho ricordato che lavoro anch'io e che è stato un vantaggio per la nostra famiglia, anche per lui. Egli ha replicato che io lo faccio solo per necessità e che quindi il mio lavoro è *una prova di solidarietà con mio marito*, in fondo *una prova di sottomissione*. . . . Io ho obiettato . . . Egli si è rivolto verso di me accoratamente, dicendo: 'Non difenderle. Tu non hai fatto come loro, mamma.' Allora in uno scatto gli ho chiesto: 'E se avessi sbagliato?'" (117–18, emphasis mine) [Today (Riccardo) said that women use their jobs for their own advantage. I reminded him that I too had a job and that it was to the whole family's advantage, to his advantage too. He said that I did it only because I had to and that therefore it was a proof of solidarity with my husband, a proof, basically, of my submissiveness. . . . I objected. . . . He turned to me in distress. "Don't stick up for them" he said. "You've never done what they have done, Mamma." "Suppose I was wrong?" I burst out (110)].

Riccardo's adoration for his mother automatically fosters another form of female disempowerment, producing similar effects to those of Dante's *angelicizzazione* of Beatrice. A closer look at the daily interaction between Valeria and Riccardo shows the emergence of the mother-son behavioral pattern first described by Jacques Lacan in his analysis of the Imaginary realm, and then critically reappropriated by feminist thinkers. Kaplan asserts that "in the Lacanian system, the child/adult . . . never forgets the world of the Imaginary, and he/she continues to desire, unconsciously, the illusory oneness with the mother he/she experienced" (1992, 30). While the daughter is forced into rearranging her object of cathexis, the son overcomes his entrance in the symbolic through the cathexis of someone who should be exactly like his mother: "Fear of castration at the Father's hands if he continues his erotic desire for the mother and the identification that this involves . . . plummets the boy into identification with his Father and with the phallus. He looks forward both to one day having symbolic power like his father, and to recuperating his mother through marriage to someone like her" (30). When Riccardo tries to praise his girlfriend's virtues to his mother, he immediately refers to the importance of a similarity between the two women: "Egli ha detto che si rifà sempre a un carattere simile al mio quando immagina quello di sua moglie; che a Marina parla sempre di me . . . " (118) [Riccardo said that he always thinks of a character like mine when he imagines his wife; that he always talks to Marina about me (110)]. On the other hand, Valeria feels that Marina is intruding in her exclusive relationship with her son: "Riccardo è entrato subito dietro di lei e già non era più mio figlio . . . stavo per dirgli: ' . . . mandiamola via'" (126–27) [Riccardo came in immediately after her and he seemed no longer my son. . . . I would have liked to say ". . . let's send her packing" (118)]. The fusional relationship that Valeria entertains with her son is often colored by moments in which nostalgia for the pre-oedipal, Imaginary stage reappears: "'Tu devi aiutarmi, mamma'. Riccardo ha ancora un che di infantile nel disegno delle labbra e la sua voce suscita sempre in me una commossa tenerezza. 'Che c'è, dimmi, che cosa è successo?'" (119) ["You must help me, Mamma." There's still something childish about the formation of his lips, and his voice makes me feel gentle toward him. "What is it? Tell me, what's happened?" (111)]. The dramatic overtones of the scene in which Riccardo admits to his mother that his girlfriend is pregnant arise exactly from a poignant employment of details related to the Imaginary sphere. While her son is relaying the tragic news, Valeria's eyes wander over his childhood toys, as if to heighten the sense of loss that she is about to experience: "'Che hai fatto? Che hai fatto?' ripetevo, piangendo . . . e alzando gli occhi al cielo . . . sull'armadio vedevo il triciclo rosso che sta lì, coperto di polvere, sin da quando Riccardo era bambino" (222) ["What have you done? What have you done?" I repeated, crying myself, and I looked up at heaven . . . on the wardrobe I saw the red tricycle that, covered with dust, has been there since Riccardo was a child (214)]. Like all good Italian sons, Riccardo, however, will never leave his mother: "'Riccardo non se ne andrà mai . . . prenderà una scusa . . . poi nascerà un altro bambino . . . Rimarrà qui vedrai. E tu hai bisogno di Riccardo'" (249) ['Riccardo will never leave . . . he'll make some excuse . . . then there'll be another baby . . . and he'll stay on, you'll see. And you need him"(242)]. By the end of the novel, he will be instrumental in bringing about Valeria's final paralysis. Because of Riccardo's child, Valeria will give up her job, her lover, and her diary, withdrawing in the silent recreation of an Imaginary fusional relationship with a grandchild that, in a moment of delusion, she will imagine hers: "Il bambino è di Riccardo. Di Riccardo e mio" (236) [The child is Riccardo's. Riccardo's and mine (228)]. The mother-son pre-oedipal *partnership*, ". . . unique to the individuals comprising it and . . . determined in their interactions from the beginning" (Kaplan 1992, 50), will be thus vicariously recreated through a new baby who ". . . se sarà una bambina la chiameremo Valeria" (239) [If it's going to be a girl, we're going to call her Valeria (232)].

Mirella's relationship with her mother is once again presented in terms that could be drawn from a study in psychoanalysis. In a significant passage, Valeria describes what could be considered a repetition of the moment in which both her children were introduced to the Symbolic: the day they discover that *la Befana* does not really exist. Such knowledge deprives them of a fundamental feature of the imaginary world of childhood. Forced to acknowledge that they are no longer under their parents' spell, both Mirella and Riccardo are virtually ushered into the adult world: ". . . Riccardo e Mirella non sono più bambini forse proprio da quando hanno smesso di credere nella Befana" (31) [Riccardo and Mirella stopped being children, perhaps from the time they stopped believing in the *befana* (24)]. While Riccardo is overwhelmed by the news, and, trying to deny its reality, remains in the shadow of the Imaginary, Mirella openly admits her hostility towards her mother, the familial figure against whom, from now on, she will define herself. "Michele accorse e . . . disse ai bambini che era molto più bello così, era molto più bello che fosse la mamma. Mirella rispose: 'no'" (32) [Michele came rushing in and . . . he told the children it was much nicer like this, much nicer that Mamma should have done it all. But Mirella said, "No, it isn't" (25)]. Resentment towards the mother is a feature that characterizes Mirella's personality; all her actions are informed by the desire not to repeat her mother's mistakes, not to follow a path that led an intelligent woman like Valeria into a life of sacrifice and silence. In "Et l'une ne bouge pas sans l'autre," Luce Irigaray presents a woman who criticizes her mother's self-obliviousness in terms which pertain to my argument. What Irigaray's narrator says, Mirella could easily say to Valeria: "I received from you only your obliviousness of self, while my presence allowed you to forget this oblivion. So that with my tangible appearance I redoubled the lack of your presence" (1981, 67). Valeria's thwarted entrance into the Symbolic, which prefigures her as lack, as someone belonging to a *sex which is not one*, is highlighted by her difficulty of expression, since the Symbolic is also the realm of language: "ma io non riesco mai a parlare, a esprimermi: Michele ha sempre avuto un carattere più espansivo del mio" (32) [But I can never talk, never express myself; Michele has always been more expansive than I (25)]. Mirella's resistance to the same realm is expressed by her vocal protest against it. Empowered by a language that she tries to revert against the discourse it speaks, Mirella has rightly chosen to become a lawyer. Her future envisions a life devoid of the moral principles bound to the patriarchal *Law of the Father.* By the end of the novel, she is ready to leave for Milan, the city of progress, where she will live with a companion she may not marry, and with whom she will establish a law partnership. While Valeria undoubtedly profits from the many inspirational conversations she has with her daughter, who acts as a real catalyst for her mother's process of awakening, it is actually Mirella herself who comes to achieve freedom through her mother. Once Valeria finally realizes that she will not be allowed to fulfill her dream of independence, the only option left is to displace her release onto her daughter, whom she urges to leave. The anaphoric structure she adopts to address her daughter heightens the dramatic urgency of the message, as if it were to stand out as Valeria's testament to Mirella, as if those were the final words uttered from a virtual deathbed. "'Vattene' Mi pareva di dover tagliare, per la seconda volta, il vincolo col quale, prima che nascesse, la tenevo legata a me. 'Vattene' ho ripetuto: 'Temo che qui ci siano molte brutte cose, molte bugie. Forse non te lo dirò più, ma ricordati che te l'ho detto stasera: salvati, tu che puoi farlo. Vattene, fa presto" (226) ["Go away." I felt that for the second time I had to cut the cord that bound her to me before birth. "Go away" I repeated. "I'm afraid there will be all sorts of ugliness and lies connected with this. Maybe I won't tell you again, but remember what I've told you this evening—save yourself, if you can. Go away, hurry" (218)]. The residual Imaginary connection between mother and daughter appears for the first time in the novel, in the shape of the umbilical cord, exactly when Valeria is about to sever it. When, after a little while, Valeria burns her diary, all that is left from her doomed emancipatory effort is a bunch of ashes, ashes from which a phoenix could rise: Mirella, whose voice will speak out for women like her mother, who have been silenced by the patriarchal establishment.

In *Epistolarity: Approaches to a Form,* Janet Gurkin Altman remarks that little interruptions of writing usually precede the final descent of the writer into aphasia, because they emphasize "the instability of [the] present, the imminent danger that threatens to interrupt the writing totally" (1982, 124). Halfway through the novel, Valeria leaves a journal entry unfinished because her husband almost catches her red-handed. The elliptical conclusion of the passage is worthy of notice because it contains a series of unanswered questions which lie at the epistemological core of *Quaderno proibito:* "Se non siamo aperti con le persone care, con le quali viviamo, giorno dopo giorno, in famiglia, con chi lo siamo? quand'è che siamo veramente noi? Forse io lo sono solamente quando . . . " (81) [If we aren't open with those we love, those we live with day after day in the family, then whom are we open with? When are we really ourselves? Perhaps I'm only really myself when— (73)]. No answer to these questions will ever be provided in the journal, which will soon be interrupted.

Bought on the spur of the moment a day that Valeria had gone to purchase cigarettes for the men in her house, the diary finally encounters the same destiny as the cigarettes: it is reduced to ashes. In the last two chapters of *Donner le temps*, Derrida analyzes a prose poem by Baudelaire, "La fausse monnaie," whose inception is also characterized by the purchase of tobacco, which is seen as a particular form of gift, as the typical present given to oneself: "*Apparemment*, c'est l'objet d'une consommation pure et luxueuse . . . un plaisir qu'on *se donne* par la voie de l'ingestion la plus proche de l'auto-affection: la voix ou l'oralité. Plaisir dont il ne reste rien, plaisir dont les signes extérieurs mêmes se dissipent sans laisser de traces: en fumée. S'il y a du don—et surtout si on *se donne* quelque chose, quelque affect ou quelque plaisir pur, il peut donc avoir un rapport essentiel, au moins symbolique ou emblématique, avec l'autorisation qu'on se donne de fumer. Telle est du moins *l'apparence*. Elle reste à analyser"(138) [*Apparently*, it is the object of a pure and luxurious consumption . . . a pleasure one *gives oneself* through the ingestive channel that is closest to auto-affection: the voice or orality. A pleasure of which nothing remains, a pleasure even the external signs of which are dissipated without leaving a trace: in smoke. If there is some gift—and especially if one *gives oneself* something, some affect or some pure pleasure—it may then have an essential relation, at least a symbolic or emblematic one, with the authorization one gives oneself to smoke. That at least is how it *appears*. But this appearance remains to be analyzed (107)].

Smoking tobacco, Derrida stresses, can also be considered as "le temps de la femme" (134) [the time of woman (103)] for the astonishing reason that the smoking room is the place forbidden to women. Furthermore, the smoking room is also associated with phallogocentrism, since it is where men ". . . fument, ils pensent à la philosophie—et *par conséquent* à éviter les femmes" (135) [. . . are smoking, thinking about philosophy—and *consequently* about avoiding women (104)]. As a matter of fact, in *Quaderno proibito* smoking is an activity which is strictly considered male territory: while both Michele and Riccardo smoke with Valeria's approval, Mirella's addiction to tobacco comes to be judged as a transgressive and unbecoming habit. When Mirella offers a cigarette to Marina, Riccardo refuses it on behalf of his *fiancée*, assuming an extremely patronizing posture that purportedly bespeaks his contempt for the *fallen* sister: ". . . è entrata Mirella . . . indossava il cappotto rosso . . . ci siamo trattenuti un po' a discorrere e Riccardo accennava al futuro, spavaldamente, tenendo un braccio sulle spalle di Marina. Mirella ha tratto le sigarette dalla borsa e le ha offerte a Marina. Riccardo ha detto subito: Non fuma. Mirella ha acceso la sigaretta, tranquillamente, ma la fiamma tremava" (128) [". . . Mirella came in . . . she was wearing the red coat . . . we stayed chatting a moment and Riccardo talked boldly about the future, his arm across Marina's shoulders. Mirella took her cigarettes out of her handbag and offered them to Marina, and Riccardo said at once, "She doesn't smoke." Mirella lighted her cigarette calmly, but the flame trembled" (119)].

Valeria's purchase of the diary, then, can only appear as a bold attempt to resist phallogocentrism because keeping a diary implies, in fact, the presence of the pen, the medium of inscription which, like cigarettes, has a phallic connotation that makes it potentially unsettling when placed in the hands of a woman. When Valeria eventually renounces the pen, giving up on her doomed attempt to resist a hostile environment, she surrenders to the pressure that the phallogocentric society put on her. The ashes to which her gift is reduced become the testimonial of her sacrifice, as Derrida explains in a context related to tobacco: "L'annihilation des restes, les cendres peuvent parfois en témoigner, rappelle un pacte et fait acte de mémoire. On n'est jamais sûr qu'elle ne participe pas de l'offrande et du sacrifice" (144) [The annihilation of the remainder, as ashes can sometimes testify, recalls a pact and performs the role of memory. One is never sure that this annihilation does not partake of offering and of sacrifice (112)].

Considering that *Quaderno proibito* itself, as a narrative, stems from ashes, it is possible to evoke the argument presented by Derrida in *Feu la cendre*, where he sees *les cendres* as the traces of an "histoire à raconter, " a *story to be told.* "Mémoire perdue pour ce qui n'est plus d'ici (15) [a lost memory for what is no longer here, (31)], ashes, through their omnipressent reference to the prototype of the *woman-as-victim*, Cinderella, become the objective correlative of Valeria's condition after the destruction of the diary: ". . . l'article absent devant telle cendre,[8] en un mot la ressemblance esquissée par cet homophone là faisait trembler d'une femme le fantôme au fond du mot, dans la fumée, le nom propre au fond du nom commun. Le cendre n'est pas ici mais il y a là Cendre" (17) [. . . the article missing before such cinders, in a word, the resemblance sketched by this homophonic *là*, "there," made a feminine phantom tremble deep within the word, in the smoke, the proper name deep within the common noun. The cinder is not here, but Cinder there is (33)].

Being the product of fire, *feu*, which in French also means *deceased*, ashes assume in the Derridean interpretation an interesting connotation which perfectly applies to *Quaderno proibito*. Not only does fire evoke the passion that rejuvenated and, at the same time, consumed Valeria during her journal days, but it also symbolizes the untimely demise of her newly achieved independence. Several times, throughout the entire novel, the diary itself comes to be associated with fire and heat. Upon her return from the tobacconist where she just bought the black notebook, Valeria feels that she is suddenly blushing and her body is being invaded by a heat wave which almost betrays her secret misdeed: "Lo tenni sotto il cappotto lungo tutta la strada, fino a casa. Temevo che scivolasse, che cadesse in terra mentre la portiera mi raccontava non so che cosa della colonna del gas. Ero rossa in viso nell'aprire la porta con la chiave. . . . Mirella entrò, disse: 'Che hai, mammà? Sei tutta rossa in viso'. 'Sarà il cappotto' risposi togliendomelo: 'oggi è caldo fuori'. Mi pareva che potesse dirmi: 'non è vero, è perché hai nascosto qualcosa nel sacco'" (8–9) [All the way home I kept it under my coat. I was afraid it would slither down while the concierge was telling me something or other about the gas, and when I unlocked our front door I was scarlet in the face . . . Mirella came in. "What's the matter, Mamma?" she said. "You're all red in the face." "It must be my coat" I said, taking it off. "It's warm out today." I felt she might say, "That's not true. It's because you've hidden something in the rag bag" (2–3)]. At the very end of the novel, the diary once again appears as a source of heat, this time because of its potentially damaging content: "Sono andata in cucina e lì, subito, ho aperto la valigia: quando ne ho tratto il quaderno ero ansiosa di posarlo, come se scottasse" (246) [I went to the kitchen and there opened the bag at once; and when I had taken out the diary, I wanted to get rid of it as if it were on fire (239)].

When Derrida affirms that ". . . la cendre n'est pas, elle n'est pas ce qui est. Elle reste de ce qui n'est pas, pour ne rappeler au fond friable d'elle que non-être ou imprésence" (23) [the cinder is not, is not what is. It remains *from* what is not, in order to recall at the delicate, charred bottom of itself only non-being or non-presence (39)], he seems to be presenting Valeria's condition, her voluntary submission to a state of *imprésence*. When Valeria decides to burn her diary, in fact, she is virtually giving up on her interior life. She reenters the space of the derridean *oikos*, silencing her needs and dooming her existence to a blank future: "Questa sarà l'ultima pagina: in quelle seguenti non scrivero' e le mie giornate future saranno, come quelle pagine, bianche, lisce, fredde. Liscia sarà la grande pietra bianca sulla quale, alla fine, tornero' a chiamarmi Valeria. . . . Di tutto quanto ho sentito e vissuto in questi mesi, tra pochi minuti, non vi sarà più traccia. Rimarrà solo, attorno, un lieve odore di bruciato. " (257) [This will be the last page. I won't write on the pages beyond it and my future days will be, like them, white, smooth, and cold. Smooth will be the great stone on which in the end I will go back to being called Valeria . . . Of all I've felt and lived in these months, in a few minutes there will be no trace at all—only, around us, a faint smell of burning (249)].

While Valeria, the fictional narrator of the novel, believes she has left no traces of her writing and of her experiences, the reader is very much aware of the contrary: *Quaderno proibito*, the novel that incorporates her narrative, rises as a phoenix from the ashes of the burned diary. Ashes, the Derridean *restance* of Valeria's fictive diary, are thus placed, in the shape of a novel, in the hands of the reader, who is summoned to accept them as a gift. When De Céspedes delivers her novel to her readers, she cannot anticipate their reactions: once the book is out in the market, it is left to its own destiny, to a potential form of dissemination which is similar to the eventual dispersion of a bunch of ashes.

While in France, where she lived for many years, Alba De Céspedes was considered an Italian Simone De Beauvoir, in Italy her works have been mostly neglected by the critics, who classify them as mere popular fiction,[9] *narrativa femminile d'evasione*. What Kaplan defines as "the established patriarchal view that popular culture is a derided terrain . . . because it is the province of women and the domestic" (1992, 72) has certainly kept works such as *Quaderno proibito* away from the canon just because of their emphasis on two peculiar traits of the so-called *woman's novel:* emotionalism and the encouragement of the reader's identification with a single heroine. Such a derogatory judgement is combined with a critique which speaks the anxiety of the phallogocentric establishment through the dismissal of subversive elements usually present in women's writing: "the largely male critics . . . focused more on broadly defined bourgeois ideology about the family in general than on the . . . [work's] specific *female* address" (66). To this effect, it is worth analyzing one of the earliest reviews of *Quaderno proibito*, an article published in a Catholic periodical called *Vita e pensiero*. In an attempt to neutralize the novel's attacks on patriarchal hegemony, the reviewer procedes to undermine Mirella's political stance in the narration: "Mirella is a different type, with a stubborn little head who knows what it wants and wants what it thinks. Her little head is well set in her aims. What she says to her mother arrogantly and condescendingly, is rather common and pretty vulgar: you are still living in the nineteenth century (I wonder what they think they are saying!)" (Casorati 1953, 146, my translation). Her feminist rebellion is reduced, in his words, to the mere materialistic desires of a shameless social climber: "And to avoid a similar life, she works with a married man who drives her around in his car, who gives her a few luxurious presents, who is going to divorce, with whom she intends to run away and make a future. That's it" (147). While both Valeria and Mirella are seen as worthy only of the reviewer's pity, the former betrays a redeeming trait in her final return to the paternal *oikos:* "One feels sorry for both; but Valeria, left to her own good and healthy emotions, redeems herself when, hearing her son's anguishing news, she already feels like a jealous mother of the child who is to be born" (147). While Casorati's chauvinistic comments probably speak for themselves, it is worth noticing that, forty years after its publication, *Quaderno proibito* still remains a best-seller which has enjoyed more than twenty editions. Its success with the public undoubtedly derives from the fact that, like many other popular culture phenomena, "it touched something deep in the cultural unconscious" (Kaplan 1992, 91).

The paradoxical *envoi* of the novel, containing a statement that negates women's ultimate access to writing—"tutte le donne nascondono un quaderno proibito. E tutte debbono distruggerlo." (256) [Every woman hides a black notebook, a secret diary, and every woman must destroy it" (249)]—even though it contradicts itself through the actual presence of the diary in the shape of a published book, opens a dilemma for the critic. How is one supposed to interpret Valeria's final descent into silence? Where does *Quaderno proibito* fall in the distinction, drawn by Kaplan, between *complicit* and *resisting maternal texts* ? If the differentiation between the two categories rests on the fact that "narratives in the . . . complicit type may appear to be spoken from the woman's position, but this is soon revealed to be that of an uncritical patriarchal function . . . [while] . . . in the second [resisting] type of texts the position is still articulated within patriarchy . . . but it assumes a feminine desire, even if its expression is constantly repressed or thwarted," (1992, 91) then De Cespedes's novel, notwithstanding Valeria's final lapse into the realm of the Imaginary, certainly qualifies as a resisting narrative.

Prohibition lies at the core of the novel, and it most clearly applies to a phallogocentric stance against the threat that women writers pose to the system: all this is clearly stated by the title, *Quaderno proibito.* Jacques Derrida affirms that a title, constituting the border, the frame of the text, represents a space where the fictive narrative encounters the outside world, where fiction meets reality.[10] His argument that each title contains a double reference, referring, on one hand, to the fiction it represents and, on the other, to the external reality evoked by the words that compose it,[11] turns the words *Quaderno proibito* into the *locus* of an extraordinary contradiction. Indeed they relate to the content of the novel, while also referring to a hypothetical notebook whose perusal is forbidden. Prohibition, in this particular case, assumes different connotations: the reader is faced with (1) a private narrative which is not supposed to be in the public domain, a notebook which could almost be safeguarded in a folder which has an *off-limit* label guarding its disclosure; (2) the potential reading of a diary which constitutes a dangerous element that, due to its power to unsettle the structure of a paternalistic society, should be prohibited because of such a revolutionary message.

This last case, in particular, comes to assume far greater importance when juxtaposed to the conclusions drawn by Derrida on a similar issue. In *Donner le temps* Derrida argues that "La fausse monnaie" captures, in its abyssal potential, the essence of literature itself. Because literature is a particular form of counterfeit money, a fictive sign that roots its existence on its imitation of reality, "La fausse monnaie" becomes its metonymical representation.[12] Likewise, *Quaderno proibito* reenacts, in its fictive content, the censorship promoted against women writers by a phallogocentric society. The opening scene of the book, where the narrator recalls the purchase of her notebook, powerfully sustains such theory. The two men present in this scene embody two different forms of phallogocentric resistance to women's writing. While the policeman embodies the law, the panoptical *Law of the Father* which surveils women and denies them any sort of empowerment, the tobacconist represents the apparent authorization given by the powers that be: a woman has a right to write, on condition that she does it secretly. The hidden notebook thus becomes the objective correlative of a phallogocentric regime that forced eminent women writers such as George Eliot and the Brontës to write under a male pseudonym. Valeria's final renunciation, and her asserting the necessity that all women burn their diary, come across, then, as an even bleaker statement contradicted, however, by its appearance in print.

When all is said and done, *Quaderno proibito* comes to represent the mirror in which a generation of women readers has painfully recognized its *malaise.* Valeria, in a moment of emotional empathy with the writing process, recognizes that her words flow on the pages of the black notebook like that river of milk which is taken, a decade later, as a symbol of the *écriture feminine:* "aspetto con ansia quest'ora, per scrivere, per dare libero corso a un fiume ricco che scorre in me e che mi duole come quando avevo troppo latte" (250) [So I wait for this time when I can write, anxious to free a rich flood flowing in me that hurts me as it used to hurt when I had too much milk (242)]. Inside the framed borders of the novel, however, this milky river is eventually redirected towards a path that leads her back to her starting point, her cage, the constricting *oikos* where she will symbolically nurture her son's child. But de Céspedes's novel, the milk of which her own words are composed, takes a different direction: it reaches the same audience that might have inspired her writing. The epigraph to *Quaderno proibito*, borrowed from Ramón de la Cruz reads: "Señor don Blas, de qué libro / ha sacado usté ese texto? / / Del teatro de la vida / humana que es donde leo" (5) [Mr. Blas, from which book / did you take this text? / From the theater of human life / which is where (what) I read (my translation)]. *Both the author and his/her addressee are readers:* the novel is only the author's reading of another text, of that theatrical *pièce* called human life. There is more to *Quaderno proibito* than just an impassioned depiction of the devastating effects of phallogocentrism. Indeed, the texture that composes Valeria's narrative betrays the presence of many interwoven symbolic patterns through which fiction and reality mirror one another in an endless process of *mise-en-abîme.*

Tale of constriction, tale of attempted escape, *Quaderno proibito* powerfully composes a complex portrayal of the secluded condition of many Italian women of the 1950s. Furthermore, De Céspedes's novel re-presents a realistic *tableau* of a society which was slowly finding its way back after the devastation brought about by World War II. And in focusing on the specific lot which awaited those women who could only glimpse emancipation without actually foreseeing its very actualization, it paves the way to subsequent narratives. Narratives that sprung in the sixties, a decade that set in motion events that led to the most dramatic changes experienced by women during the twentieth century. Fictional journals authored by Doris Lessing, Dacia Maraini, and Simone de Beauvoir, analyzed in the following chapter, will bear witness to such events.

2

Neurotic Cassandras: Lessing, Maraini, Beauvoir, and Their "Crazy" Diaries From the Sixties

> Who are these women we admired so much? In the strange cultural landscape of 1960 they loomed up, Cassandras of women's experience, an experience that was everywhere silenced, concealed and denied . . . a generation of women—and men—ransacked their work for "truths" about the human condition, and, especially, for the truth about women. Yet their work aroused anger and hatred at the same time as they were idealized . . . to whom did they speak, secretly and silently? (Wilson 1993, 57)

With these powerful lines, Elizabeth Wilson opens "Yesterday's heroines: on rereading Lessing and de Beauvoir," a powerful analysis of the writings produced by the two eminent women writers. Authors of literary works which have been officially acknowledged as landmarks in the history of feminism, both Beauvoir and Lessing have captured, in their texts, the essence of women's condition in one of its darkest ages. During the sixties they produced some of their most refined works, describing in literary terms what Betty Friedan had identified in *The Feminine Mystique* (1963) as "the problem that has no name." Lessing's *The Golden Notebook* and Beauvoir's "La femme rompue" particularly addressed this issue in a most effective fashion. At the same time that their texts were being published with great acclaim, another woman writer, in Italy, was trying to confront similar questions without encountering the same success: Dacia Maraini.

Doris Lessing's work had received critical praise as early as in the fifties, when she published both *The Grass is Singing* (1950) and the first three of the five volumes that compose the cycle known as *Children of Violence.* The realism of her first novels had not prepared her readers, however, for the formidable example of postmodernism that she produced in 1962, *The Golden Notebook,* a book that eventually gained her worldwide fame. When Simone de Beauvoir published "La femme rompue" in installments in *Elle* in the fall of 1967, she was already famous for her groundbreaking treatise on the woman's condition, *Le deuxième sexe*, which had appeared in 1949. A leading intellectual of the existentialist movement, Beauvoir had also published, among other fictional and nonfictional works, *Les mandarins* (1954), a novel which became an instant classic.

Dacia Maraini, on the other hand, had started her career in the early sixties with a novel whose title perfectly described its period of publication, *L'età del malessere* (1962). The *malaise* she depicted in her novel was not only that of its adolescent protagonist, but that of an entire generation shaken by existentialist torment. Small was the following that Maraini's early production gained her, because little was the esteem that Italian readers and critics generally granted to women writers. As her writing took an experimental path, Maraini's fame grew dimmer and dimmer, only to be reestablished in the seventies, when the feminist movement finally made its presence felt in the land of phallogocentrism. *A memoria*, published in 1967, definitely stands out in Maraini's early production because of its innovative complexity, and because of its particular portrayal of the female condition.

Like *The Golden Notebook* and "La femme rompue," *A memoria* is both stylistically innovative and politically engaged. My analysis of these three works will show how Beauvoir, Maraini, and Lessing all chose to represent female anxiety in the sixties, the age of female *malaise*, through the symbolic depiction of different aspects of female neurosis.

The Golden Notebook by Doris Lessing

> After breakfast I took my shopping basket and walked along the Earl's Court Road. [. . .] Then I walked across the street into a stationer's shop, and went to a counter loaded with notebooks similar to these four I have. Yet they were not what I wanted. I saw a large thick book, rather expensive, and opened it, and it had good thick white paper, unlined. The paper was pleasant to touch, a little rough, but silky. It had a heavy cover, of dull gold. I had never seen a similar notebook, and I asked the assistant what it was manufactured for, and she said that an American customer had ordered it especially made for him, but had not come back for it. He had paid a deposit, so it wasn't as expensive as I expected it to be. Even so, it was expensive, but I wanted it, and I brought it home with me. (605)

Drawn to the purchase of a golden notebook by an unexplicable urge, Anna Wulf, the protagonist of Doris Lessing's *The Golden Notebook* (1962) reenacts the same scenario depicted at the inception of

De Céspedes's *Quaderno proibito.* Times have changed, however, and Lessing's text bears no trace of the obstacles encountered by Valeria on her way to the acquisition of the black and shiny *quaderno.* Instead of opposing resistance to Anna's desire to buy the notebook, the stationer actually quotes a discount on its price, a discount prompted by the incongruous behavior of a male customer, for whom the golden notebook had been originally manufactured. In a different decade, in a decade where women are slowly starting to take stock of their lives, those same women can come to profit from the mistakes of their male counterparts. The same authoritative figure who seemed to deny Valeria her right to write, now willingly seems to be granting it to Anna, if only because a distracted man has apparently withdrawn his bid to the same right, out of sheer carelessness. Unlike Valeria, the Italian frustrated housewife who takes up writing as a clandestine venture, Anna is a woman whose writing has been publicly acknowledged. Both women buy notebooks to turn them into diaries but, while Valeria's purchase of the *forbidden copybook* marks the beginning of her diaristic effort, Anna's decision to buy the golden notebook is a prelude to the end of the same activity. Intended to substitute the four notebooks that have been keeping track of her life and thoughts, this fifth journal eventually leads Anna to abandon diary writing in favor of a new enterprise, the composition of her second novel.

Divided in five segments, a potential version of Anna's novel, called "Free Women," is alternated to sections of the five notebooks she keeps. Two parallel narratives are thus established since the beginning of *The Golden Notebook.* A short realist novel written in the third person is juxtaposed to fragmented entries of notebooks, transcribed in a first-person narrative voice which changes its register and its intent as it moves from one journal to the other. At first, both narratives seem to be focusing on the same story, presenting it through different lenses, alternating the so-called objectivity of the realist novel with the more subjective perspective which underlies diary writing. However, as the book progresses, consistent differences in their plots reveal their independent status. Be it Anna's fictional adaptation of her recent past or an altogether differently authored narrative, "Free Women" still enacts an effective counterpoint to the presentation of similar events as portrayed in Anna's notebooks.[1]

The story of Anna Freeman Wulf slowly unravels in the pages of Lessing's novel. A British Left-wing writer who spends her youth in central Africa, where she is part of a Communist clique, Anna Freeman gets married to a member of the revolutionary group, Max Wulf, and has a child by him, Janet. A divorce soon follows, and, upon her return to England, Anna joins the British Communist Party, which she subsequently abandons. With her friend Molly she shares much more than political commitment and disillusion: like Anna, Molly is a "free woman," married and divorced, mother of a rebellious and tormented young man, Tommy. Author of *Frontiers of War*, a successful novel based on her stay in Africa, Anna lives off its royalties while struggling with a writing block, which leads her into therapy with a Jungian analyst whose approach she strenuously critiques. The end of a long affair with a Czech refugee, Michael, leaves her shattered, marking the beginning of her breakdown. With Janet gone to boarding school, the Communist Party eventually abandoned, her friendship with Molly slowly withering away, Anna is now free to experience her descent into hell, a descent she undergoes with her new lover, Saul Green, an American writer who suffers from a serious case of schizophrenia. Their long trip into darkness comes to an end as they finally realize the common necessity to resume writing: bestowing on each other the "gift of writing" by composing each other's first line of their new novels, Anna and Saul finally part. Paradoxically enough, the line suggested by Saul, "The two women were alone in the London flat."[2] coincides with the beginning of "Free Women,"[3] the conventional novel whose sections have been interspersed throughout the entire book. Opening Lessing's novel with its first section, and thus with the line just quoted, "Free Women" acts as a veritable frame to the text, closing *The Golden Notebook* with a section that ends on the line: "The two women kissed and separated" (666). A comment on the enigmatic nature of postmodern writing, *The Golden Notebook* thus leaves the reader pondering on the causes and effects of the circularity of its narratives, the interwoven nature of which comes to be inevitably questioned.[4]

Five notebooks and a short novel: all these elements combined come to constitute the bulk of Lessing's masterpiece, a work by now established as "a talismanic production of the decade in which it was published, whose moral debates it both anticipates and confirms" (Fullbrook 1990, 155). Divided by color, the notebooks are initially only four: black, red, yellow, and blue. In the black notebook Anna talks about herself as writer, in the red notebook she addresses her life as political activist, in the yellow notebook she writes short stories inspired by real life events, while the blue notebook is her real diary. Witnessing Anna's desire to keep things separate, the four notebooks are meant to represent her own attempt to fend off the chaos of the contemporary world. With her breakdown, however, all fences come crashing down: those divisions, barriers she has surreptitiously built in order to stay sane, eventually tumble down, "I could feel that the walls of myself were thin or in danger" (477). Enter, then, the golden notebook, the fifth diary in which unity is finally achieved, if only on a superficial level. The other four notebooks left aside, Anna decides to keep only one diary, facing the chaos she dreaded for so long, "I'll start a new notebook, all of myself in one book" (607). And the darkest stages of her descent into madness eventually come to be represented in this fifth journal. Its unlined, unruled paper is a reminder of its potential to contain the inscription of chaos without the artificial imposition of order that Anna compulsively needed in her previous diaristic experiment. As breakdown slowly turns into breakthrough, it actually evolves into a disruption of boundaries, into a collapse of those same distinctions that, while safeguarding Anna's sanity, were also keeping her away from the epiphanic revelations brought about by the Shakespearean "reason in madness."

While breakdown certainly stands out as the main theme of Lessing's novel, to the extent that the author herself felt the need to stress it in her 1971 preface,[5] another textual strand intimately related to it, that of separation, deserves critical attention. The color bar, the class bar, the social bar that divides the intellectual from the masses, gender division, division of genres, division of notebooks, the division that separates an author from its literary creation, the division that separates language from truth, the divided self: apparently different yet thematically related, each split leads into the other. This way, Lessing weaves her postmodern web, which holds the reader captive as it unveils the many "degrees of separation" that pervade the society she sets out to describe.

The black notebook, poignantly entitled "The dark," is dedicated to Anna's first novel, *Frontiers of War*, in which her long experience in Africa is rewritten through nostalgic eyes. As the romanticization of the material turns the book into a successful commercial venture, idealistic Anna starts feeling that her memories have lost that quality of truthfulness which could have made them less appetizing to the capitalistic market. In the black notebook, the pages of which are split in half, one section headed *Source*, the other headed *Money* (57), she records both her own attempt to recapture the true essence of her African memories and the many attempts, made by people in the show business, at a further commercialization of her novel. Over and over, she finds herself forced to reject ludicrous proposals for the adaptation of *Frontiers of War*, because of the adaptors' blatant dismissal of the political content of the novel. Over and over, she finds herself questioning the true nature of her African memories, memories which seem to lose their objectivity once they are put down on paper (153). As she sets out to recuperate the truth in writing, Anna comes to face the limits of linguistic representation, thus encountering a dramatic split, that between language and the world it is called to portray. Language and its slippery nature again come to be questioned when, attempting to describe an old acquaintance, Anna resorts to terms that she inherently despises, because of their nonreferential quality: "I've thought about that often since. I mean, about the word nice. Perhaps I mean good. Of course they mean nothing, when you start to think about them. A good man, one says; a good woman; a nice man, a nice woman. Only in talk of course, these are not words you'd use in a novel. I'd be careful not to use them. . . . And so I'll write again that George was a good man" (109–10). Once words like "good" and "nice" start betraying their abstract nature, the entire language, with them, becomes subject to a revision. All the premises are laid for the more drastic questioning of the role of fiction, by convention based on principles of characterization, principles that have lost their effectiveness if words can no longer fulfill their denotative role.

Anna's narrative, centering on the activities of the Marxist circle in which she operates during her days in central Africa, dwells on the color bar as well as on another bar, that which separates intellectuals from both the black working class and white capitalists. Incomprehension reigns within and among the three social groups: Anna's story appears more as a tale of friction and suffering than as a nostalgic *remembrance of things past.* What seems most relevant, for the purpose of my analysis, is the extent to which racial and class tensions come to be projected onto another sphere, that of gender. When Willi, the fictional counterpart of Anna's former husband, expounds on the necessity to restrain the temper of a "difficult" woman, he adopts a language that is highly charged with racial overtones. He maintains that the woman deserves "a good hiding," a derogatory phrase usually adopted by Colonialists when discussing their intent to educate the "natives." Anna's attempt to neutralize the reactionary potential of such linguistic terms by dismissing their usage as Willi's innocuous appropriation "for general use" and by confining their etymological explanation in parentheses is quite striking: "(The 'good hiding' was a Colonial phrase . . . but Willi had appropriated it for general use)" (98). Intellectually patronized by the chauvinism still present in the *progressive* minds of her Marxist friends, Anna shares the burden of such a treatment with her friend Maryrose, a woman who offers uncommon resistance to political jargon, a traditional instrument of male empowerment. Refusing to partake of a linguistic code that bespeaks phallogocentric elitism, Maryrose eventually succumbs to silence and Anna voices no complaint on her behalf. In public, both characters are almost forced to acknowledge their inferiority, and only the smile that they exchange in private betrays a common understanding, the common realization that they would need to oppose some form of passive resistance: "She was sitting near me, and she turned her head in the dark of the car to smile at me" (91). The two women who exchange a smile in the dark, in a darkness that symbolically reveals their subdued condition, are women whose political voices were silenced in the name of their beauty. In this respect, both Maryrose and Anna are sisters of Dante's Beatrice: like her, they are turned from thinking souls into ethereal, and silent, angels. Similar words to those addressed to Maryrose are also directed at Anna: "'Anna,' he said, or chanted. 'Anna, beautiful Anna, absurd Anna, mad Anna, our consolation in the wilderness, Anna of the tolerantly amused black eyes'" (120), and Anna can only feel misread, misunderstood, almost mutilated by such statements. Having to partake of the same destiny that befalls the other women of the colony, the female members of the revolutionary intelligentsia submit to a social code that demands their reduction to passive objects of desire. What separates them is the degree of awareness of their own condition. When young June Boothby, the daughter of the owner of the Hotel Mashopi, finally reaches puberty, it becomes a duty of these women to shelter her from the aggression of men who could take advantage of her sudden restlessness, or make of her a laughingstock, ". . . we wanted to protect her from their laughter. . . . There is a female chivalry, woman for woman, as strong as any other kind of loyalty" (96–97).

Split being the nature of communist organizations, *separated* being Anna's group from Africa and Africans, *discriminated against* being the condition of women who lived by the Marxist dogma, Anna's black notebook can only appear as a dark, bleak statement on a status quo of division, entrenchment and stagnation . . . all to be taken up again in her next notebook, entirely dedicated to, and named after "The British Communist Party."

The struggle to keep chaos off the pages of this notebook is not as evident from its inception as it was in the black one, where Anna's first entry followed "doodlings, scattered musical symbols, treble signs that shifted into the £ sign and back again; then a complicated design of interlocking circles" (56).[6] The black notebook, dealing with art, memory, and nostalgia for a world she has left behind, covers an area of Anna's life that is deeply tormented and unclear. Less chaotic, colored by a different kind of ambiguity, is the tie that binds her to Marxist ideology and to the British Communist Party. Anna's entries on the notebook date from the fifties, a period of extreme unrest for Communists all over the world. During this period, the Cold War reaches its climax, the Rosenbergs are tried and electrocuted for state treason, the first H-bombs are being experimented with, McCarthy keeps conducting his ruthless witch-hunt and Americans leave their country and take refuge all over Europe. But most of all, faith in communism is being shaken by the Prague trial, the Soviet invasion of Hungary and the official acknowledgement, during the Twentieth Party Congress, of the cruelty of the Stalinist regime. The early entries, concentrating on Anna's doubts regarding her real commitment to Communism, unexpectedly lead to her decision to join the party at a moment when many people are leaving it out of disillusionment. She joins the party in spite of her closeness to the sufferings of her lover Michael, whose beliefs have been shattered by the Soviet conduct in his home country. She does it out of a desire to regain a lost sense of unity, "I came home thinking that somewhere at the back of my mind when I joined the Party was a need for wholeness, for an end to the split, divided, unsatisfactory way we all live. Yet joining the Party intensified the split . . ." (161). The split, the same sense of separation and isolation do not disappear, however, as she becomes a member of the CP, and her only solace lies in the social work she conducts while canvassing the streets of suburban London for the upcoming elections. In her door-to-door service, Anna comes to learn what hides behind the closed doors of many a gray suburban home: a world of female disempowerment is suddenly disclosed, a world of extreme poverty and disillusion, a "country . . . full of women going mad all by themselves" (167). As this other form of dispossession comes to the fore, it immediately monopolizes Anna's attention: most of her red notebook will be dedicated to the unhappy lives of these women. It is quite striking how, even when it reaches its most political heights, Lessing's novel never fails to operate a thematic connection between collective and individual issues, issues which always, somehow, refer back to women's condition. The day Stalin dies, Anna shares her disquieting pain with her friend Molly. Still in awe of the ruthless dictator, she comes to the realization that Stalin represented the "great man" every woman needs to have in her life, the man whose *greatness* remains intact even after his questionable actions are unveiled. And Anna's thoughts on Stalin perfectly apply to her personal involvement with past and present lovers, Max, Michael, or Saul. In the yellow notebook, which contains a sketch of a new novel, "The Shadow of the Third," such line of reasoning becomes even clearer as Anna's mouthpiece, Ella, takes a very similar stand. When Ella gets dumped by her lover Paul, a figure who is strikingly similar to Michael, Anna realizes how both women have brought on themselves the failure of their relationships because of their tendency to let their partners, the "great men" they have created, "put their intelligence to sleep,"

> And yet I, Anna, like Ella with Paul, refused to see it. Paul gave birth to Ella, the naïve Ella. He destroyed in her the knowing, doubting, sophisticated Ella and again he put her intelligence to sleep, and with her willing connivance. (211)

Much has been written about the similarities between Anna and Ella: both of them leave their husbands after giving birth to a child, both of them have a strong friendship with another woman, both of them write novels, both of them break down after an intense affair with a "witch-doctor." In *Rereading Doris Lessing: Narrative Patterns of Doubling and Repetition*, Claire Sprague grounds her analysis of *The Golden Notebook* on the figure of the double, the Conradian "secret sharer" who appears repeatedly throughout Lessing's fiction: "I should like to suggest an additional way of defining the merging and separation of characters in *The Golden Notebook*, one that proposes these permeable selves as another structural pattern that works effectively and together with the narrative pattern. In other words, structure inheres in the disposition of protagonists as much as in the collision and interweaving of the five notebooks and the Free Women sections" (1987, 66–67). Molly Hite, however, discourages such reductive moves, claiming that Ella should be analyzed as an independent character: "Anna's and Ella's stories invite comparisons with, rather than reduction to, one another . . . it is often hard to naturalize Ella's experiences as Anna's inventions or projections. Ella's life seems as detailed, as absorbing, and ultimately as important as Anna's" (1989, 83). Depicted, at some point, as a failed projection of her author, Ella seems to demand her own independence from Anna: "I see Ella, walking slowly about a big empty room, thinking, waiting. I, Anna, see Ella. Who is, of course, Anna. But that is the point, for she is not. The moment I, Anna, write: Ella rings up Julia to announce, etc., then Ella floats away from me and becomes someone else" (458). At the same time, though, the name *Ella* acts as a powerful reference to the "motive of the *third*," which pervades Anna's novel to the extent that it figures in its title. The equivalent, in Italian, of the subject pronoun *she*, the word "ella" *evokes* the figure of the third, personifying in Lessing's novel Anna's alienated self. It powerfully symbolizes Anna's attempt to analyze her own life through the projection of her fears and sufferings onto someone else, onto an idealized figure[7] representing "the woman altogether better than I was" (637). It is from this perspective, then, that Anna's creative writing comes to be understood, by analogy, as springing from the same source as Ella's, who describes her novels as the product of intense soul-searching, as the actual transcription of something that was deep inside of her (174).

Writing for a counseling column in a women's magazine, Ella comes to face, like her creator, the daily misery of the female population. Lonely, dissatisfied, and frustrated, the many women who write to Ella are only one step away from breaking down, and try to fend off depression and chaos through compulsive shopping or ill-directed charity work. The knowledge that she is somehow conducting an unconventional sort of social work keeps Ella at her workdesk, within an institution that, however, she rejects because of its empty trend-setting activity. Enslavement to fashion, recycling of sterile clichés, exhortation to dangerous daydreaming . . . these are the weaknesses of a women's magazine, the same weaknesses that Lessing will later denounce in *The Diaries of Jane Somers*.

As Anna inevitably faces the advent of her breakdown, so does Ella, and for similar motives. The writing of crisis takes the shape of fragment, at least in the yellow notebook: words fail their task as they are summoned to depict the extreme end of alienation: Ella retreats into silence as her creator sets out to explore the world of insanity. The blue notebook, which is meant to act as a "private journal," witnesses Anna's struggle with psychoanalysis and with mental sanity. Its color suggestively evokes "the blues," a constitutional sadness, a tormented condition that pervades its owner. Many of her sessions with a Jungian therapist, Mrs. Marks, are described in minute details, and include Anna's frequent complaints against a method of analysis that reduces personal experience to archetypes and myths. In resisting her therapy, Anna voices the importance of her own being-in-time, of her own belonging to a particular period in time, a period of unparalleled crisis. And that crisis invests not only the individual but also the world at large. A different woman, a new woman, a "free woman," Anna feels like she is treading on uncharted territories for women (472). Later in the notebook, in the midst of her breakdown, she identifies herself as embodying "the position of women in our time" (579). The entire notebook appears to be dealing with questions of time: dates are carefully reported throughout most of the diary, but they are suddenly interrupted when the crisis becomes extreme, in a symbolic strengthening of the descent into timelessness that the breakdown entails. Two different conceptions of time are juxtaposed as Anna sets out to transcribe, in its most minute details, an entire day of her life, the day in which she abandons the CP, Michael finally leaves her, and, last but not least, she gets her menstruation. As the impossibility of registering conventional time soon becomes evident, however, another time finds its unexpected inscription: her biological time, woman's time, "I realise my period has caught up with me" (359). Evidence of a vulnerability that Anna prefers to repress, her menstruation is described as the bleeding of "the wound inside my body which I didn't choose to have," (365) a wound against which she voices her resentment. Resentment, the reader learns in the same entry, is part of women's condition: "I learned that the resentment, the anger, is impersonal. It is the disease of women in our time. I can see it in women's faces, their voices, every day, or in the letters that come to the office. The woman's emotion: resentment against injustice, an impersonal poison. The unlucky ones, who do not know it is impersonal, turn it against their men. The lucky ones like me—fight it. It is a tiring fight" (333). Anna's luck derives from the fact that she is a *free woman*, and, like all the free women that populate Lessing's fictional universe, she is granted a kind of awareness that escaped women from previous generations. About this issue, Fullbrook knowingly argues that

> Lessing's women find themselves in positions where they have been persuaded to think of themselves as creatures of a personal, private realm, free to pursue individual happiness at a time when many of the familial and sexual imperatives that have traditionally structured women's lives are dissolving. . . . In Lessing's work, the change has happened and the women have no choice but to come to some kind of terms with it. As the women characters shed parents, husbands, lovers, children, take up jobs, work in politics and in the arts, as they move, in short, into the kinds of autonomy and self-definition that women writers earlier in the century had so strenuously claimed as needs for women, they confront new problems, new aspects of bondage and unease. . . . As they live through the historical dissolution of their traditional roles they confront central questions of liberty, responsibility and happiness with fresh eyes, and with no guidelines to hand. (1990, 147)

Once her affair with Michael is over, Anna has a few flings with other men, who all seem to be reacting in peculiar ways to the loosening of the ties that used to bind women to old moral codes. Either accused of being a castrating witch or treated as object of sadistic games, Anna, the new woman, threatens the virility of her lovers. Rarely, if ever, is her writing acknowledged as a positive achievement: be it dismissed or begrudged, it still becomes the object of male contempt, a form of contempt which hides, however, a constant fear of castration at the hands of the woman who holds the pen. When Saul, another blocked writer, enters her life, Anna is still in the midst of her writing paralysis, which has been further propelled by the lack of self-esteem brought about by previous frustrating encounters. As they guide each other through their breakdown, however, both Anna and Saul eventually overcome their temporary impairment and resurface *with a tale to tell.* The inner golden notebook, which testifies to the crashing of the artificial barriers that compartmentalized Anna's life, contains the haunting narration of most of their breakdown, during which they experience the world in the absence of boundaries. In their hallucinatory dreams, they overcome gender, race, and class boundaries, reemerging from their all-encompassing delirium with a new awareness, the awareness of the limits of human perspective on life. Conscious that their linguistic tools and their subjective outlook on life will never enable them to portray "truth" in its multifaceted essence, they still feel compelled to follow their "call" in life, believing that their writing will eventually save them (638). As Anna initially laments her inability to resume writing, Saul exhorts her to flesh out the story she has been recently considering, "a short story: or a short novel: comic and ironic: A woman, appalled by her capacity for surrendering herself to a man, determines to free herself" (636). It is a gloomy story that emphasizes the drawbacks of women's freedom while actually commenting on women's actual "unfree" state. And its first line, suggested by Saul, coincides with the opening line of "Free Women," the short novel present in Lessing's text, a novel which actually offers a bleak portrayal of female freedom.[8] What mostly distinguishes "Free Women" from the notebooks is the different emphasis placed, in the narration, on outer and inner "events." While the notebooks, especially the blue one, concentrate on Anna's tormented journey through crisis and madness, the short novel mainly focuses on Anna's relationship with Molly, projecting the same tensions onto her environment. Little space is allotted to the description of Anna's breakdown, which ends upon her encounter with Milt, a man who, unlike Saul, does not act as her "partner in torment." It is Molly's son, Tommy, who plays a central role in "Free Women," a role that becomes particularly important once his suicide attempt impairs his sight. Prey to existentialist angst, Tommy is initially presented as a young man caught as a pawn in the intense struggle between a capitalist father and a communist mother. His face betrays his torment, he has "the look of being buttoned in, a prisoner of his own nature" (33). Like so many of his contemporaries, he has learned to repress emotions: later in the novel, Anna refers to the universal quality of this *malaise* by adopting similar terms to those which defined Tommy's appearance when describing her own generation: "That's what's wrong with us all. All our strongest emotions are buttoned up, one after another" (625). Expecting some sort of oracular revelation from Anna, who should explain to him the "meaning of life," Tommy reads the woman's notebooks, and the knowledge he derives from them drives him to attempt suicide. Alive but blind, Tommy seems to have finally achieved peace and stability,[9] yet his already haunting presence becomes even more overbearing as he wanders about his mother's house silently controlling, with eyes that cannot see, all its inhabitants. During one of her visits to Molly, Anna describes Tommy's haunting presence in acute details:

> The two women went up to the room that had been Molly's bedroom, and was now a sort of bed-sitting-room. There they sat, thinking in spite of themselves of the mutilated boy just below them, who was now the centre of the house, dominating it, conscious of everything that went on in it, a blind but all-conscious presence. (377)

Installed at the very heart of the house, from which he exerts his position of silent watchdog, Tommy seems to be depicted as the guardian of Jeffrey Bentham's *panopticon*, the powerful instrument of social surveillance analyzed by Michel Foucault in *Surveiller et punir* (1975). As they sit uncomfortably in Molly's bedroom, the two women feel the encumbering presence of the boy's dark stare, which subtly conditions their behavior. According to Foucault, "All that is then needed is to put an overseer in the tower and place in each of the cells a lunatic, a patient, a convict, a worker or a schoolboy" (200). Like the madman, the patient or the schoolboy, Lessing's Anna and Molly feel the restraining power of the panoptical stare. As the panoptical structure, translated into a wider discourse, acts as "generalizable model of functioning; a way of defining power relations in terms of the everyday life of men" (205) Tommy's inquisitive, yet blank stare establishes itself as a metaphor for phallocentric patronization of women. However, the sightless gaze acts as a symbol of male inability to "see" properly, a quality which seems to pertain to all the male characters of Lessing's novel, all stereotypical in their close-mindedness. His impaired vision forbids him to "comprehend" what he sees, he remains a victim of his own "mutilation," a mutilation which is not only physical, but also metaphoric, the loss of sight being considered as a metaphor for castration, as Freud amply demonstrated in "Das Unheimliche" (1919). Should Tommy's blindness be seen as a form of emasculation, then the "scene of castration" would be represented by his reading of the notebooks; brought about by Anna's penmanship, his impairment comes to actualize the threat represented by women's writing. Yet, from "Free Women" the reader learns that Tommy represents a far more threatening presence than Anna does: it is she who feels "exposed" while the boy is going through her notebook, her writing metonymically turning into her body, vulnerably laid in front of the male voyeur. His gaze first focuses on the notebooks, "She saw him turn his heavy head on the pivot of his thick short neck and look at her notebooks lying *exposed* on the trestle . . . " (264, emphasis mine) yet soon it is Anna who is "exposed," and, as the feeling of "exposure" shifts from writing to the female body, Tommy's frenzied perusal of the notebooks comes to be described as a metaphoric rape:

> Anna sat still, terribly exposed, forcing herself into immobility. She was suffering, remembering the intimacy of what she had written. And he read on and on, in a stubborn fever, while she simply sat there. Then she felt herself go into a kind of stupor of exhaustion, and thought vaguely: Well, what does it matter? If this is what he needs, then what does it matter what I feel? (272)

Tommy's fever is contrasted to Anna's stupor, she is paralyzed by his actions, standing aghast as he violates the privacy of her diaries. Abandoned to her emotional exhaustion, she acts as a rape victim, opposing no more resistance to her aggressor, and withdrawing into silent stupor. Tommy's attempted suicide, and his blindness, then, could be read, under this perspective, as the just penance for his misdeed.

In the inner golden notebook, another man happens to look at Anna's notebook: Saul Green. When he inquires, as Tommy did, on the reason why Anna keeps four notebooks, he understands what Anna means when she answers, "Obviously, because it's been necessary to split myself up" (598), because he shares her alienation. Like her, he keeps diaries that eventually become the objects of Anna's perusal: as she looks through his notebooks, Anna is searching for clues that will lead her to understand Saul better. Saul, however, has preempted Anna's move by keeping a journal in which he only inscribes lies: the impossible task of capturing truth in writing, the already discussed fallacy of representation comes again to the fore through Saul's parodically transgressive act. It is Saul, the writer of the anti-diary, who eventually tells Anna that she should leave the journal practice aside: "Instead of making a record of my sins in your diary, why don't you write another novel?" (604) Writing should be directed outwards, it should not be a self-serving habit, and that would only be accomplished by writing a new novel. The exchange of a first gift, that of the first line of their new novels, is accompanied by a second gift, that of the golden notebook, eventually offered by Anna to Saul. Saul is the first to bestow "the gift of writing" and the temptation to read such a move in Derridean terms is practically irresistible: is writing going to be a remedy, is it going to save Anna from madness? Or is it actually doomed to act as a poison, dragging her further down in despair? And is Anna, by surrendering her precious golden notebook, that which gives the name to the entire novel, actually giving all of herself in return for the *pharmakon?* These and other questions remain in the mind of the reader as s/he confronts the many splits that will lead to new and challenging interpretations of a text destined to puzzle entire generations of readers with its complex portrayal of Anna Freeman Wulf, "a woman inside time" (584), Lessing's haunting representation of the "free woman" of the sixties.

A memoria by Dacia Maraini

> 8 dicembre
> "Sai da quanti anni siamo sposati?" "Da otto. Perché?" "Siamo sposati da otto anni." "Da quanto?" "Da otto anni." "Sono molti." "Troppi?" "No. Sono giusti." "Che vuol dire giusti?" "Sono quelli che sono. Né troppi né pochi." "Siamo sposati da quasi sei anni." "Sono sei anni che siamo sposati?" "Quasi." "Sono molti." "Troppi?" "No. Sono giusti." "Cosa vuol dire giusti?" "Che vanno bene cosí." "Fra un mese saranno dieci." "Dieci cosa?" "Dieci anni che siamo sposati." (7–8)
>
> [December 8. "Do you know how long we've been married?" "Eight years. Why?" "We've been married for eight years." "For how long?" "Eight years." "That's a lot." "Too long?" "No. It's a fair amount of time." "What does fair mean?" "That it's just what it is. Not too much, not too little." "We've been married for almost six years." "Have we been married for six years?" "Almost." "That's a lot." "Too long?" " No. That's a fair amount of time." "What does fair mean?" "That it's fine as it is." "In a month, it will be ten." "Ten what?" "Ten years that we've been married."][10]

The stychmomythic lines exchanged by Maria and Pietro at the inception of Dacia Maraini's *A memoria* (1967) immediately introduce the reader to a fictional world ruled by contradiction, alienation and, most of all, forgetfulness. Maria, who soon thereafter comes to be identified as the diarist, is a woman suffering from an uncommon form of mental disease: dysmnesia, lack of social memory.[11] As a consequence, she seems to have lost self-consciousness, not being able to link the past with the present, or to make any form of rational connection. Deprived of the knowledge that lies at the basis of cultural, intellectual, or affective life, Maria appears as a robotic creature exclusively driven by instincts. In her journal she transcribes conversations coldly, without specifying the interlocutors, or she mechanically registers her daily activities, always as though from the outside, and usually in a contradictory fashion. Such bizarre diary entries are also punctuated by the interspersion of a series of letters she receives from Giacomo, her husband Pietro's colleague who, while disguising himself as Pietro's best friend and admirer, desperately attempts to seduce her. In the five months covered by the journal, the reader witnesses a series of events that culminate in the death of both protagonists preceded by Pietro's long agony caused by cancer of the bowels. While her husband is still alive and suffering, Maria goes from one adulterous encounter to another, always playing the role of the temptress with young men that she picks up during her aimless wandering in the streets of Rome. Soon after her husband's untimely demise, however, Maria suddenly withdraws from the world, as if deprived of her only reason for existing: her former restlessness is replaced, in the last few entries of her diary, by the impossibility of leaving what becomes, in a short amount of time, her deathbed. A handful of characters revolves around the singular *ménage* established by Maria and Pietro. Giacomo plays the third cusp in an impossible triangle, voicing lustful craving for Maria while betraying a latent homosexual desire for Pietro. On the borders of this triangle lie three uncommon families: three mothers uncannily characterized by a voracious hunger, two greedy siblings, Pietro's brother Davide, and Giacomo's sister, nicknamed *la piattola*, the leech. There are no fathers, since both Maria's and Giacomo's are dead while Pietro's hardly ever makes his presence felt.

What immediately strikes the reader upon the completion of the novel is the rigid differentiation between male and female characters: prisoners of their bodies, women are all instincts and voracity, from Maria's uncontrollable sexual drives to the intimately related ferocious desire for food of the three mothers. On the other hand, intellectual speculation appears to fall entirely in the male domain: both of them high school teachers, Pietro and Giacomo are the only characters who seem to be endowed with the ability to think. Such a contrast comes to be established in the novel since its beginning, with Pietro's reiterated claim that he can remember everything of his past, "Io invece ricordo tutto" [I remember everything, instead] (20) in response to Maria's often repeated "Non ricordo niente" [I don't remember anything] (20).

Maria's mental condition assume symbolic overtones, especially when her behavior is analyzed in light of statements made by Maraini in an interview published in *diacritics*. Asked by the interviewer if the present period could be considered as a time of transition for women, Maraini said that "It's a change from *preistoria* to *storia*.[12] . . . *Preistoria* is characterized by an unconsciousness: letting yourself live, living by instinct, or even by reason, but a reason fairly well closed up in that particular moment. Instead, the characteristic of *storia* is reflecting on yourself at the moment you're living, while you look at yourself live. This is *storia*, which is a continuity of memory. *Preistoria* is, precisely, outside of *storia*. Its day is sufficient unto itself; it has no memory. Women are entering *storia* in our era" (Anderlini 1991, 159).

Written in 1967, *A memoria* portrays women's *preistoria*, since it was penned before the official advent of feminism in Italy. Indeed, while writing in her diary, Maria, the woman with *no memory*, does not reflect on her actions, merely transcribing them as if they had been accomplished by somebody else. In order to show such detachment in the most effective way, Maraini adopts the technique *du régard*, the peculiar trait of the French *nouveau roman*. Maria's daily actions are described with extreme precision by an I/eye that is only concerned with external mechanics, an I/eye which hardly ever contemplates the possibility of enriching writing with any sort of psychological nuance. In an effort to render reality in the most meticulous fashion, the description often turns on itself, accruing and changing some of the details. While the descriptive journal entries certainly bring to mind the *nouveau roman* as practiced by Alain Robbe-Grillet, the passages exclusively devoted to conversations employ stylistic devices borrowed from the *nouveau roman* as practiced by Nathalie Sarraute. Indeed, different dialogues are interwoven in these scenes, and *conversation* and *sous-conversation*, typical elements of the Sarrautian novel, come to be juxtaposed; no information is provided about the identity of the interlocutors, who, at times, remain anonymous throughout the entire passage. No room is allotted to the inscription of their impressions, they have no depth, they are all surface.

Among the many novels written by Maraini, *A memoria* is certainly the only one that has been consistently avoided by the critics because of its utmost obscurity. Impossible even to summarize, this book seems to reject critical exegesis. No explanation of the events is ever provided, the entire novel seems to be wrapped into a veil of mystery and of silence that bespeaks the deep sense of despair that subtly pervades it.

In this book, the harshly realistic quality of Maraini's writing is intimately related to an avantgardistic project that attempts to depict reality in its incomprehensibility, in its disorder, in its innate contradiction. Maraini herself will comment:

> Paradoxically, it was, above all, the avant-garde that proposed new forms of naturalism. . . . Today's naturalism . . . uncritically mimics a reality that has become incomprehensible. A senseless world that produces in its observers those effects of malaise, of loss, of delirium that are considered essential for the modern artist.
>
> But we're still talking about naturalism. About abstaining from moral and political judgment. The writer, in brief, declines to intervene upon narrative matter, declines to offer a subjective angle on things. He limits himself to giving back the disorder, as is. His work consists in miming, through verbal and syntactic irregularity, the irregularity of the real. (1987, 34–35)

The presence of Robbe-Grillet and Sarraute is powerfully evoked in these haunting statements, along with that of another master of western modernism, Samuel Beckett. *Waiting for Godot* (1952), *Endgame* (1957), and many other of his works, patently resist any interpretation, "no concessions are made to the comfort of readers, in terms both of form and of the conventional consolation of fiction" (Alexander 1990, 54), and what the readers face is thus a most unusual confrontation with a work of art which stems from profound existential despair. Maria and Pietro's stychmomythic exchanges are potent reminders of Vladimir and Estragon's endless conversations, which are both dramatic and comic at the same time, and which constantly repeat themselves without ever achieving proper closure. Instead of reaching a climactic stage, these conversations only spiral down into silence, in the same way that both Pietro and Maria eventually fall into the aphasic state that precedes their death. Failure to communicate is powerfully evoked by Maraini and Beckett through a similar device: neither character of the two couples ever listens to the other one. Like Didi and Gogo in *Waiting for Godot*, Maria and Pietro seem to be uttering monologues, instead of participating in a dialogue, and the fragmentary nature of their discourse is only one instance of the fragmentary quality of the entire narrative, composed of short entries grouped in three different sections. Fragmentation indeed appears as a stylistic and thematic characteristic of one of these sections, that which contains Giacomo's letters, which are striking for their uncanny punctuation, that elliptically breaks down sentences in meaningless syntagms: "E' qui il nodo. Il cuore proliferante e bruciato. Io sento il fumo a un miglio. Perché il saperti. Cosí e cosí. Tu sai. Lo vuole. Vuole che tu. Insomma vorrebbe che anch'io . . . " (65–66) [The knot is here. The burning and proliferating heart.

I can feel smoke at a mile's distance. Because to know you. So and so. You know. He wants it. He wants you to. Basically he would expect me as well . . .]. As a matter of fact, division and fragmentation at the formal and stylistic levels serve to reconfirm the internal rift experienced by the female protagonist, who could be considered an ideal example of the Laingian *divided self.*

Like many characters from Beckett's texts, Pietro and Maria live at the margins of society. A failed existentialist, Pietro rejects his materialistic family to the extent that he does not allow it to assist him in his long agony; a wild nymphomaniac, Maria appears to be able to communicate only through her body. When, at the end of the novel, Maria's mother decides to send her daughter to see a psychiatrist, Maria refuses to be treated, avoiding a possible societal normalization of her behavior. In several instances Maraini voiced her opinion about women's madness, defining it as an act of resistance against the strain imposed on them by a paternalistic society:

> Madness is not adjusting to the world. Women find themselves, objectively, in a non-adjusted condition, because this is not a world made to a woman's measurements. It's made to a man's measurements. So many women don't fit in it, and the damage that this does to some women is so severe that some go crazy. Some do not hold. You could say that it is actually the most sensitive who go crazy, the ones who feel the most strongly this violence that is being done to their psyches, to women's psychological integrity, by the male world, which is very powerful. My play *Clitemnestra* is the story of female madness, as rejection, incongruence, nonrelationship with the male world. Also, if you look deep enough, you can find this theme of madness in other texts of mine. (Anderlini 1991, 150)

Through the estranged perspective of the madwoman, Maraini thus launches an attack against societal values, and the opacity of her work only reinforces such a political stance. Leo Bersani defines opacity in Beckett's work as the necessary element that turns artistic products into *acts of resistance* because "they refuse to serve the complacency of a culture that expects art to reinforce its moral and epistemological authority. We could even speak . . . of an art at war with culture" (1993, 8). In refusing to adjust to the world, both Beckett's and Maraini's characters establish their subversive role, and bear out the subversion already enacted through stylistic techniques proper to the avant-garde.

Formally subversive, Maraini's novel places equal subversive potential in its female protagonist as threat to patriarchal society. Maria's sexual aggressiveness is a potent reminder of the danger she incarnates as a deviant member of a society that has built its foundation on the objectification and submission of women. In Catholic Italy, religion has always played a fundamental role in subjecting women to a condition of inferiority, especially through its strenuous reinforcement of sexual taboos: for this reason sexual promiscuity appears as the most transgressive act that a woman can possibly perform in such a society. Maria's revolutionary misdeeds take on an even stronger symbolic relevance because of her first name, which binds her to the image of the Madonna. Furthermore, the fact that the novel's first entry falls on 8 December, the day of the Immaculate Conception, only enhances the role of such a connection. In her introduction to *Parlare con Dacia*, Ileana Montini discusses at length the role of the Virgin Mary within Catholic and feminist contexts:

> Mary is an ambiguous figure, on one hand she represents *wisdom* and on the other she represents women's dutiful submission as symbolized in the fideistic acceptance of the mistery of incarnation. To disobedient Eve is counterposed obedient Mary. The order unsettled by Eve is reestablished by Mary. . . . Mary's *place* in the Church depends on divine maternity. What characterizes her is her willing and total "consecration" of herself as God's *Handmaid*. . . . She is the image of the true woman, whose relationship with God must pass through the mediation of Man. (1977, 94–95; my translation)

Instead of being an *obedient Mary*, Maraini's protagonist definitely comes closer to the image of the *disobedient Eve*. Always, in the description of her adulterous encounters, she is depicted as the agent of a castrating threat. Due to their youth, the *ragazzi* seduced by her share an uncommon sexual vitality as well as an extreme frailty, which usually becomes evident once they undress. The Achilles' heel of the heterosexual macho is symbolically unveiled as these men shed their clothes, revealing their own fallibility, inevitably defined by the inadequacy of their genital apparatus. A penis that cannot aspire to the role of the Lacanian phallus because it cannot match its symbolic "size," the shrinking male member betrays the presence of fear at a moment when it should least appear: under the castrating eyes of Maria the temptress,

> "Mentre mi spoglio, tu voltati dall'altro lato." "Perché?" "Adesso vado nel bagno, tu non ti voltare.". . . "Siediti sul letto. Vuoi una sigaretta?" "Ti dispiace se chiudiamo gli scuri. Io alla luce, mi sento impacciato.". . . "Vieni vicino. E' buio, non vedo niente." "Quando fa cosí , è tutto rovinato." "Chi fa cosí?"
> "Lui, il verme." "Chi?" "Non mi toccare. Mi sento tutto rattrappito e indolenzito." (52–53)

["Turn on the other side, while I undress." "Why?" "Now I'll go to the bathroom, don't turn."... "Sit on the bed. Do you want a cigarette?" "Do you mind if I shut the blinders? I feel awkward when there's light in the room."... "Come closer. It's dark, I can't see anything." "When he does that, it all goes to pot." "Who does that?" "He, the worm." "Who?" "Don't touch me. I feel all shrivelled and in pain."]

As Freud showed in his analysis of Hoffman's tale of male disempowerment in "Das Unheimliche," (1919) the female gaze can act as the purveyor of castration and the scene excerpted from Maraini's novel appears to be proving the same point. In the only passage in which she describes herself, Maria faces her image in the mirror as she is about to open the door of a shop: "La mia figura mi viene incontro dalla vetrina . . . la piccola faccia dai tratti duri, fortemente marcati, si muove sul collo magro come una testa di uccello rapace . . . alla maniera di un uccello affamato" (116) [My image comes towards me from the shop-window . . . the small face with hard features moves on the neck which is as thin as the head of a rapacious bird . . . as if it were a starving bird]. Her features resembling those of a preying animal, *un uccello rapace*, Maria is portrayed as a menacing presence, threatening because of her animal lack of awareness of those societal norms that she unconsciously defies as if in compliance with the primitive, *prehistorical* law of the *survival of the fittest*. The young prey on which she feasts are already marked by previous encounters with the *enemy*, they have scars on their bodies to prove it, scars that speak of their vulnerability as well as their ability to overcome the adversary: "Il ragazzo adesso è nudo. Si china sul lenzuolo, la testa affondata nel cuscino, le ginocchia piegate. . . . Adesso viene verso di me. Una cicatrice rossa gli attraversa la coscia destra . . . in mezzo al petto gonfio brilla una medaglia d'oro con l'effige della Madonna" (156) [Now the boy is naked. He bends on the bedsheet, his head buried in the pillow, the knees bent . . . now he comes towards me. A red scar runs across his right thigh . . . a golden medal with the effigy of the Madonna shines in the middle of his swollen chest]. Even though the fetal posture of this body betrays the *ragazzo*'s innocence, revealing his initial unwillingness to participate in the sacrificial coitus, the presence of the red scar on his thigh acts as a *memento* of his past encounters. Furthermore, the effigy of the Virgin on the medal plate definitely comes across as a polisemic signifier: as a religious token, it is both a reminder of his youth and naïveté and a talisman on which the *framed* image of Mary acts as the symbol of the phallocratic disempowerment of women. However, because of the uncanny equation between Maria and the Madonna, the previous symbolism could be reversed, thus making the *medaglia* come to signify its opposite, representing a mark of the young man's idolatrous submission to the quintessential man-eating witch.

However, as the unfolding of her sexual escapades progresses, Maria slowly sheds her aggressiveness, assuming an ancillar position of inferiority. Her process of self-destruction, already initiated through sexual promiscuity, reaches its climax during her encounter with a young bartender, an opportunistic *ragazzo di strada,* whose assertiveness dethrones Maria from her active role of seducer. Refusing to eat the apples that Maria is offering him, he proclaims his superiority over atavistic temptations: " 'Cosa hai da mangiare?' . . . 'Ci sono le mele.' 'Che me ne faccio delle mele?'" (199–200) ["What do you have to eat?" . . . "There are some apples." "What would I do with apples?"] and, by asking her to surrender her precious ring, " 'E' bello questo anello, allora me lo regali?'" (201) ["This ring is beautiful, will you give it to me, then?"] he eventually leaves the scene as the phallocratic conqueror, as an epic hero who, upon killing the mythical dragon, returns home with a symbolic prize. In another relevant scene, Maria suddenly turns into Mary Magdalene, washing the hair of a poor teenager that she has accidentally met. The path that led her from the virtual freedom experienced in the days of her wild promiscuity to the eventual framing in the role of the redeemed prostitute can be safely identified as a slow process of normalization performed on her by society. One more step needs to be taken, however, before she can be acknowledged as a full-fledged societal member, and it is the normalizing step *par excellence:* psychotherapy, which should enable her to overcome her diversity and thus bring about her rehabilitation. Her inability to give in, to surrender her wild side, appears as an ominous indication of her will to self-destruct. Until her husband died, Maria seemed to be allowed any sort of infringement against the behavioral rules established by the community, but once she is alone, either she conforms or she perishes. Abandoned to a destiny that she appears to choose, she retreats from the world and slowly drifts into a solitary death, which she still experiences in the same unconscious fashion with which she has lived all her life: "Scrivo la data. Sei giugno. Apro il quaderno, scrivo la data sei giugno. Sei giu . . . " (223) [I write today's date. June sixth. I open the notebook, I write today's date June sixth. Sixth of Ju . . .]. What makes this entry even more striking is that its last two words actually do acquire a different meaning in their truncated state. Not only does *Sei giu* represent a failed attempt to write *sei giugno,* but it also means, through a most significant Lacanian slippage, "You are down," where "down" is a synonym of "depressed." Could despair be inscribed in a text in a stronger fashion?

While Maria, in her lack of self-awareness paradoxically stands up against a phallocratic society that demands her submission, all the other female characters in the novel seem to have voluntarily chosen to remain in the shadows. Abiding by the Catholic *dictatum* that requires them to depend on their men, these characters manifest their repressed instinctual subversiveness through compulsive hunger. Like the ancient goddesses whose matriarchal reign preexisted the advent of patriarchy, they still request sacrificial offerings from their male companions, offerings of food which are ritually served in order to appease them. In the following scene, Pietro is depicted as bringing pastry to Maria's mother. As usual, the passage contains several contradictory versions of the same scene and in each of its versions Maria's mother eats a differently shaped type of pastry:

> 12 dicembre
> Pietro ha posato il pacco sulla tavola. . . . Ha posato il vassoio davanti a mia madre . . . Pietro le ha indicato una sirena di marzapane. Mia madre ha addentato la coda della sirena, dipinta di azzurro e di argento. . . . Pietro . . . ha posato il vassoio davanti a lei, sulla tovaglia . . . ha indicato una pasta intrisa di liquore. Mia madre ha allungato le dita. La pasta trasudava umore colloso. Mia madre l'ha portata alle labbra, stringendola fra il pollice e l'indice. Un rivolo di liquore rossiccio le è scivolato sul mento. (29)
>
> [12 dicembre. Pietro puts the pack on the table . . . he puts the tray in front of my mother. . . . Pietro points her to a marzipan mermaid. My mother bites into the mermaid's tail, painted in blue and silver. . . . Pietro . . . puts the tray in front of her, on the table-cloth . . . he points to a pastry full of liquor. My mother stretches her fingers. The pastry exhuded a gluey humor. My mother takes it to her lips, holding it tight between her index and thumb. A little red stream of liquor drips on her chin. . . .]

And the different versions of the same story follow a rhythmic iteration that recalls ritualistic overtones:

> Un momento dopo è rientrato reggendo un vassoio di cartone dove erano allineate una diecina di paste. . . . Pietro ha allungato il braccio verso un corno di pasta sfoglia da cui straboccava una crema densa e gialla, molto grassa. Con due dita si è aperto un varco fra le labbra di mia madre. Le ha spinto il corno fra i denti. . . . Pietro le ha indicato una pasta quasi nera, rinchiusa in un involucro di caramello bruciato. Mia madre l'ha stretta fra due dita. Nel fare questo gesto la crosta trasparente si è spaccata, due lame di zucchero cotto, dal bordo filettato di giallo si sono sollevate verso il suo mento. Pietro ha allungato un braccio; con il pollice ha spinto due lame brune nella bocca di mia madre. (29–30)

[A moment later, he comes back holding a tray containing a row of about ten pastries. . . . Pietro stretches his hand towards a crescent roll from which spills a dense and yellow cream, very greasy. With two fingers, he makes room for the pastry between my mother's lips. He pushes the roll down her throat. . . . Pietro shows her a blackish pastry, enclosed in a wrapping of caramel. My mother holds it with two fingers. When she does this, the transparent crust breaks in two, two blades of cooked sugar, with a yellow border, move up towards her chin. Pietro stretches his arm; with the thumb he pushes the two dark blades in my mother's mouth.]

The first pastry is in the shape of a mermaid, which can be read as a symbol of female threat to men. When Maria's mother bites off her tail, she replicates the voluntary mutilation that Andersen's mermaid underwent in order to be with her male companion, performing a sacrificial act of female self-disempowerment. Both the second and the third pastry seem to be offered through a staging that resembles a ritual offering of the male phallus. While in its first version the woman takes the pastry by herself and the liquid that drips from it has the color of blood, in the other version the man shoves it in her mouth and its liquid, *una crema densa e gialla, molto grassa*, has different color and consistency. What seems to be portrayed, in the first case, is an act of male castration, followed by the ingestion of the member, as if to signify female empowerment through incorporation of the sign of power. In the second stance, instead, it is the woman who is subjected to a symbolic submission through the virtual staging of oral sex, an act through which she acts as the disempowered provider of pleasure. The blackness of the last pastry, and the sugar blades which compose its shape, certainly render it another bleak symbol that ominously repeats women's dark condition: when Pietro pushes the two blades down into his mother-in-law's mouth, he definitely performs another violating gesture. The highly charged symbolism of the food offering is differently portrayed, however, in the case of the other female characters: both Pietro's and Giacomo's mothers are portrayed as voracious women who do not hesitate to steal food from their children's plates. Pietro's mother selfishly feasts on chicken while her son is dying at the hospital: "'Non ti mangiare tutto il pollo, mamma.' 'Credevo che l'aveste già preso'" (144) ["Don't eat all the chicken, mother." "I thought you had already taken it"]. Giacomo's mother is remembered by him as a ghostly animal-like creature who thrives on meat: "Mia madre, pover'anima. E' viva dico. Non credere. Né si cura di me. D'altronde. Pover'anima. Che mangiatrice. Non fai in tempo a riempirle il piatto. E' ghiotta di carne. Te lo giuro. Si mangia mezzo chilo di carne al giorno." (47) [My mother, poor soul. She's alive I mean. Don't think.

And she doesn't care about me. But of course. Poor soul. What an eater. You have barely finished to fill her plate that. She craves meat. I swear it to you. She eats a pound of meat each day]. Her presence is so menacing, so castrating, that her son cannot stand to look at her:

> Mia madre mi guarda. Non ti piace? dice. Dalla a me. Lo so. Non posso alzare gli occhi. Perché incontrarla mi è. Mi disgusta. Insomma. Alzo forse alla fine. I piedi forse. Le mani. Ma gli occhi no. Beh, lei si è già ripulita il piatto suo. E vedo una forchetta che vola. Rapidissima. Dove vai forchetta del cavolo? Ha agguantato un brandello di carne. Il mio piatto vuoto. Anche il suo. Perché io non la vedo. Ma so che mastica. Che ferocità! E il suo pallore, la sua calvizie, quasi senza denti. Mi capisci. (47)

> [My mother stares at me. Don't you like it? she says. Give it to me. I know. I can't raise my eyes. Because meeting her eyes is. It disgusts me. Anyway. In the end I raise. Maybe my feet. My hands. But not my eyes. Well, she has already cleaned her plate. And I see a fork flying. Incredibly quick. Where are you going, you damn fork? It snatches a chunk of meat. My empty plate. Hers too. Because I don't see her. But I know she's chewing. What ferocity! And her pallor, her baldness, almost toothless. You see what I mean.]

and the chunk of meat, the *brandello di carne* that she is holding actually seems to have been snatched off his own flesh. Colorless, hairless, and toothless, she is evil incarnate while personifying lack and deprivation at the same time.

Characterized by their hunger or by their restlessness, by their promiscuity or by their ruthlessness, the women of *A memoria* all share a profound segregation from the world of thought, all being imprisoned in their confining body. All actions and no thought, they make perfect characters for a bleak fairy tale, a mythic fable on the war of the sexes in prefeminist Italy. Indeed a magic aura surrounds Maraini's novel: the naturalistic streak of many a description does not clash with the rich symbolism that pervades a language that still remains, notwithstanding its many connotations, strikingly simple. The endless repetition of sentences and entire paragraphs entices and hypnotizes the reader, who is presented with a vision of the world as seen through Maria's estranged eyes. This idea is further reinforced by the presence, at the very heart of the novel, of an intriguing rewriting of Calderon de la Barca's *La vida es sueño*, a play which comments on the restraining power of societal values while destabilizing the boundaries between reality and dream. In a long passage where the lines uttered by the performers can hardly be discerned from the comments made by the characters of Maraini's novel, a significant interweaving of the two texts occurs. The two characters of the play, Sigismondo and Rosaura, are portrayed in terms that would easily define Pietro and Maria. While the man is introduced as a failed thinker, the woman is depicted as an active presence, as a threatening figure: armed with a sword that connotes her aggressiveness, she is alone. Both bent on revenge against phallocracy, Rosaura and Maria are indeed alone in their quest, since their men seem to be either absent or too weak to help them. In both cases, revenge is stated in the obscure, haunting dreamlike fashion that characterizes the style of Maraini's novel. Maria's erratic prose and her hypnotic convolution are powerfully reinforced by Maraini's paraphrasis of the final lines of Calderon's play "Il più gran bene è niente; perché la vita è sogno e i sogni sono sogni" (131) [The highest virtue is nothing; because life is a dream and dreams are dreams] lines which are meant to face the hypnotized reader of *A memoria* with a statement that inevitably questions the fictional status of reality and fiction. If life is just a dream then what is the difference between fiction and reality? And how does Maraini's desperate portrayal of the women's *prehistoric* condition comment on reality? And how does Maria's lack of awareness, her going through life as if it were a dream, change its meaning in the light of such new perspective? These are only some of the questions present in the mind of the reader at the end of this book, a book that, like all true avant-garde novels is supposed to disturb its audience, unsettling its beliefs and instilling what Marguerite Alexander called, in reference to Beckett's work, "the shock of recognition" (1990, 61). As the chart of Maraini's intellectual landscape gets drawn, as the intricate web of literary voices of protest and resistance finally unveils, what becomes evident, in its bleakness, is the absence of any Italian source of influence: Robbe-Grillet, Sarraute, Beckett, Sartre all spoke, in revolutionary fashion, of an existential *malaise* that keenly applies to the tormented condition of Italian women before feminism, but none of them was Italian, and none was ever really concerned with the feminist cause. And Calderon's voice, so different from that of the avant-garde, yet so powerful because of its rich texture, is another cultural reference that excludes Italy. No inspiration, the author seems to be implying, could ever be derived from the same intelligentsia which gave such powerful contribution in laying the foundations of the phallogocentric constriction, erecting the bars of those symbolic prisons women never chose to inhabit.

La femme rompue by Simone de Beauvoir

> Lundi 13 septembre. Les Salines.
> C'est un extraordinaire décor, cette ébauche de ville abandonnée aux lisières d'un village et en marge des siècles. J'ai longé une moitié de l'hémicycle, j'ai monté l'escalier du pavillon central; longtemps j'ai contemplé la sobre majesté de ces bâtiments édifiés à des fins utilitaires et qui n'ont jamais servi à rien. Ils sont solides, ils sont vrais; cependant leur délaissement les transforme en un simulacre fantastique: on se demande de quoi. (121)

> [*Monday 13 September. Les Salines.*
> It is an astonishing setting, this rough draft of a town lying deserted here, on the edge of a village and outside the flow of the centuries. I went along one half of the hemicycle and climbed the steps of the central building; for a long while I gazed at the quiet splendor of these structures that were put up for functional purposes and that have never been used for anything at all. They are solid; they are real: yet their abandoned state changes them into a fantastic pretense—of what, one wonders (123)

The description of the *Salines de Ledoux*, a utopic industrial city designed by Claude Nicolas Ledoux in the eighteenth century and subsequently built on the outskirts of Arc-et-Senans, opens the diary of Monique, the narrator of "La femme rompue," a novella written by Simone de Beauvoir in 1967. Having just accompanied her husband to the airport, from which he departed on a business trip, the middle-aged woman treats herself to a slow drive back home. She takes a road that guides her through the French countryside and, eventually, leads her to the abandoned buildings which were once supposed to actualize the visionary dream of an architect: such a dream, however, was doomed to remain unfulfilled. What is left is just a simulacrum, an empty monument witnessing the defeat of an idealistic endeavor.

Confronted with Monique's first few remarks on the spoils of the *Salines*, little does the reader know about the symbolic role that, as the narration unfolds, they will inevitably come to assume. In a journal that covers about six months of her life, the protagonist transcribes her slow *descente en enfer*. Soon after her return to Paris, she is abruptly faced with the news of her husband's repeated betrayals: her dreams untimely shattered, she grapples with a reality she cannot force herself to accept. Her entire life spent as guardian of the quintessential *foyer*, Monique suddenly finds herself alone, abandoned by a cheating husband and by two grown-up daughters who have fled the familiar nest in order to start their own independent lives. The journal chronicles her many desperate attempts to rekindle a flame that is forever extinguished: countless conversations with friends and strangers (graphologists, astrologers, psychiatrists, and even a gynecologist) dwell on her strenuous quest for advice and explanations. Forced to acknowledge her own responsibility in the failure of her marriage, Monique eventually terminates her diary as she is about to cross the threshold to a new life as a single, independent woman.

Early in the narrative, it becomes clear that Monique's dreams encounter the same sad destiny of Ledoux's visionary construction: infidelity turns her husband Maurice into a mere simulacrum of the caring companion he once was: "Je me disais: 'Il ne reviendra pas.' . . . Il n'est pas revenu. Pas lui: et un jour, il n'y aura même plus son simulacre à mes cotés" (223) [I said to myself then, *He will not come back*. . . . He has not come back. Not him: and one day there will no longer be even this semblance of him at my side (224–25)]. Likewise, her house, which she always saw as a love-nest, eventually becomes another simulacrum, having lost its function as warm environment to the ideal *ménage:* "Je ne reconnais plus l'appartement. Les objets ont l'air d'imitations d'eux-mêmes." (152) [I no longer recognize the apartment. The things in it have the air of imitations of themselves. (153)] And the furniture, which had once filled the house with warmth and joy, have now turned into mere skeleton (232). Like Ledoux's buildings, Monique's *foyer* has a utilitarian aspect: as all *foyers*, it partakes of that special relation to economics depicted by Jacques Derrida in *Donner le temps.*[13] The very word *interest*, belonging both to the economic and to the affective semantic fields, plays a central role in Monique's own depiction of her role as dependent housewife: " Me voilà, à quarante-quatre ans, les mains vides, sans métier, sans autre intérêt que toi dans l'existence. . . . —Mais Monique! m'a-t-il dit . . . J'ai énormément insisté, il y a sept ans, pour que tu prennes ce secrétariat . . . —Passer la journée loin de la maison et des enfants, pour cent milles francs par mois, je n'en voyais pas l'intérêt, ai-je dit" (206) [—Here I am at forty-four, empty-handed, with no occupation, no other interest in life apart from you . . . —But Monique! he cried, looking astonished . . . I urged you as strongly as I possibly could to take that job as secretary . . . —I couldn't see any point in spending the day away from the house and the children just for a hundred thousand francs a month, I said (207)]. Displacing interest away from her own life only to reverse it on her family involves a different kind of interest, the utilitarian accrual of a symbolic debt that her husband and daughters should thus owe her: "Et je sais qu'en effet j'attends beaucoup des gens; je leur demande peut-être trop.—Evidemment. Comme tu vis beaucoup pour les autres, tu vis aussi beaucoup par eux . . . " (202) ["And I know that in fact I do expect a lot from other people: maybe I ask them too much.—Obviously. Since you live very much for others, you also live a great deal through them . . . (204)].

Monique's emotional dependence on her family, aptly represented by the juxtaposition, in the previous quote, of the two verbs *vivre pour* and *vivre par*, is a potent reminder of an apparently similar situation depicted in *Quaderno proibito*. Like Valeria, Monique has invested all her life on her family, but differently from the former, the latter never really yearns for her own independence. While de Céspedes's novel revolves around Valeria's struggle for a Woolfian *room of her own*, Beauvoir's fictional diary concentrates on its protagonist's endless remodeling of a *living room*, a term constantly mentioned in English even in the French version of the text. Valeria searches for solitude, Monique, instead, tries to escape from it. Valeria would even settle for a room as big as a closet, if only to escape momentarily the presence of her family: ". . . sogno di avere una camera tutta per me. I domestici, anche se lavorano tutto il giorno ininterrottamente, a sera dicono: 'Buona notte' e hanno il diritto di chiudersi in una camera, in uno sgabuzzino. Io mi accontenterei di uno sgabuzzino" (67) [. . . I dream of having a room all to myself. Servants, even if they work all day without stopping, say "Good night" in the evening, and have the right to shut themselves up in their bedroom, even if it's only some tiny hole. I'd be happy with any little place (59)]. On the contrary, Monique concentrates her efforts on the rearrangement of a *livingroom*, a common room where the family should reunite around the fireplace or around a large table, a place which should enable the broken couple to come together one more time (143–44). To the autonomous setting of a *room of her own*, Monique then prefers not the passionate intimacy of her bedroom, but the asexual warmth of the *livingroom:* unlike Valeria, in fact, she seems to have given up on her sexual drives (196). At the end of her diary, Valeria mentions that a couple's silent wake, in bed, bespeaks the exemplary quality of a marriage. Indeed, such silent wake betrays the necessary element of compromise proper to all successful unions: ". . . di questo continuo fingere di dormire e rimanere svegli nella propria angoscia, senza che il compagno se ne avveda, è fatta la storia di un matrimonio esemplare" (255) [. . . this continual pretense, and staying awake in one's private torment, without the other noticing, makes up the story of a perfect marriage (247)]. In "La femme rompue," the same silence only reveals a slow drifting apart of husband and wife, accentuating the increasing incomprehension that connotes their last few weeks of cohabitation: "Je suis restée éveillée longtemps; lui aussi m'a-t-il semblé. Que pensait-il?" (149) [I stayed awake a long while; so did he, it seemed to me. What was he thinking about? (151)] Instead of bearing witness to their lovemaking, the bedroom becomes the stage of the most climactic scenes in their separation: Maurice finally confesses his betrayals to Monique while she is in bed, and it is still in the bedroom that, subsequently, he confronts her with a series of accusations which clearly denounce his long repressed anger towards his wife. In her husband's absence, Monique retreats to the same bed for days on end, refusing to leave it until he returns: awoken from a long sleep to an unbearable reality: "Ton plus grand tort, lui ai-je dit, c'est de m'avoir laissée endormir dans la confiance. Me voilà, à quarante-quatre ans, les mains vides . . ." (205) [The biggest thing you did, I said, was to let me lull myself in a sense of false security. Here I am at forty-four, empty-handed . . . (206–7)] she tries to recapture an artificial appeasement through sleeping pills, tranquilizers, and alcohol. On a deeper level, her desire to continue sleeping is paralleled by the many lies she unconsciously writes on the diary in order to paint a reality less painful than it actually is. The conviction that her husband will soon grow weary of his longtime lover leads her to justify his betrayal as a mere "histoire de peau" (137) [a question of direct desire (139)]. Monique's current delusional state forcefully parallels her previous existence, similarly conducted in a dream-like fashion (223). Upon learning the truth, Monique ponders the motives that pushed Maurice to make his confession, thus betraying her desire to remain in the dark. And the image of darkness plays an extremely important role in the depiction of Monique's despair. Dark as the night is the condition of women who cannot understand the motives behind their husbands' betrayals, as Simone de Beauvoir wrote in *Tout compte fait* (1972):

> I had recently received the confidences of several women in their forties whose husbands had left them for others : in spite of the differences of character and circumstance, there were interesting likenesses in all these stories—the women could not even remotely understand what was happening to them ; they thought their husband's behavior contradictory, abnormal and deviant, and the rival unworthy of his love ; their world was falling to pieces and they ended up by no longer knowing who they were. . . . They were struggling in complete ignorance . . . and I had the idea of speaking about their darkness and making it evident. (124)

As a matter of fact, darkness becomes Monique's refuge during her husband's absence: "Hier soir quand Maurice est rentré, j'étais assise dans le living-room, dans le noir, en robe de chambre" (236) [Yesterday evening when Maurice came home I was sitting in the living room, in the darkness, wearing my dressing gown (237)]. Like Valeria, Monique derives her own sense of identity from her companion: abandoned by him, she is nothing, she is left in the dark: "Moi, j'ai perdu mon image. Je ne la regardais pas souvent; mais à l'arrière-plan elle était là, telle que Maurice l'avait peinte pour moi. . . . Il fait noir, je ne me vois plus" (238) "As for me, I've lost my own image. I did not look at it often; but it was there, in the background, just as Maurice had drawn it for me. . . . It is dark: I cannot see myself anymore (239)].

On one hand, Maurice appears as the purveyor of light, and his absence is synonymous with darkness and angst. Once he is gone, the apartment turns from love nest into an oppressing prison: Monique feels as if the four walls were closing in the same way they did in Poe's "The Pit and the Pendulum" (242). On the other hand, Maurice himself becomes the personification of darkness: he brought about Monique's despair, leaving her in pain and obscurity. Maurice is ". . . tout ce qui est mal, tout ce qui me nuit" where the polisemic *nuit*, signifies both *night* and a form of the verb *nuire*. Furthermore, his somber eyes,which immediately attracted her when she first met him, eventually become the ominous symbol of his impenetrability, an impenetrability proper to all men: "C'est le 'mystère masculin', beaucoup plus impénétrable que le 'mystère féminin'" (197) [It was the "masculine mystery," far more impenetrable than the "the feminine mystery" (199)]. In "Lettera a Natalia Ginzburg," Alba de Céspedes described women's sorrow as a fall in a dark pit, a pit in which women are always thrown by their men:

> Del resto—tu non lo dici, ma certo lo pensi—sono sempre gli uomini a spingerci nel pozzo; magari senza volerlo . . . sì, devi ammetterlo, sono proprio gli uomini a spingerci nel pozzo. I figli pure sono uomini, e i fratelli e i padri; ed essi tutti con le loro parole, e più ancora con i loro silenzi, ci incoraggiano a cadere nel pozzo smemorante ove loro non possono raggiungerci e noi possiamo esser sole con noi stesse. (1948, 106)
>
> [After all—you do not say it, but certainly you think it—it is always men who push us down the pit; even without wanting it . . . yes, you have to admit it, it is really men who push us into the pit. Sons are still men, and brothers and fathers and all of them with their words, and even more with their silence, they encourage us to fall into the pit of forgetfulness, where they cannot reach us and we can be alone with ourselves. (my translation)]

Similarly, as Monique mourns the end of her marriage, she describes herself as the protagonist of an "affreuse descente au fond de la tristesse" (203) [hideous fall into the abyss of sadness (205)], a vertiginous and endless fall in the abyss, “Je perds les pédales. Je tombe plus bas, toujours plus bas” (232) [I am losing all grasp on things. I am falling lower, lower all the time (234)], “On peut toujours descendre plus bas, et plus encore, et encore plus bas. C’est sans fond” (238) [You can always go lower, and lower still, and still lower. There is no bottom] (239). In one of her dreams, her despair comes to be symbolically represented by a breathless run in a dark, narrow corridor which closes in on her, thus evoking again Poe’s short story (193). Displacing the void which is inside of her onto her surroundings, Monique eventually describes her livingroom table, which once was so meaningful to her, as a heavy and hollow object, “La lourde table du living-room: elle est creuse.” The same adjective, *creux*, later reappears in the text as the only possible way of defining Monique’s lonely life: “J’avais toujours des choses à faire. Maintenant, tricoter, cuisiner, lire, écouter un disque, tout me semble vain. L’amour de Maurice donnait une importance à chaque moment de ma vie. Elle est creuse. Tout est creux: les objets, les instants. Et moi” (210) [I always used to be busy. Now everything—knitting, cooking, reading, putting on a record—everything seems pointless. Maurice’s love gave every moment of my life a meaning. Now it is hollow. Everything is hollow—things are empty: time is empty. And so am I (212)]. Deprived of her *raison d’être*, Monique feels as if she were losing consistency: along with the objects around her, she turns into one of “The Hollow Men” portrayed by T. S. Eliot, “Shape without form, shade without color, / Paralysed force, gesture without motion (1925, 1:11–12).

In a passage quoted from Charbonneaux-Lessay, Gaston Bachelard describes the empty shell as symbol of the body deprived of its soul: “Ancient symbolics used the shell as a symbol for the human body, which encloses the soul in an outside envelope, while the soul quickens the entire being, represented by the organism of the mollusk. Thus, they said, the body becomes lifeless when the soul has left it, in the same way that the shell becomes incapable of moving when it is separated from the part that gives it life” (1958, 116). In “La femme rompue,” Monique initially depicted her house as a homely, protective shell out of which she hardly felt the need to wander: “Avant, je ne sortais pas beaucoup de ma coquille mais quand je le faisais, je m’intéréssais à tout: les paysages, les gens, les musées, les rues. Maintenant je suis une morte” (251) [Before, I used not to come out of my burrow very often, but when I did I was interested in everything—the countryside, people, museums, the streets. Now I am a dead woman (252)]. From the woman who, at the beginning of the novella, loved staying at home yet enjoyed to appease her occasional "envie de soleil et d'air," (191) Monique eventually chooses to hide forever into her empty house, which has now become a personification of the Bachelardian *lifeless shell.* Like a body bereaved of its soul, her house *sans* Maurice has turned into a different shell. It is a shell made of dirt, a shell that eerily resembles the antichamber to death: "La chambre pue le tabac froid et l'alcool, il y a des cendres partout, je suis sale, les draps sont sales, le ciel est sale derrière les vitres sales, cette saleté est une coquille qui me protège, je n'en sortirai plus jamais. Il serait facile de glisser un peu plus loin dans le néant, jusqu'au point de non-rétour" (222) [The bedroom stinks of stale tobacco and spirits; there are ashes everywhere; I am filthy; the sheets are filthy; the sky is filthy behind the filthy windows: this filth is a shell that protects me; I shall never leave it again. It would be easy to slide just a little further into the void, as far as the point of no return (223)].

It is only on a surface level, though, that the warm *foyer* depicted at the inception of the journal suddenly turns into a lifeless shell. Devoted wife and mother, Monique appears as the innocent victim of her husband's infidelity and, her life shattered by Maurice's undeserved betrayal, she is left prisoner of her memories, her regrets, and her solitude. Seen from a different perspective, a perspective that assumes the narrator's unreliability, Beauvoir's text tells quite a different tale.[14] It is Monique's gynecologist and counselor who first alerts the reader of the possibility that there might be a different side to this coin: Maurice's version of the story should be taken into account because "Ces histoires de rupture, racontées par la femme, on n'y comprend jamais rien" (197) [There is never anything to be understood in these cases of separation when they are recounted by the wife (199)]. A clear reference to the title of Beauvoir's text effectively turns Lambert's statement into a veritable key to the epistemic core of the novella. With this statement in mind, many of Monique's previous assertions come to reveal their utmost ambiguity: her casual admission to the imprecision of her written reports, "Je disais pêle-mêle tout ce que je pensais de Noëllie et aussi de lui. Oui, je me rappelle vaguement" (186) [I poured out everything I thought about Noëllie and him. Yes: I have a confused recollection of it (186)], reappears later in the text in a stronger, yet double-edged fashion: "Mais peut-on se fier à sa mémoire? J'ai beaucoup oublié, et il semble que parfois même j'ai déformé les faits. (Qui a dit: 'Il n'y a rien de changé'? Maurice ou moi? Sur ce journal j'ai écrit que c'était lui. Peut-être parce que je souhaitais le croire . . .)" (213) [But can one trust one's memory? I have forgotten a great deal, and it would appear that sometimes I have gone so far as to distort the facts. (Who was it who said, "There is nothing changed"? Maurice or I? In this diary I wrote that it was he. Perhaps because I wanted to believe it . . .) (214)]. Forgetfulness seems to be the excuse through which Monique justifies her partial recounting of the events, yet the intentionality of some of her misrepresentations reveals itself in quite a subtle and telling fashion. Placed between parentheses meant to emphasize its marginality, Monique's admission of guilt is also followed by three suspension points that only emphasize her desire to leave things unsaid. The inattentive reader, that same reader who will sympathize with Monique without questioning her actions, will thus disregard the narrator's elliptical and marginalized admission of unreliability.

Rereading one's diary undoubtedly constitutes one of the most common *topoi* of diary-fiction, and it is usually meant to foster insightful comments on the limits of linguistic representation. Beauvoir's Monique does it with uncommon rage and frustration, recording the event with words that once again betray a fundamental ambiguity:

> Pendant deux semaines je n'ai rien écrit sur ce cahier parce que je me suis relue. Et j'ai vu que les mots ne disent rien. Les rages, les cauchemars, l'horreur, ça échappe aux mots. Je mets des choses sur le papier quand je reprends des forces, dans le désespoir ou l'espoir. Mais la déconfiture, l'abrutissement, la décomposition, ce n'est pas marqué sur ces pages. Et puis elles mentent tant, elles se trompent tant. Comme j'ai été manoeuvrée. . . . Il n'y a pas une ligne de ce journal qui n'appelle une correction ou un démenti. . . . Oui, tout au long de ces pages je pensais ce que j'écrivais et je pensais le contraire; et en les relisant je me sens complètement perdue. Il y a des phrases qui me font rougir de honte. (222–23)

> [For a fortnight I have written nothing in this notebook because I read over what I had written before. And I saw that words say nothing. Rages, nightmares, horror—words cannot encompass them. I set things down on paper when I recover strength, either in despair or in hope. But the feeling of total bewilderment, of stunned stupidity, of falling apart—these pages do not contain them. And then these pages lie so—they get things so wrong. How have I been manipulated! . . . There is not a single line in this diary that does not call for a correction or a denial. . . . Yes: throughout these pages I meant what I was writing and I meant the opposite; reading them again I feel completely lost. There are some remarks that make me blush for shame. (223–224)]

Still certain of being exploited by her devious husband, Monique actually admits to having provided a biased reading of the most recent events. What appears most striking is Monique's inability to take responsibility for her own actions. She has not lied intentionally: it is her own words that failed her, it is the very pages of her journal that construct a different reality. And the adoption of a passive construction makes Monique's resistance to agency ever so clearer. Even when it is her own remarks that make her blush for shame, these very remarks seem to have a life of their own, independent from the person who uttered and should thus be held responsible for their impact on others. Not surprisingly, she portrays herself as being equally victimized by her own slippery language as well as by her husband's unjust machinations. Prey to her own unconscious, prey to the lies imbued in linguistic representation, prey to an evil husband, Monique constantly eludes responsibilities by placing the blame on external factors.

Early in her diary, Monique concludes one of its entries by stating her firm intention never to humiliate herself in order to win her husband back: "Je ne te disputerai pas à Noëllie" (161) [I shall not fight with Noëllie over you (162)]. It becomes immediately clear, however, that this simple sentence is actually aimed at reaching the opposite effect: its performative force subverts Monique's larger statement, thus deconstructing her own intention. Indeed, as the events unfold, Monique actively resorts to all sorts of tricks in order to keep her husband away from his lover, making plans that slowly come to resemble veritable war strategies: "Non, je ne dois pas essayer de suivre Noëllie sur son propre terrain, mais me battre sur le mien. . . . J'ai passé la journée à mettre de l'ordre dans nos armoires" (179) [No, I must not try to follow Noëllie on to her ground, but fight it out on my own. . . . I spent today tidying our wardrobes (180)]. Turning the *foyer* into a battlefield, Monique seems to be taking stock of her own ammunitions through the *inventaire* of her husband's clothes and underwear. The wardrobe, packed with neatly arranged handkerchiefs, socks, and sweaters, communicates to her a sense of calm and potency, bespeaking the control she still believes to be exerting over her husband's life. About wardrobes and their content, Gaston Bachelard writes that "In the wardrobe there exists a center of order that protects the entire house against uncurbed disorder. Here order reigns, or rather, this is the reign of order. Order is not merely geometrical; it can also remember the family history" (1958, 79). Under this perspective, then, Monique's *armoire* comes to represent the order of the *foyer*, symbolizing a family history which should act as a cohesive agent against the threat represented by Noëllie, the lover, the enemy, the embodiment of those disorderly forces which could fatally upset its content. Everything that concerns Noëllie betrays, in

Monique's eyes, her profound immorality. A divorced woman, she is a mischievous agent of family disruption. The careless mother of an only daughter, she seems to lack the most basic caring instincts. As ruthless lawyer, she also represents the career woman who makes her living by profiting from other people's misfortunes. Being a total antithesis of Monique, she could not possibly be constructed as a bigger threat to the orderly institution of the *foyer*. Noëllie's independence, her success, her youth: these are the actual reasons that make Noëllie *cheap*, as she eventually says in a moment of extreme rage (168). Noëllie is everything Monique never was and, probably, never will be; left by Maurice, all Monique has left is a wardrobe full of clothes, a *living room* where she will reign in solitude, a *foyer* whose flame has long been extinguished.

In a fundamental passage of "La femme rompue" the wardrobe returns to assume its symbolic presence, this time to signify, however, the imminent demise of the orderly world it represents. In the midst of a dramatic confrontation with Maurice, Monique asks him to leave, opening the wardrobe and throwing out some of his clothes: "J'ai sorti sa valise de l'armoire, j'y ai jeté pêle-mêle du linge, j'ai décroché des cintres. . . . C'était comme un affreux psychodrame où on joue à la vérité. C'est la vérité, mais on la joue" (185) [I pulled his suitcase out of the wardrobe, I flung clothes into it higgledy-piggledy, I unhooked coat hangers . . . It was like a dreadful psychodrama in which they play at truth. It is the truth, but it is being acted (186)]. Hysterical despair dominates the scene, a scene in which Monique eventually learns about her husband's long dissatisfaction with a marriage which has held him hostage in the hands of "une castratrice" (186). As the painful truth is finally unveiled, Monique once again resorts to her homely weapons: the wardrobe, repository of domestic happiness, is ravaged with anger and a suitcase is extracted, as if to represent a symbol of departure and abandonment. Metaphoric signifiers for the obedience and faithfulness sworn by the couple in the marriage vows, the belts are poignantly unhooked from the hangers which held them firm: Monique is thus showing, through these images, the disruption that Noëllie has caused in their lives. Much more needs to be said, however, before their union is finally broken: some dirty *linge* needs to be aired, more skeletons need to be dragged out of the closet. As Monique takes the *linge* out of the wardrobe, Maurice, finally exasperated, vents his long repressed frustration, confesses to repeated adultery and calls her a castrating wife and mother.

Un affreux psychodrame où on joue à la vérité, such an ominous statement does refer to much more than Monique's long confrontation with her husband. Indeed, it seems to offer an appropriate commentary to the entire novella, summarizing in its elliptycal strength the realistic intent of the Beauvoirian creative effort, while retaining the dramatic, yet ironic dimension proper to a narrative which, disguised as a desperate plea for human sympathy, actually undermines its most evident meaning through subtle rhetorical and structural devices. Be it the story of the unjust sufferings of a broken woman, a *femme rompue*, or the chronicle of a rightly punished phallic mother and wife, be it the diaristic account of the fast transformation of a love nest into a lifeless shell or the tale of the destruction of a spider web aptly disguised as a warm *foyer*, "La femme rompue" remains a valid document of the female condition in a prefeminist era.

Finally convinced that her husband will never return to her, Monique concludes her diary on her return home after a trip to America, where she visited one of her daughters. As she crosses the threshold of her apartment, now turned into that Woolfian *room of her own* she has never desired to obtain, Monique sits in the *livingroom* which once represented the heart of her *foyer*. She looks at the table that was supposed to witness many joyous family events and, eventually staring at two closed doors she ponders on her future:

> Mais je sais que je bougerai. La porte s'ouvrira lentement et je verrai ce qu'il y a derrière la porte. C'est l'avenir. La porte de l'avenir va s'ouvrir. Lentement. Immancablement. Je suis sur le seuil. Il n'y a que cette porte et ce qui guette derrière. J'ai peur. Et je ne peux appeler personne au secours.
> J'ai peur. (252)

> But I know that I shall move. The door will open slowly, and I shall see what there is behind the door. It is the future. The door to the future will open. Slowly. Unrelentingly. I am on the threshold. There is only this door and what is watching behind it. I am afraid. And I cannot call to anyone for help.
> I am afraid. (253–54)

Blocked by fear, yet pushed by mere survival instinct, Monique is about to cross a threshold. "A threshold," Bachelard reminds us, "is a sacred thing" (1958, 223) and, as a sacred *locus*, it inspires awe and fear. Monique's fear is fear of the future, of a future which will reserve for her, and for other women after her, better conditions of living, better options, options which will not necessarily bind a woman's life to that of her male companion.

BURNT BY THE BLACK SUN

> Let us keep in mind the speech of the depressed—repetitive and monotonous. Faced with the impossibility of concatenating, they utter sentences that are interrupted, exhausted, come to a standstill. Even phrases they cannot formulate. A repetitive rhythm, a monotonous melody emerge and dominate the broken logical sequences, changing them into recurring, obsessive litanies. Finally, when that frugal musicality becomes exhausted in its turn, or simply does not succeed in becoming established on account of the pressure of silence, the melancholy person appears to stop cognizing as well as uttering, sinking into the blankness of asymbolia or the excess of an unorderable cognitive chaos. (33)

Monotony and repetition, identified as defining elements of the manic depressive's speech by Julia Kristeva in *Soleil noir* (1987), mark the utterance of Maraini's Maria and Beauvoir's Monique, while vaguely defining Lessing's Anna as well. Brief sentences, often devoid of any contextual relation to the conversation of which they are part, dominate Maria's speech; endlessly recurring, Monique's accusations against Noëllie and Maurice are voiced through long obsessive statements.

A gradual withdrawal into aphasia precedes Maria's death, and it could be read, in Kristevan terms, as a defense mechanism that effects a dramatic retreat from a hostile environment, that, in Maria's case, of patriarchal society: ". . . when all escape routes are blocked, animals as well as men learn to withdraw rather than flee or fight. The retardation or inactivity, which one might call depressive, would thus constitute a learned defense reaction to a dead-end situation and unavoidable shocks" (34). Death, as Kristeva points out in another passage of her essay, appears as the ultimate form of withdrawal, brought about by the subject's inability to partake of the "symbolic dimension," that dimension which Maria never manages, or wants, to inhabit: "If, on the contrary, the symbolic dimension proves to be insufficient, subjects find themselves back at the dead-end of a helplessness leading to inaction and death" (36). The death drive, thus, takes over as the subject reveals his inability to be part of society, an inability which Kristeva relates to the lack of memory which constitutes Maria's most peculiar pathological symptom: "The death drive appears as a biological unfitness for sequentiality and integration (no memory)" (18).

On the other hand, Monique's last step into depression is inscribed in a long and chaotic journal entry, the only entry which has no precise chronological referent, being headed "6 février, puis sans date"

(Beauvoir 235) [6 February: then with no date (236)]. The timelessness of the darkest stage of breakdown is similarly portrayed in *The Golden Notebook*, where Anna's writing suddenly loses coherence, and follows the chaos of her thoughts. Both characters face, when rereading their own journals, the emptiness of the linguistic signifier, and, thus, the gratuitous nature of language. As Kristeva remarks, all this is intimately related with the subject's state of depression: "Persons in despair become hyperlucid by nullifying negation. A signifying sequence, necessarily an arbitrary one, will appear to them as heavily, violently arbitrary; they will think it absurd, it will have no meaning. No word, no object in reality will be likely to have a coherent concatenation that will also be suitable to a meaning or referent" (51). The descent into a dark abyss, which is so often stressed by both diarists, is another symptom of their inability to master the chaos that surrounds them: "The chasm[15] that settles in between subject and signifiable objects is translated into the impossibility for concatenations to signify" (51). And those elements which once appeared as fundamental in their lives suddenly lose their much cherished value: the oak table which stood at the warm center of Monique's precious *foyer* suddenly becomes hollow, *creux*, and Anna's writing activity, which used to be so central in her existence, eventually becomes pointless. As they lose their sense of purpose, non-sense and emptiness invade their life: "Objects and signifiers, denied to the extent that they are identifies with life, assume the value of nonmeaning: language and life have no meaning" (51).

Brought about by an unexpected separation from the beloved, Anna and Monique's crises deeply affect their sexuality: as they start doubting their ability to give pleasure to their partners, the two women feel sexually inadequate. Kristeva identifies this stage of female depression as that of "female castration": "Loss of the erotic object (unfaithfulness or desertion by the lover or husband, divorce, etc.) is felt by the woman as an assault on her genitality and, from that point of view, amounts to castration. At once, such a castration starts resonating with the threat of destruction of the body's integrity, the body image, and the entire psychic system as well" (81). Both struck by unexpected menstrual bleeding, Anna and Monique face such threat to their physical (and sexual) integrity exactly as their partners are finally leaving them . . . it is only a matter of time before their mind will start betraying them as well.

Anna, Maria, and Monique share common or similar neuroses. They are split apart by schizophrenic attacks, deprived of their ability to function due to the lack of social memory, thrown in the midst of profound depression, hiding from a harsh reality in a pathological form of denial. Their neuroses signify their inability to adjust to patriarchal societies that are faced with the threat represented by the possibility of female emancipation. At the eve of the advent of feminism, these three women either struggle with old roles or face the drawbacks hidden in new ones. While Lessing's England certainly allows a certain degree of freedom to women, a freedom which however extols a high price on those who demand it, Beauvoir's France and Maraini's Italy are still societies where, in the mid-sixties, patriarchy almost reigns undisturbed. Some women, like Monique, have internalized its ideological *diktat* to the extent that they have become their own worst enemies. No room is allotted, no sins are forgiven to those who have rejected its law, and who have lived their life on the outskirts of society: for women like Maria, in a country like Italy, a solitary death is all that is written in the cards.

3

The War Years: Maraini's Angry Look at the Seventies

> I always see this great spectacle: in half of the world, when the sun reaches its zenith, then in narrow cells of an immense beehive, millions of women, isolated from one another, all bend at the same time performing monotonous food rituals—preparing, cleaning, chopping, cooking. (Guiducci 1983, 5)]

This is the opening statement of Amanda Guiducci's essay on the female condition, aptly entitled *Donna e serva: Storia non sentimentale della degradazione femminile* (1983). Like many busy bees, Guiducci's housewives perform their chores in a repetitive, monotonous ritual, a ritual that bespeaks a married woman's submission to her lord and master. All it takes is a brief list made of four verbs in the infinitive, four impersonal expressions, four markers of actions whose subject is, however, hidden and displaced: *preparare, pulire, sminuzzare, cuocere.* Could the alienation of millions and millions of women be described in more powerful terms? These women bend over their chores as the sun, symbol of the phallogocentrism that entraps them, reaches its zenith. They are deprived of their own individuality, dispossessed of their own agency, held captive in the isolation of the four walls that delimit a home whose curtains often disguise the invisible presence of sturdy prison bars.

In "L'arte d'amare," the long poem that opens Dacia Maraini's *Donne mie* (1974), motherhood is equated to death:

> And instead you are dead. You lost your life
> in the moment you let your flesh be torn apart
> by the soft and shiny head of
> your first adored son who smells like paraffin. (22)

yet, despite her death, a mother still remains tied to endless domestic chores:

> If a dead woman then also does the chores,
> and washes and irons and sews and responds "yes Sir,"
> then there you have found the solution to family enigmas. (22)

Another list of verbs coldly displays the many duties that enslave women to the *foyer:* the terms that describe Maraini's dead mother appear to be strikingly similar to those adopted by Guiducci in *Donna e serva.*

Only one year after the publication of *Donne mie*, Maraini authored a fictional diary entitled *Donna in guerra.* Both texts were written in the midst of the decade that witnessed the most strenuous fights for the emancipation of women. And both texts can indeed be considered Maraini's most effective contribution to the feminist debate. As Vannina, the young protagonist of *Donna in guerra*, describes the first long and uneventful days spent on vacation with her husband in Addis, a small island in southern Italy, dry lists of household chores make their reappearance on the printed page:

> Alle dieci mi sono messa a sparecchiare. Ho lavato i piatti. Ho sgrassato le pentole. Ho sciacquato i bicchieri. Ancora non mi sono abituata alla cucina stretta e lunga col pavimento di mattonelle rotte. (4)

> [At ten I started clearing the table. I washed the dishes, scoured the saucepans, rinsed the glasses. I haven't yet got used to the long narrow kitchen with its floor paved with broken tiles. (4)]

Like one of the bees portrayed by Guiducci, Vannina still remains, while on vacation, a woman defined by those duties that patriarchal society demands of her.[1] While her husband Giacinto wanders around the deep Mediterranean Sea fishing with his buddy Santino, Vannina remains confined to the small apartment which comes to constitute her unescapable realm of action.

However, in the five months covered by her diary, Vannina undergoes a profound transformation, a veritable awakening to her subjugated condition. The narration begins with her arrival in Addis and follows her encounters with the inhabitants of the island. While her husband immediately strikes a profound and ambiguous friendship with Santino, a young and beautiful fisherman, Vannina first meets with Tota and Giottina, two mysterious matriarchs who introduce her to the dark secrets of the island. Soon thereafter, she becomes very close to Suna, the disabled young woman who eventually draws her away from Giacinto. Towards Suna gravitates a series of men who belong to an extremist movement: through them, Vannina comes in contact with the underground world of political terrorism.

At the end of her vacation, she follows Suna to Naples, where she suddenly becomes involved in the activities of the group, which she eventually abandons after bearing witness to the kidnapping of the director of a prison. Upon her return to Rome, where she lives with her husband, Vannina resumes her old life, returning to the elementary school where she teaches. This time, however, the woman who steps into the classroom is a very different person. Empowered by her new sense of awareness, she refuses to comply with the patriarchal norms that demand of an educator to shape its own pupils according to its gender-biased rules, and thus embarks on a rebellious process of re-instruction of youth. As the novel draws to its end, Vannina finally stands up to her husband who, intimidated by her barely achieved independence, has gotten her pregnant despite her open resistance. Vannina's decision to have an abortion marks her final emancipation from Giacinto, whom she eventually abandons in order to pursue a new life, "Ora sono sola e ho tutto da ricominciare" (269) [Now I am alone and I must start everything again from the beginning (282)].

Addis, Naples, and Rome: Vannina's journey moves along these three places that mark her progress from the private space to the public sphere. Addis is where most of the action occurs: of this island, Maraini chooses to portray its most secluded and enclosed spaces while offering, at the same time, an extremely bleak portrayal of its phallocentric environment. The two most widely discussed areas of action are the small apartment in which Vannina and Giacinto are spending their cheap vacation, and the *lavanderia* where Tota works, the place which witnesses Vannina's strange encounters with her two female friends, Tota and Giottina. When she first describes the house, Vannina likens it to a tadpole, because of its irregular shape.[2] Its gloominess is aptly reinforced by the presence of a black curtain that separates the kitchen from the bedroom. Still ensnared in the phallocentric trap, Vannina finds the court, where a tall wall closes in on her: "In compenso abbiamo un bellissimo cortile, chiuso dentro un muro alto tre metri, segreto come un giardino arabo" (4). [To make up for it we have a beautiful courtyard, enclosed by ten foot walls, as secret as an Arab garden (4)]. Beautiful like an exotic garden, the *cortile* is also suffocating like an Arabic *harem*, bespeaking, as it does, her very imprisonment in the private sphere of the *foyer*. The court is essentially an orchard where vegetables grow, the same vegetables which constitute basic components of the meals she is expected to prepare. Beautiful flowers only decorate this corner of the house, a claustrophobic corner designed to act as yet another stage to her domestic duties: "Ci cresce il basilico, l'erba medica, la mentuccia, il pomodoro. E poi ci sono anche i gerani, bianchi e violetti, le zinnie, e gli anemoni" (4) [In it grow basil, alfalfa, mint, and tomato plants. There are also some white and violet geraniums, zinnias, and windflowers (4)]. The banana trees that stand at its center act as a powerful phallic image of domination: "Al centro, come un cuore verde e lucido, un gruppo di banani. Lustri e pallidi, si muovono con un rumore di gomma strusciata" (5) [In the centre, like a green, glistening heart, grows a cluster of banana trees; lustrous and pale, the leaves rustle with a noise like brushed rubber (5)]. Under the protective shade of these trees, Vannina often finds solace and repair, far from a madding crowd to which she feels she does not belong: "Abbiamo preso il caffè in cortile, all'ombra dei banani" (3) [We had coffee in the yard, in the shade of the banana trees (3)].

Yet, the magic garden immediately appears not to shelter her much: the objects thrown by her neighbors over the wall which separates their properties appear as a sign of intrusion which eventually turns into a symbolic act of violation. Fish, a wounded cat, and a used condom still filled with sperm eventually replace the ball that initially crosses the wall. Her frequent complaints have little effect: they are met with excuses, lies, and open derision. As Suna will eventually point out, such forms of abuse only recur because of Vannina's inability to intimidate people: "Qualsiasi cosa fai, non riesci a mettere paura, sei troppo mite" (111) [Whatever you do, you never succeed in scaring anyone, you're too meek (114)]. The wall of fear is, then, the real wall behind which Vannina hides, and her inability to overcome its towering presence turns her into vulnerable prey to the sadistic impulses of the males around her. While secluded, her own apartment still remains inherently dangerous: not only do these criminal neighbors often invade it, but it is also the place where domestic violence occurs. Indeed, it is in this house that, confronted with the news that Vannina slept with another man, Giacinto reacts by hitting her in the back: "Poi improvvisamente, mentre pulivo il lavello, mi è arrivato un pugno sulla schiena. Non ho fatto in tempo a voltarmi. Mi è venuto addosso come un cane inferocito" (104) [Then all of a sudden, as I was wiping down the kitchen table, I felt a punch in my back. I didn't have time to turn round before he came at me like a savage dog (106)]. A different sort of aggression, that which more subtly affects the woman's psyche, is enacted in the same place by another man, Vittorio, the leader of the leftist group with which she suddenly becomes involved through Suna. Barging into her house in order to get to Suna through Vannina, he starts ordering her around and Vannina duly complies, falling under the spell he casts with a voice which hides, under its sweetness, strong paternalistic attitude. Giacinto, Vittorio and his friend Faele discuss Communist ideology while Vannina is left to accommodate their every need: at one point, one of them utters a vulgar sentence which constitutes, however, an interesting rewriting of a popular Italian proverb. While the original saying, "Tira più un pelo di figa che cento paia di buoi," states the extent to which women and their sexual attractiveness lead men into action, the version offered in the text asserts the contrary, reaffirming phallocentric domination and influence over women:

> - Tira più un pelo di cazzo che cento paia di buoi, lo sapevi? Sono scoppiati a ridere. Faele ha staccato un pezzo di foglia lustra del banano, l'ha sbriciolata fra le dita nervosamente. Vittorio ha spento il mezzo sigaro contro un blocchetto di tufo e poi se l'è infilato in tasca. (107)
>
> ["One hair of a man's prick is stronger than a hundred oxen, did you know that?" They burst out laughing. Faele broke a piece of shiny banana leaf and crumbled it nervously in his fingers. Vittorio put out his half-smoked cigar against a stone and slipped it into his pocket. (110)]

The men's laughter further reinforces female disempowerment, as does the indication that this conversation is occurring under the phallocentric *locus* par excellence, the banana tree. Prisoner in a house that acts as the objective correlative of her subjugation, Vannina remains, while in her house in Addis, accomplice to her own victimization. Unable to question a system that denies her freedom, she stays in what Doris Lessing called, in a different context, *prisons we choose to live in.*

Dangerous and demeaning, because still falling within the male domain, the house is counterbalanced by a different space, that of the laundry where Vannina meets with Tota and Giottina. Marked as a feminine space whose threshold is never crossed by a male foot, Giottina's shop is depicted as a dark cave where fumes of bleach create a peculiar atmosphere: "La lavanderia è una stanza lunga e buia, ricavata da una grotta scavata nel tufo. . . . La roba pulita penzola dal soffitto, appesa a cordicelle di nailon. Sono stata assalita da un odore violento di varechina che mi ha tolto il fiato" (9) [The laundrette is a long, dark room, carved out of rock and containing two enormous washing machines . . . The clean laundry hangs from the ceiling, drying on nylon lines. As I entered I was assailed by a violent stench of ammonia that took my breath away (9)]. Clean laundry is left hanging in a spectral fashion, its whiteness standing out in the dark environment, its ghostlike presence akin to that of the characters evoked in the sordid tales of the two women. Giottina and Tota are both presented as heavyset matriarchs whose features are as enigmatic as the stories they relentlessly narrate: "Giottina assomiglia a Tota. Ha il corpo come un fagotto. Le braccia corte, forti, abbronzate; la faccia senza età, gli occhi grandi, languidi" (9) [Giottina looks just like Tota. Her body is a bundle, she has short, strong, sun-tanned arms, an ageless face and large, listless eyes (9)]. Ageless priestesses of a pagan cult, they take pleasure in spinning narratives which focus on sexual perversions; their storytelling acquires ritual overtones as the voices of the two women alternate with short, stychmomythic utterances:

> - Alla villa Trionfo l'amore si fa sputazza.
> - La sputazza si fa semenza.
> - La semenza si fa veleno.
> - La serva si fa padrona.
> - Portasse le monete d'oro cucite nel vestito.
> - Camminasse come il diavolo, sui piedi in punta.
> - Li vedesti quando scendono per la passiata?
> - La padrona innanze, come una reggina, il marito dietro a tre passi e la serva in fondo, con i bracciali che fanno tirintin, tin, tin.
>
> Le voci si alternano, rapide, guizzanti, senza mai coprirsi. Un ritmo gioioso e caldo. Casco dentro un sogno afoso e serpentino. (13)
>
> ["At the Villa Trionfo love-making has turned into whoring." "Whoring has turned into sperm." "Sperm has turned into poison." "The maid becomes the mistress." "She carries gold coins sewn into her dress." "And walks like the devil on tiptoe." "Did you see them when they came down for a stroll." "The mistress in front like a queen her husband three steps behind and the maid last with her tinkling bangles." The voices alternate with each other, swift, darting, without ever overlapping, a joyful, undulating rhythm. I listen to them, forgetting the heat. (13)]

Vannina is thus lulled into a hypnotic dreamworld where class and gender roles are strangely reversed, where slaves turn into masters and women subjugate their men, tying them up and reducing them to mere puppets: "Isso non fa niente, il marito meschinello, rimane così vestito e le due serpente si baciano, si baciano, si strusciano, e lui rema, lo coglione, la camicia zuppetta insudorata, la cravatta a penzoloni, non dice niente il meschinello, rema e va" (13) ["The man doesn't do anything, poor sod, just stays still, all dressed up like that. And the two serpents kiss each other, pet, rub against each other, and he rows on, the prick, his shirt soaking with sweat, his tie dangling down, he doesn't say a word, the idiot, he just rows and rows" (13)]. Emasculated to the extent that his tie, like a symbolically limp penis, is left hanging, *a penzoloni*, the male protagonist of this tale is only one of the many disempowered men who appear in these women's tales. Like him, all men are left aside, constricted to a voyeuristic role that, however, does not allow them to turn women into hapless objects of their gaze. Hopelessly staring at their unreachable objects of desire, these men appear to be extremely conscious of their doomed condition. Fantasies of female empowerment thus unravel in the deep recess of the earth, in the smoky cave where, in their oracular fashion, Tota and Giottina reside, in a netherworld towards which Vannina feels inexplicably drawn:

> Non entrerò piú lí dentro, ho detto. Ma so che ci tornerò. E' un teatro buio e afoso dove si improvvisano inquietanti giochi dell'immaginazione. Giochi rustici, spericolati, pieni di una sensualità agra, selvatica che mi affascina nonostante la nausea. (14)
>
> [I won't go back there again, I told myself. But I know I would. It's like a dark theatre where they improvise disturbing fantasies, reckless games full of bitter sensuality that fascinate me in spite of the nausea. (14)]

With the two women Vannina ventures, for the first time, into the mysterious hills of Addis. In this unique foray into the outside world, Vannina embarks on a dramatic ascent to the house of an American woman who left all her earthly belongings in order to conduct an ascetic life away from civilization. The foreign hermit, however, shall not welcome the three women, only her dead body awaits them in the hut: Tota and Giottina, then, perform a strange funerary rite witnessed and subsequently recorded by Vannina. Occurring on 15 August[3], the day that celebrates the Virgin's ascent to heaven, *l'Assunzione*, this trip immediately acquires mystic overtones. When the two women step into Vannina's house, they refuse to inform her of the whereabouts of their excursion; both dressed in black, they hold Vannina by her arms, as if they were holding her hostage. A disfigured portrait of the Virgin appears on the way to the hilltop, as Vannina voices her desire to rest by a fountain, where she hopes to quench her thirst. The fountain, however, has gone dry for fifteen years, and the holy image it bears on its top only reinforces a Wastelandian atmosphere: "Sopra la fontana secca c'è un minuscolo tabernacolo di mattoni. Dentro, una statuetta della madonna dalla faccia mangiata e bucherellata che sembrava avesse il vaiolo" (74) [Above the dried-up fountain there was a minute niche made of bricks. Inside was a small statue of the madonna with such a riddled face it looked as if she were suffering from small-pox (75)]. As their pilgrimage progresses, Vannina re-experiences the harshness of a landscape that assumes religious overtones once thorns start bruising her legs: "Il sentiero si è fatto piú stretto. Siamo state costrette a metterci in fila indiana . . . i rovi ci graffiavano le gambe" (75) [The path became narrower and we had to walk in single file . . . There were no trees, no shrubs, no shade, only brambles which scrtched our legs . . . (75)]. Even the walking rhythm of the two women reminds Vannina of a mystic event: "Tota e Giottina, ora che avevano rallentato l'andatura, avevano acquistato qualcosa di ieratico, di religioso nel loro modo di procedere, quasi stessimo raggiungendo la meta di un pellegrinaggio santo" (76) [Now that they had slowed down, Tota and Giottina had acquired something stately, almost sacred in the way they advanced, as if we were about to reach the end of a holy pilgrimage (76)]. It is from the hilltop that Vannina suddenly assumes a new perspective on her life: as she looks down towards the village, she becomes aware of her usual state of confinement: "Tutta quell'aria libera, quel vento, quegli orizzonti aperti mi hanno dato un senso di vertigine. Abituata a stare sempre chiusa fra le mura del mio cortile, avevo perso il senso dello spazio. Ho serrato gli occhi feriti dalla luce. Avevo un dolore al petto. Ho sentito subito la stretta delle due mani amiche" (75) [All that air, the wind, the wide open horizon, made my head spin. Accustomed as I was to being shut in between the walls of my courtyard, I was overcome by the sense of space. I had a pain in my chest and the fierce light assaulted my eyes. I closed them and immediately felt the grip of two friendly hands (76)]. The friendly hands that hold her, pushing her forward toward a symbolic ascent toward the full recognition of the mystery of womanhood and motherhood, lead her away from her former seclusion and take her into a hut where new discoveries are about to occur. In witchlike fashion, Tota and Giottina precede their entry into the cabin with a ritual that combines sacred and profane elements. As they cross the threshold, the two women begin a mysterious chant, in which they invoke the resurrection of the soul of the dead woman. Their prayer refers to Christ's physical suffering, yet it is not clear whether they are only describing Christ's abused body or they are actually juxtaposing it to that of the dead hermit:

- Anima candida, cuore addolorato, vai con la morte, vai senza vita.
- Madonna, aiutala a sortire dal corpo.
- Il sangue pesa, l'anima piange.
- Gesù mio, acchiappala per mano.
- Cuore sanguinante.
- Tempie martirizzate.
- Mani inchiodate.
- Piedi crocifissi.
- Costato avvelenato dal fiele.
- Bocca bruciata dall'aceto.

- Prendila, signore, piccolo re.
- Portala via con te. (76)

> ["Poor innocent soul, afflicted heart, may your death be peaceful." "Holy Mary, help her to free herself from her body." "The blood is heavy, the soul is weeping." "Jesus, seize her hand." "Heart bleeding." "Hands nailed." "Feet crucified." "Temples tormented." "Chest poisoned by gall." "Mouth burned by vinegar." "Take her, Lord, my Prince." "Take her away with you." (77)]

Which is the body in pain that they are evoking? Who is the bearer of such suffering? Is it Christ or is it the woman Vannina will soon discover laying lifeless on a bed, a woman whose ample naked body strangely resembles that of Tota and Giottina? What appears evident from the text, in fact, is that this woman partakes of Christ's same divine aura: her eyes, which refuse to close, "Tota le ha calato le palpebre. Ma gli occhi sono tornati ad aprirsi, lentamente sembravano guardare proprio me" (77) [. . . Tota lowered her eyelids. But her eyes slowly opened up again and seemed to stare straight at me (77)] come to symbolize the power to see, and act, beyond one's death, a power that she once again shares with Christ. Tota and Giottina can be then identified as priestesses of a synchretic cult which, mixing pagan and Catholic elements, results in the adoration of a modern personification of the Earth Mother, the Goddess which historians and mythologists have often seen as a pagan version of the Virgin Mary. Both archetypal mothers, these two figures differ, however, because the empowered status of the former clearly contrasts with the disempowered condition of the latter, whose sacred role in the Catholic world only stems from the fact that she is the mother of Christ. Divested of her earthly garments by Tota and Giottina, the dead woman appears to hide, in the deepest recesses of her body, a talisman:

> Era un grosso fallo d'oro da cui pendeva un sacchetto di maglia d'argento. Dentro la maglia si intravvedeva qualcosa di rosso. Ho premuto le due estremità della cerniera e mi sono trovata nel cavo della mano due uova di corallo della grandezza di un fagiolo. (78)

> [It was a large gold phallus from which a small silver net dangled. Inside the mesh I caught a glimpse of something red. I pressed the two ends of the clasp and there in the palm of my hands were two coral eggs the size of beans. (78)]

The golden phallus, that Giottina immediately steals from Vannina's hands and subsequently places in her breast, can thus be read as a magic symbol of empowerment, conferring supremacy to women, bearers of the phallus, over disempowered, virtually castrated men.

Before they abandon the hut, the three women pause to read a bundle of letters that they discover among the few things owned by the old American. In these epistles, a son informs his distant mother of the untimely demise of his own child, and of his unhappy marriage. He harshly accuses the old lady of having failed him as a mother: "'Cara mamma, oggi è nato George, gli abbiamo dato il tuo nome per ricordo di te, lo so che a te non te ne importa niente, ma è un modo di sentirti vicina'" (79) ["Today George was born, we called him that because of you. I know that you don't care but it's a way of feeling close to you" (79)]. Another contradiction is thus introduced in the text: why does the woman, who represents a divinity of a matriarchal cult, hide a talisman shaped after the male phallus? And why, if she is meant to represent an archetypal mother, is she depicted as a bad parent? All this could certainly be interpreted, within the larger context of the novel in which it is placed, as a sign of the failure of such myths and such archetypes. Tota and Giottina, in fact, while appearing as quintessential matriarchs, often condone in their speech domestic abuse: discussing Santino's father, who probably constitutes, within the text, the most abhorrent figure of male chauvinism, they justify his terrible actions by stating that, notwithstanding his violent actions, he is a good man:

> Qualche volta la prende a pugni, è manesco quell'uomo, non cattivo, ricco, buono, religioso, bravo, devi vedere quando vanno a messa tutta la famiglia, la domenica, sono favoriti, belli, devoti, bravi, una famiglia molto rispettata insomma. (40)

> ["Sometimes he punches her with his fists—he's a violent man. He isn't bad, though, he's a decent man, rich, pious, good-natured. You should see them when they go to Mass on Sunday, the whole family together, they're the best people in town, good-looking, devout, hard workers, oh yes, they're a very respected family." (40)]

All these elements certainly deflate the transgressive quality of these women's discourse: their words lose power once they betray their contradictory nature. Voices from the netherworld, from the dark caves of the earth, Tota and Giottina come to represent the voices of female atavistic revolt. And they also signify, through their confinement in the darkness, the doomed nature of such rebellion, in a symbolic reenactment of the defeat of matriarchy at the hands of the patriarchal world. Giottina and Tota do not offer Vannina any potential weapon which could enable her to achieve her own independence from men: their words are sterile, and their orgiastic tales belong to a dreamworld that comes to life only among the fumes of bleach of Giottina's haunted laundry.

Vannina's apartment and Giottina's laundry, however, are not the only places that delimit Vannina's field of action in Addis: a third location often appears, the *piazza*, the town square dominated by a bar aptly named *Mondo*. Representative of the real world, of a universe that essentially revolves around men, this bar is a place where Vannina never wanders unaccompanied by her husband. There, young men endlessly stroll, boasting of their beauty and selling their bodies to rich old women whose charm has long vanished. Always in control, even when they prostitute themselves, men always remain in charge of the female gaze:

> Arrivano a due a due, camminando mollemente. Sono giovanotti sui vent'anni, di una bellezza appariscente, curata. Portano pantaloni attillati, camicie aperte sul petto abbronzato, zoccoli alti, catenine d'argento ai polsi, ciondoli d'oro al collo. Si guardano intorno senza vedere, con occhi languidi e distratti. Hanno i capelli schiariti dalla camomilla, lunghi sul collo, a ciocche, o a riccioli lucidi che scivolano pigramente sugli occhi. Passano fra i tavolini fingendo di non accorgersi di niente. Ma i loro sguardi rapaci hanno già scovato in un lampo chi cercano: delle donne anziane, eleganti che seggono sole negli angoli più bui. (16)

> [They arrived in twos, strolling along idly. They are young men in their twenties, affected and sophisticated. They wear tight-fitting trousers, shirts open to their tanned chests, wedge-heeled clogs, silver chains at their wrists, gold trinkets at their necks. They look around without seeing, with dreamy languid eyes. Their hair is lightened with camomile rinse and they wear it down to their necks or in shiny curls falling indolently over their eyes. They make their way through the tables, feigning indifference. But their roving eyes track down what they're after in a flash—some smartly dressed middle-aged women sitting alone in a dark corner. (16)]

Vannina's first description of the bar's customers provides the reader with a detailed presentation of gender roles and common attitudes of the Italian working class: "Donne grasse che parlano a mezza voce, guardinghe, pigre, furtive. Uomini flaccidi, panciuti, la camicia aperta sul petto peloso. Seguono con languida intensità tutte le ragazze che passano. Fanno commenti a voce alta" (7) [. . . fat women chatting idly in low voices; flabby, pot-bellied men, their shirts opened up to their hairy chests. With indolent intentness they follow all the girls that pass by and comment on them in loud voices

(7)]. The contrastive nature of this passage essentially relies on two features that differentiate women from men: the voice and the gaze. While men establish their superior status by mastering both features, being loud and openly voyeuristic, women, to the contrary, speak softly and avert their eyes from the public arena. The same distinction applies to the younger generations: "I figli di questi genitori sono in genere asciutti, inquieti, la pelle annerita dal sole, il sedere in vista dentro pantaloni attillatissimi. Portano occhiali scuri e magliette dai colori squillanti. Le figlie sono più rotonde e guardinghe. Si muovono in gruppo, scontrose, impacciate, parlando a voce bassa fra di loro. Non si truccano, portano i capelli abbandonati sulle spalle, la gonna corta sopra le ginocchia. Ai piedi zoccoli altissimi" (7) [The sons are mostly lean, restless, sun-tanned, encased in extra tight-fitting trousers, their buttocks conspicuously in evidence. They wear dark glasses and brightly-colored T-shirts. The daughters are plumper and more wary. They move about in groups, unsociable, ill-at-ease, talking amongst themselves in low voices. They wear their hair shoulder-length, no make-up, thigh-length skirts and sandals with very high heels (7)]. While the young men flaunt their attractive bodies in revealing clothes, their female counterparts hide behind their friends, trying not to become the source of any sort of attraction. In Maraini's novel the male body is always the center of attention: in this case, it appears as a phallic body, a body which proclaims, through its vain exhibition, the superior nature of its owner. Objects of desire that are supposed to attract the attention of the female bystanders, these bodies are carefully arranged and displayed in order to exploit and further disempower the women who are eventually cast by their spell. Like true businessmen, these men make great fortunes and support entire families by selling their phallic bodies to rich and lonely women. Unlike female prostitutes, they appear to be the pride and joy of the entire population of Addis, which flaunts its male beauties as one of its most cherished resources.

Man, thus, remains the proverbial hunter even when he disguises himself as prey. An island of fishermen, Addis is the place where fishing, a subspecies of hunting, appears to be the main habit of most men, locals and tourists alike. Quite poignantly, Maraini decides to open Vannina's diary on a passage that describes her husband's love for fishing:

> 1 agosto 1970
> Giacinto è andato a pescare. Si è alzato alle sette. Prima ancora di lavarsi la faccia ha allineato per terra i suoi attrezzi da pesca; li ha puliti uno per uno con lo straccio intinto nel petrolio (3).

> [1st August. Giacinto has gone fishing. He got up at seven. Even before washing his face he lined up his fishing tackle on the floor and cleaned it item by item with a rag dipped in paraffin. (3)]

The act of arranging and cleaning the fishing equipment can be easily interpreted as an empowering act of masculine performance: later in the text, Vannina describes Giacinto as a "ragazzo indeciso e solitario," (3) [. . . a lonesome, uncertain boy (3)] whose sleeping posture denotes fear and vulnerability, "Giacinto dorme. Se ne sta rannicchiato tutto nudo sul letto, nascondendo il sesso fra le ginocchia. La schiena curva, la testa incassata fra le spalle, le gambe piegate esprimono una accanita difesa. Di che cosa, non lo so" (6) [Giacinto's asleep. He's curled up naked on the bed, hiding his genitals between his thighs. He's hunched back, his head deeply set between his shoulders, his bent legs, all express a tenacious self-defence. Against what, I wonder? (6)]. His naked body, though, is quite different from that of the male prostitutes: in Giacinto's case, it bespeaks his frailty and not his phallic power, as clearly implied by the fact that his penis is hidden from sight. Assuming a fetal position, Giacinto thus appears, ever since the inception of Maraini's novel, as a dephallicized man, as a seeker of the lost phallus which can only be regained through a universally acknowledged rite of manhood: fishing[4]. Empowered by the fishing instruments, Giacinto can thus stage a virility which otherwise he seems to lack. His friendship with Santino, his fishing buddy, presents extreme homoerotic overtones. From the moment Santino shows up at their doorstep, Giacinto permanently reverts his attention from his wife to his newfound companion. Like him, Santino has childlike qualities, "E' alto, più di Giacinto, bello di una bellezza infantile, capricciosa," (14) [He was tall, taller than Giacinto, with the beauty of a spoilt child (14)] like him, he does not boast a phallic body, "Il ragazzo non parlava. Mangiava, sorrideva, tenendo le gambe allacciate sotto la tavola" [The boy didn't speak: he ate smiling to himself and keeping his legs crossed under the table (14)].[5] Like Vannina, Santino appears to be in awe of Giacinto, "Santino lo stava a sentire serio, attento, gli occhi sgranati" (14) [. . . Santino listened to him, serious, attentive, his eyes wide open (14)]. Great tenderness characterizes their exchanges, "Santino ha preso la tazzina, si è chinato sull'amico, l'ha svegliato sfiorandogli gli occhi con le dita" (15) [Santino picked [the cup] up, bent over his friend, and woke him up by a gentle touch of his finger on his eyelids (15)]. Evident codependency is immediately established between the two men, whose pseudo-virile bonding openly excludes Vannina: "Poi lui e Giacinto si sono stesi sulla sedia a sdraio, *all'ombra dei banani*"

(15, emphasis mine) [Afterwards he and Giacinto stretched out on the deck-chairs in the shade of the banana trees (15)]. Happy because they had a fruitful fishing venture, the two men return home, in another occasion, and start behaving like a true couple: "Erano allegri. Hanno voluto pulire loro il pesce, e anche preparare la tavola lanciandosi i piatti, i bicchieri, le posate, con delle grandi risate festose" (113) [. . . they were both in good mood. They insisted on cleaning the fish themselves. They tossed the plates, glasses, and cutlery at each other with cheerful laughter (115)]. Fishing, in fact, actually strengthens their strange bond, as Maria Comninou clearly explains in "Speech, Pornography, and Hunting": "For hunters, game animals provide sport and a means of validation of their manhood or brotherhood with other hunters" (1995, 135). By the same token, Santino's occasional absence inevitably saddens Giacinto, who feels abandoned. It is only fitting, at that point, that a dejected Vannina eventually sleeps with Santino's younger brother, Orio. Upon learning the news, Giacinto feels doubly betrayed, because in Orio his wife has chosen, as a lover, a symbolic alterego of his own platonic object of desire, Santino. It is once again relevant that, at first, Giacinto does not have the strength to react to his wife's adultery; before he can actually attack her, he needs to empower himself by touching his fishing rifle: "Avrei voluto continuare, ma ho capito dalla sua faccia che preferiva non parlarne più. Mi sono messa a lavare i piatti. Lui se n'è andato in camera da letto. L'ho sentito trafficare col fucile subacqueo. Poi improvvisamente, mentre pulivo il lavello, mi è arrivato un pugno sulla schiena" (104) [I would have liked to carry on, but looking at his face it was clear that he wasn't prepared to talk about it any longer. I started washing the dishes. He went into the bedroom. I heard him bustling about with his spear gun. Then all of a sudden, as I was wiping down the kitchen sink, I felt a punch in my back (106)]. In "Woman-Battering and Harm to Animals," Carol Adams affirms that "when a man hits a woman, he has not lost control—he achieves and maintains control: *It is not so much what is done but what is accomplished.* Not only is he achieving and maintaining control, but he is reminding the woman of her subordinate status in the world" (1995, 57). By hitting his wife, then, Giacinto reassumes control of the situation and, having reestablished a balance in their relationship, he feels entitled to switch abruptly from abuse to lovemaking: "Mi ha riempita di pugni, di calci, di morsi. Poi di colpo mi ha abbracciata" (104) [He covered me with punches, kicks and bites. Then suddenly he put his arms around me and hugged me (106)].

The constant association of fishing to a violent form of sexual intercourse, one that empowers man while disempowering its prey, is again stressed by Vannina's description of the two shops that Giacinto finds most attractive: the swimwear shop, and its adjacent fishing shop. The former, significantly called "Pussy Pussy Bang Bang," always presents different decorations in its shop windows, "costumi appesi a rami di corallo, oppure adagiati su un fondo marino bianco e struggente, o galleggianti su un mare in tempesta. . . . Giacinto è affascinato da quei fondali marini dai colori bizzarri e clamorosi. Un miraggio iridescente in cui ciondolano piccoli pezzi di stoffa misteriosi e invitanti" (22) [. . . costumes hanging from coral branches, or placed carefully on a white sea-bed, or floating on a stormy sea. . . . Giacinto is fascinated by these vividly coloured sea-beds. They are an iridescent mirage in the middle of which dangle tiny inviting garments and mysterious bits of fabric (22)]. Projecting his sexual fantasies onto the objects so cunningly displayed in a shop window, Giacinto falls prey to this mirage of phallic empowerment: "Giacinto si è fermato un momento davanti al Pussy Pussy Bang Bang. Degli slip a fiori rosa svolazzano sull'albero di una nave di cartone, a mo' di vela" (43) [Giacinto stopped for a minute in front of the Pussy Pussy Bang Bang shop. Some pink floral slips fluttered from the mast of a cardboard ship, like a sail (43)]. In a different fashion, a similar effect is produced by the array of fishing equipment displayed in the other shop. In this case, however, Giacinto does not happen to project his sexual fantasies, yet he dreams of finding ways to compensate for his lacking virility: "Una bacheca zeppa di oggetti da pesca: maschere nere e gialle, pinne azzurre, tute subacquee rosse e verdi, coltelli di plastica galleggianti. Sono sempre le stesse cose, ammucchiate in maniera caotica, ma Giacinto non si stanca mai di guardare" (22) [. . . it's a showcase full of fishing gear: black and yellow masks, light blue flippers, red and green diving suits, plastic knives that will float. It's always the same stuff, but Giacinto never tires of looking at it . . . (22)]. What appears most evident in these passages is that Giacinto is construed as the only desiring subject in the couple: Vannina, on the other hand, expresses neither desire nor interest in anything. Until she meets Suna, who suddenly confronts her with the grim reality she has chosen to live, Vannina remains happy with what little she has.

A confusing arrangement of different objects once again attracts the attention of the couple when they have dinner at Santino's house. Vannina precedes her portrayal of a family unit strictly ruled by the laws of phallocracy with a suggestive description of the house in which they live: "E' una casa di un secolo fa, di pietra chiara, ha le finestre piccole, i muri spessi, delle strisce di muffa che la macchiano per lungo. Le porte sono vecchie e tarlate" (28) [The house is over a century old, of white stone, with small windows, thick walls and damp patches staining it all along its length. The doors are red and full of woodworm (28)]. The small windows, as well as the thick walls, already prefigure the house as a prison, as a fortress where two women are held captive: Santino's mother and sister. The spots that cover its walls, as well as the damaged doors, signify the profound corruption of most of its male members, namely Santino's father and his older brothers, whose criminal and sadistic persecution of women is soon unveiled. Orio, the youngest, naïve brother ushers them in, and then abandons them in the living room. Here begins Vannina's perusal of the many objects that furnish this strange place:

> Il divano è foderato di finto leopardo. Accanto c'è una poltrona di plastica rossa con una grossa bambola bionda seduta sopra a gambe larghe . . . sopra una mensola tirata a lucido fanno spicco alcuni oggetti vistosi: una madonna dentro una conchiglia gigantesca, uno scarpone di ceramica pieno di fiori finti, una bottiglia di profumo in forma di mela, una barca egiziana che serve da portacenere, un cannoncino di ottone che fa da accendisigari. Alle pareti sono appesi quadretti con damine del settecento a passeggio nei giardini del parco reale di Napoli. (28)

> [. . . a sofa lined with imitation leopard skin. Next to it there's a red plastic armchair on which sits a big blond doll with its legs wide apart . . . The top (of the sideboard) is highly polished and on it is an array of garish objects: a madonna inside a gigantic shell, a ceramic boot filled with artificial flowers, a bottle of perfume shaped like an apple, an ashtray like an Egyptian boat, a cigarette lighter in the form of a small brass cannon. On the walls hang small paintings representing seventeenth century damsels strolling round the gardens of the royal park of Naples. (28)]

Such collection of kitsch *bibelots* certainly deserves to be carefully analyzed. The fake leopard skin which covers the sofa already betrays the hegemonic presence of the hunter's mentality, extended metaphorically to the hunting of women as signified by the blond doll, poignantly arranged with her legs wide open. Different images of femininity are encountered: from the objectified woman as sexual prey represented by the doll, to the idealistic portrayal of *femminilità* from another era, as witnessed by the painting of the Neapolitan dames. Like the doll, these dames are materially and symbolically framed, as a reminder of the framing power of phallocentrism. The statue of the Madonna, representing female chastity, is counterbalanced by the presence of the apple-shaped bottle of perfume, symbol of the archetypal temptress, Eve. The former is enwrapped, and thus framed by a shell, while the latter discloses its threatening power in the liquid contained, and thus again framed, in a bottle. Be it the image of purity or sin, be it idealized beauty or objectified prey, woman is always represented, through these objects, as victim. And for every victim, of course, there needs to be evoked the presence of a victimizer: the large shoe that contains fake flowers is an image of oppression as much as the ashtray and the lighter, both strictly connected to the phallic image *par excellence*, the cigarette.

Sheer brutality connotes most male members of Santino's family: his father is immediately likened to a wolf: "Il padre alza la testa dal piatto. Ha i denti lucidi, bianchi, da lupo" (30) [. . . the father raises his head from his plate. he has sparkling, white, wolf-like teeth (30)] while his older brothers all seem to be different from Santino and Orio because of their aggressive masculinity: ". . . alti, bruni, l'aria spavalda e sicura. Hanno facce svogliate, tratti vigorosi, spalle da nuotatore, ma nessuno è bello come Santino o come Orio. Qualcosa di brutale gli aggronda le facce giovanili" (30) [. . . tall, dark, they look cocksure and confident. They have listless faces, strong features and swimmer's shoulders. But none of them is as good-looking as Santino or Orio: there is a hint of brutality tainting their youthful faces (30)]. The food they are so voraciously devouring is, naturally, fish, which plays such a symbolic role in the entire novel. Metaphor for the male penis, as evidenced in Orio's speech, as well as metaphor for the quintessential male prey, woman, *fish* comes to symbolize the Lacanian phallus, that which all men are bound to try and regain through their relationships with women, quintessential bearers of the phallus itself. Possession and abuse of women, then, essentially partake of the same symbolic role played by fishing and hunting: they all reaffirm male virility, they all reenact a primal scene in which men try to win back their lost phallus. Asked by their father to entertain their guests with tales that bespeak their male prowess, Santino's older brothers recount, under their father's glowing eyes, the atrocious rape of two foreign women. While the gang rape of a rich German woman is mainly described in order to reassess, once again, the phallic power of Addis's young male prostitutes, the violation of a young English tourist is disclosed in a tale that aptly comments on the symbolic connection between women and fish.

> - La incoccio che nuota da sola a cento metri dalla riva . . . ci avviciniamo ancora, quella naviga come un pesce e noi dietro, la spingevamo fuori, al largo; nuota nuota, si agitava, poi quando è stanca, la tiriamo su di peso, era livida, batteva i denti, allora dico: hai visto a che serve scappare a un bello giovanotto come me? prima l'asciugo bene bene, poi l'afferro per il collo e le tiro le mutande . . . si dimenava come un'anguilla, mordeva, graffiava; dico: va bene, ora lo sai che faccio visto che non mi vuoi? ti butto a mare . . . l'ho scaraventata in acqua . . . il mare si ingrossava . . . lei ha

preso paura, si affannava, nuotava e beveva, piangeva e si mangiava le lagrime. Quando la vedo che non ce la fa più infatti la pesco, la tiro su, l'asciugo, la strofino e me la chiavo là sul fondo della barca che pareva un pesce morto." (32–33)

["I bump into this bird as she's swimming along a hundred yards from the shore . . . we get closer. . . . She sails along like a fish and we follow behind. We were gradually edging her off shore. She swims and swims and tosses about, then when she's really tired we hoist her bodily into the boat. She was sort of livid blue color and her teeth were chattering, so I say: "Do you see now that it's no use running away from a handsome lad like me?" First I dry her well, then I grab her by the neck with one hand and pull her knickers off with the other . . . She started wriggling like an eel, biting and scratching. I say: "Okay then, if that's how you want it. You know what I'm going to do? Throw you back in the water". . . I grabbed her and slung her back into the water. . . . the sea was getting rougher . . . she got really scared, she was struggling and panting, taking in mouthfuls of sea-water, crying and swallowing her own tears. . . . When I see that she really can't cope any longer, I heave her up into the boat, dry her and screw her right there in the bottom of the boat. Well, it was all the same as screwing a dead fish." (32–33)]

Initially depicted as capable of swimming like a fish, the poor victim is followed and caught in a trap like a veritable prey; like the helpless animal which refuses to surrender to the fisherman, the woman tries to escape the figural net thrown by her abuser. Once she is finally pulled into the boat, she is treated again like a fish who is about to be killed: holding her by the neck, the man pulls her bikini down with the same mechanical gestures performed by the fisherman who takes the hook off his prey. Like an eel that still refuses to die, the woman poses resistance, by moving and shaking uncontrollably. One last act of cruelty leads the aggressor to throw her back into the sea, only to take her back once she is absolutely unable to resist her rapists. Santino's brother actually refers to this last action by using, again, terms that belong to the semantic field of fishing: he *fishes* her back and, once the violation is performed, she appears to resemble a *dead fish*.

While the young men recount such tales of violence, Vannina also registers the different reactions of the two women of the family. Santino's mother is clearly disgusted by the speech, yet her complaints meet no answer. *Donna e serva* like the typical housewife studied by Amanda Guiducci, this woman holds no power over her children. Even her daughter appears to be so ensnared by phallogocentric discourse that she actually laughs at her brothers' sordid stories: "I fratelli ora ridono compiaciuti, a bocca piena. Solo Santino rifiuta di partecipare allo spettacolo, ma in modo assente, passivo. Laura ride, approva con timidezza" (35) [The brothers are now laughing with their mouths full. Only Santino refuses to participate in the performance, but in a passive, detached way. Laura shows her approval by laughing a bit uncertainly (36)]. Santino, however, is different: he does not support his brothers' actions, nor does he approve of their attitude, yet he does not voice his discontent. Like his friend Giacinto, who feels outraged by what he just heard but has no strength to denounce his indignation, he remains silent. Adams and Donovan say, in their introduction to *Animals and Women*, that ". . . in reality there is no neutral place from which to observe evil. To observe in silence is to be complicit" (1995, 3). Santino and Giacinto, then, are no less guilty than the perpetrators of such abhorrent crimes: their passivity and their silence eventually validate a behavior that should be forcefully condemned.

Only four days later, Vannina learns from Santino that his father has just died: while no details are offered on the cause of his death, large space is given to the unexpected turmoil arisen among his brothers because of the inheritance,

> - Non fece testamento perché non credeva di morire: Gigi ha tirato fuori una carta che dice che lascia tutto a lui che è il maggiore, Toto dice che se la scrivette da sé solo mettendosi d'accordo col notaio che è il padrino suo, Armando gli ha sparato con la pistola di papà, ma non l'ha preso, ora sta tutto per aria, ci hanno messo di mezzo gli avvocati, gli esecutori testamentari. (52)
>
> ["He didn't leave a will. Gigi has produced a piece of paper that says he left everything to him as the eldest son. Toto says he's hand in hand with the notary, who is his godfather, and wrote it himself. Armando took a pot shot at him with dad's pistol, but missed. Now they've dragged in the lawyers and everyone's at daggers drawn." (52)]

The three brothers, subsequently described at the funeral as "truci e gentili" (55) [threatening and gentle (55)], thus enact a battle amongst themselves that automatically excludes the weakest members of the family: the two women and the two younger brothers, "Gigi odia la mamma. . . . La casa Laura dice che è sua, ma tanto vale poco, è vecchia e cade a pezzi, ma poi non gliela daranno perché dice che è minorenne" (52–53) ["Gigi hates my mother . . . Laura says the house is hers. . . . It isn't worth much anyway, it's old and falling apart, but anyway they say she can't have it, she's under age" (53)].

In his essay on Racine's plays, Roland Barthes (1963) discusses the primeval fights that ensued after a patriarch is killed by his own sons, a primeval fight which lies at the very roots of modern society. Like the protagonists of the Barthesian hoard, the three brothers engage in a dispute that further objectifies the two women, who are treated like mere loot. Savage and primeval overtones are again evoked in this circumstance when, at the funeral, a group of *mammane*, old women who were paid to cry and despair at burials, bursts into the middle of the ceremony and enacts its strange performance: "Due donne hanno cominciato a piangere a voce alta. Un'altra donna ha mandato un grido profondo, cattivo, da lupo affamato. Altre vecchie le hanno fatto coro. C'è stato un movimento di corpi neri, alcune si sono inginocchiate per terra, altre hanno preso a strapparsi i vestiti. Il funerale stava per scatenarsi in una cerimonia antica, selvaggia" (54) [Two women began to cry loudly. Another womean gave a deep, sinister scream like a hungry wolf and this was repeated by several other women. Then there was a bustle of dark bodies, some kneeling on the ground, others starting to tear their clothes. The funeral was on the point of turning into an archaic primitive ritual (55)]. Like those Indian wives who proved their subservience to phallocracy by throwing themselves into fire at the funeral of their husbands, these women frantically mourn the death of a man who spent his entire life humiliating and persecuting them.

While this episode offers an intriguing portrayal of a world dominated by the primeval "Law of the Father," another passage in the novel aptly depicts a more contemporary aspect of the same law. In response to a particularly violent attack from their neighbors, a desperate Vannina finally reacts by throwing empty bottles on their side of the wall; what she does not expect, however, is that they answer back by reporting the event to the local police station. Summoned to appear in order to provide her own version of the events, Vannina comes face to face with a bureaucratic system which strenuously protects paternalistic interests: "Erano tutti molto gentili. Mi dicevano: si segga, si accomodi . . . meno male, dico . . . invece poi sono venuti i dolori" (95) [They were all very kind. They said: "sit down, please, take a seat . . ." Thank goodness, I thought, . . . but later the trouble started (97)]. After showing initial politeness and respect, the *carabinieri* soon become rude and disrespectful. The local authority is embodied by a man whose empty speech, full of nonsensical jargon, voices an obvious critique of the unreliable world of justice in Italy. Such a figure immediately brings to mind a character from Alessandro Manzoni's *I promessi sposi* (1842), Dottor Azzeccagarbugli, the lawyer who discourages the poor protagonist, Renzo, from claiming his own rights by quoting abstruse sentences in Latin, a language the uneducated man will never understand. Both Manzoni's and Maraini's characters obviously embody and represent a law which only protects the rich and the noble. Like his famous predecessor, the *maresciallo dei carabinieri* who questions Vannina adopts an encoded, yet empty language which is meant to exclude her from comprehension and self-justification. The version of the events that he expects Vannina to subscribe openly declares her full responsibility, while actually dismissing her neighbors' fault (97). And when Vannina dares to voice her disagreement, she encounters a wall of resistance essentially represented by the *maresciallo*'s stupid syllogisms, which are constantly aimed at establishing her guilt:

> - L'hanno ferita parimenti le bottiglie lanciate da loro?
> - No.
> - Vede? si capisce che costoro si sono assicurati che parimenti lei non era alla portata del tiro in modo da non ferire nessuno, ergo logicus est.
> - Ma nemmeno io ho ferito nessuno, se no avrei sentito dei gridi, qualcosa.
> - E qui si sbaglia, signora cara, perché lei ha ferito parimenti ergo et simpliciter l'anziana signora Stella Di Pepe . . . che . . . ha dovuto parimenti farsi ingessare il braccio.
> - Ma il braccio ingessato ce l'ha da tanti giorni . . . lo sanno tutti in paese. (96)
>
> ["Did the bottles they hurled injure you?" "No they didn't." "You see? Obviously they made sure that you weren't within reach of their missiles, so they wouldn't hurt anybody, ergo logicus est." "But I didn't hurt anyone either, or else I would have heard screams or something." "And there you're wrong, my dear lady, you did injure someone, ergo et simpliciter, signorina Stella di Pepe . . . who . . . had to have her arm put in plaster." "But she's had her arm in plaster for several days . . . everyone in the village knows that!" (98)]

Entrenched behind a false logic which is clearly stated by the Latin words he obsessively reiterates, the detective thus abides by the paternalistic diktat which excludes women from the law and from the world of logic itself. Indeed, his recourse to Latin, one of the two languages of the founders of the phallogocentric world of Western Metaphysics, most clearly bespeaks Vannina's disempowered state. He, who cannot utter a sentence without repeating at least once the word "parimenti," thus comes to remind Vannina of the lack of parity between the sexes. The female sex, producer of what Vittorio calls, in a discussion with Suna, "logica alogica, tipicamente femminile" (73) [typical female logic (73)], is thus meant to be silenced, its devoicing essentially due to women's supposed inability to grapple with the superiority of male thought.

At the Bar Mondo, the reactionary core of Addis, the place where male domination is mostly felt, Suna makes her first appearance in the novel. As she negotiates her way to one of its many tables, heads turn and mockingly observe her: her extreme beauty, in fact, is counterbalanced by her physical disability. Conscious of the effect produced on the people around her, she still manages to hold her own:

> La ragazza viene avanti arrancando sulle stampelle. Gira intorno gli occhi provocatori. Veste di rosso. Porta dei gelsomini. Gli sguardi di tutti si fissano impietosi . . . qualche bambino scoppia a ridere apertamente . . . la ragazza si fa strada tra i tavolini battendo le stampelle sull'asfalto, la testa alta, le spalle muscolose, i capelli morbidi come una cascata fresca e selvaggia. (8)

> [The girl plods forward on her crutches, sweeping her soft, provocative eyes over the scene. She is dressed in red and wears jasmine in her hair. Everyone's gazed is now fixed . . . with a mixture of compassion and curiosity. One or two children burst into laughter. . . . The girl threads her way through the tables, stumping her crutches on the asphalt with her muscular shoulders, holding her head up, her hair as soft and fresh as a waterfall. (8)]

Of all the elements that Vannina registers in her initial description of Suna, two of them deserve critical attention: her provoking eyes and her red dress already prefigure, in fact, her strong personality, essentially characterized by a defiant attitude towards the system. Red is the dress she wears at the bar, red are the shoes she will wear on several occasions. In *The Edible Woman*, Margaret Atwood frequently connotes the redness of her protagonist's favorite outfit as a sign of her vulnerable position in society. In *The Handmaid's Tale*, written by the same author, the red uniform that all the handmaids are forced to wear inspires a similar interpretation. Red, after all, is the color that mostly attracts the attention, it is the color that mostly captivates the voyeuristic gaze, it is the color that mostly alerts the wandering eye of the male hunter. Red, it should not be forgotten, is the color of blood. Yet Suna, as the reader soon learns, defies any stereotype that wants women subdued, a stereotype which requires even stronger submission from a woman who is physically impaired. As a matter of fact, in a society that demands her disempowerment, Suna's strenuous resistance to female objectification is what actually hinders her from being symbolically able to walk among chauvinist men and demure women. In this, she resembles Baudelaire's albatross (1857), who, harrassed by the arrogant sailors that have captured it on a boat, is exiled from the sky and unable to walk on the earth because of its gigantic wings. Two distinct passages in the novel clearly draw such similarity. At one point, it is Vannina who describes her as a big, gawky bird: "Lei è corsa via arrancando. La lunga gonna nera svolazzante, le maniche ampie, cadenti, frangiate; sembrava un grosso uccello che si trascina sulle ali" (161) [She ran off limping, her long black skirt and large fringed sleeves ballooning out behind like a great black bird dragging itself along on its wings (168)], but earlier in the novel it is Giottina, jealous of Suna's threatening closeness to Vannina, who tries to warn her friend by saying "attenta alle alazze di chi non può volare" (62) ["Watch out for the evil wings of the one who can't fly" (168)]. While the women around her define her as a bird that cannot fly, Suna chooses instead to liken herself to a mermaid:[6] half-woman, half-fish, like her Andersenian alter ego, she is chased by men who eventually reject her. In love with Santino, pursued by Vittorio, Suna ends her days in complete loneliness and like two Andersenian characters, the Little Mermaid and the protagonist of "Red Shoes," she meets an untimely demise. Like the ballerina of the filmic rendition of "Red Shoes" she jumps off a balcony, in a symbolic attempt to fly or, maybe, to return to the sea whence she came. As some commentators have remarked, Suna plays a contradictory role within the novel: while strenuously defending women's emancipation, she openly demonstrates how her life revolves around two men, her father and Santino.[7] Her self-proclaimed resemblance to a mermaid turns her into a quintessential object of male desire. Her father cannot seem to release his longlasting hold on her. Santino, torn between his platonic infatuation with Giacinto and his passion for another woman, can never bring himself to sever his ties with Suna. Vittorio, persistently rejected by Suna, appears to be obsessed with her. Indeed, being half-woman and half-fish, she constitutes the perfect prey, combining the elements that every male hunter seeks in order to restore his dwindling virility. All the men in her life, however, eventually put her aside. Her father's actions blatantly declare his undevoted attention to another woman, his second wife. Santino goes to jail and, from there, he stops communicating with her, while Vittorio finally regains control of his passion by marrying a frigid Swiss virgin. Suna's last few days are thus spent in solitude, with the company of a record she obsessively plays, Bellini's *Norma*, an opera which dwells on the story of a druid priestess who breaks her sacred vows for a man that eventually betrays her. A common destiny unites Suna and Norma: they both die with the shameful awareness that they sacrificed their beliefs for the love of a man who deserted them.

Ever since her first conversations with Vannina, in fact, Suna comes across as a strong advocate for women's rights: hers are the first words that denounce Giacinto's neglection of his wife's needs,

> - . . . Sono sicura che Giacinto non ti accontenta in amore.
> - Come fai a dirlo?
> - Lo vedo da come ti prende il braccio quando viene al bar, lo vedo da come ti parla, da come ti guarda; mi dispiace dirtelo ma tuo marito di te non è innamorato per niente, ti vuole bene sí, ma pensa ad altro. (64)

> [". . . I'm sure that Giacinto doesn't satisfy you sexually." "How can you say that?" "I can see it from the way he holds your arm when you come into the bar, I can see it from the way he talks to you, the way he looks at you. I'm sorry to tell you this but your husband is not in love with you in the least. He's fond of you, maybe, but his mind's elsewhere." (64)]

Hers are the words that defend the forgotten sexuality of older women in Italian society, as witnessed by her discussion with Vittorio,

> - Ha mai avuto un amante tua madre?
> - Ma che dici? . . . quella mia madre è una vecchia, mica è una donna.
> - Appunto, una vecchia, senza sesso e senza cervello, una vecchia che pulisce il culo a tutti voi.
> - Logica alogica, tipicamente femminile. . . . (73)[8]

> ["Has your mother ever had a lover?" "What are you jabbering about? . . . this mother of mine is an old hag, she isn't a woman." "That's it, you've said it. An old hag, without sex and without brains, an old hag that wipes all your bums clean." "Typical female logic." (73)]

And, more importantly, hers are the words that push Vannina to leave her husband, if only for a short period of time, in order to follow her to Naples,

> - Partiamo domani.
> . . .
> - Lo dirò a Giacinto.
> - Non puoi decidere di testa tua?
> - E' mio marito.
> - Lo dici come se fosse il tuo padrone. (138)

> ["We're leaving tomorrow.". . . "I'll ask Giacinto." "Can't you decide for yourself?" "He's my husband." "You say it as if he were your master." (141)]

A similar path, however, conducts the two women to different points of arrival. While in Addis, Vannina is a woman who never questions male authority. Her marriage with Giacinto is tightly held together by the symbolic strength of his paternalistic arms and even with Vittorio, she feels compelled to behave in a subservient fashion, because that is what she calls "a woman's task,"

> Era quello che si aspettavano da me, era naturale, era il mio compito di donna. Mi sono accinta a fare come diceva Vittorio, con mansueta disinvoltura. (108)
>
> [It was just what they expected from me, naturally, it was my role as a woman. Meekly I set about doing what Vittorio had demanded from me. (110)]

In Naples, however, Vannina is finally on her own. The distance from her husband allows her to develop a different sense of independence, while the closeness with Vittorio and with his terrorist group makes her finally aware of his immense shortcomings. Paternalism, she learns, informs the behavior of all men, even of those, like Vittorio, who publically declare their desire to go against the establishment.[9] This subtle critique of the leftist arena had already appeared in *Donne mie*, where Maraini had voiced her contempt for the pseudo-feminist stance of Italian comrades,

> So, bitter comrades, know that it is not enough / to eliminate social classes, and abolish private ownership. / Man's exploitation of other men will end, but / not the trivial and grandiose, instinctive and ancient / male exploitation of women. (1974, 18)

A new Vannina, who is finally starting to reconsider her role in society, thus experiences her stay in Naples as a moment of awakening. Suna, instead, comes face to face with a disappointing reality: not only is she deserted by the men she loves, but she also encounters enormous resistance from the male members of the extremist group that she is so determined to support. Considered inadequate for active participation in the group's management, she is asked to perform a "feminine" duty: with Vannina, she conducts a survey among the clandestine glove makers who work in Naples. The two women thus embark on endless tours of the poorest neighborhoods of the city, going from home to home, witnessing the extreme ignorance and the bereft condition in which these women are left. In *The Golden Notebook*, Doris Lessing portrayed a similar situation when she sent her protagonist on a political canvassing trip around the streets of London; like Lessing, Maraini here denounces the effects of an iniquitous establishment which systematically denies women any sort of social assistance. While Lessing's Anna feels empowered by her encounter with these women, who all welcome her interest, Suna fails to establish a real connection with her interviewees, who all place enormous emphasis on her physical disability and on her bourgeois background. At the same time that Vannina starts regaining confidence, Suna thus experiences a dramatic loss of self-esteem: it is at this point that she inevitably starts flirting with suicide. Abandoned by Santino, disgusted by the behavior of every other man, she suddenly feels drawn to another woman, Mafalda, only to encounter failure one more time. Expelled by the group because of her sexual orientation, she is subsequently left by her last partner. Vannina, by then, has returned to Rome: Suna's withdrawal is registered in the diary through the insertion of the letters she sends her Roman friend, while her suicide is narrated by a sad missive written by her father. It is interesting how, as Suna slowly withers away, she actually becomes a source of strength and inspiration for Vannina. The authorial choice to alternate Suna's letters with Vannina's regular entries clearly demonstrates how, to a certain extent, the two friends have become one person, their voices suddenly interweaving in a narration of suffered female empowerment. It is Suna's death that strangely brings about Vannina's rebirth: this is the message which, somehow, seems to lie at the core of *Donna in guerra*'s last pages.

In one of her last letters, Suna's voice suddenly becomes extremely powerful as she desperately asks her friend not to give in to her husband: "Come va con Giacinto? se non ti va di fare l'amore, non farlo, il cazzo può aspettare, tu no. Hai aspettato anche troppo, stupida, con le tue fisime di moglie buona e ubbidiente" (245) [How's it going with Giacinto? If you don't feel like screwing, don't. His prick can wait, you can't. You've been waiting too long, in fact, with your fad of being the kind and obedient wife (258)]. Little does she know that Giacinto will actually read her letter, and that this will actually push him towards his last, and most supreme act of violence against his wife. Indeed, in a desperate attempt to regain possession of Vannina, Giacinto decides to get her pregnant against her own will:

> - Fai un figlio come vuole natura, pianti quel lavoro di merda di cui non te ne frega niente, facciamo pure contenta quella burina di mia madre che sempre mi dice a quando? a quando? Mica ti voglio costringere, sia chiaro, io voglio solo che ritrovi te stessa, amore mio, voglio che torni quella Vanna di prima, di quando ti ho sposata, naturale, innamorata, dolce, timida, laboriosa, gentile. (247)

[But it's natural to have a child, then you can give up that shitty job that you've never liked, we'll even please my boorish mother who keeps on asking: "When's it due then? When?" I don't want to force you into it, Vannina, of course not, I only want you to find yourself again, my love, I want you to go back to what you were before, when I married you, so natural, so spontaneous, so much in love, sweet, shy, so hardworking. (259)]

If his suave, paternalistic voice declares his intention not to force her into motherhood, his action are quite different; nature, and what is naturally, biologically feminine inform his discourse, and his actions alike. Climbing on top of her while she is asleep, he impregnates her like an animal, following what he probably sees as a "natural" way of forcing the events. What Giacinto has not realized, though, is that his wife has really become another person: she is now a "woman at war," a woman who has finally decided to challenge the confining roles that society has assigned to all women.

Once an educator profoundly disillusioned with her power to bring about social change, Vannina realizes that she can make a difference in shaping the attitudes of the new generations when she is confronted with her students' repressed violence. What is more, it is what happens in her classroom that eventually leads her to sever her ties from her husband by choosing to have an abortion. The portrayal of such an important event begins with Vannina's transcription of a dictation that she is soon forced to interrupt. The rhymes she is dictating forcefully depict the traditional roles of women in society:

Ai suoi bambini perché siano buoni
la mamma canta le vecchie canzoni,
le sue vecchie canzoni di fanciulla
che già cantò la nonna alla sua culla.
. . .
I bimbi attenti spalancano gli occhi
stanno a sentire scordando i balocchi,
e mai non son stanchi di ascoltare
la dolce voce e le canzoni care,
la mamma dalla faccia di madonna . . . (255)

[To keep her children happy / The mother sits and sings / A song she learned from Granny / An old old song that brings / Memories from the cradle / . . . / The children listen quietly, / They open wide their eyes. / They're never tired of listening / To her sweet lullabies. / They love to see their mother, / Calm and madonna-like . . . (268)]

Candid and unproblematic images of motherhood are accompanied to a sense of continuity represented by the connection between mother and grandmother. Both of these figures are presented as bearers of an oral tradition that unfolds in tales meant to lull children to sleep. Like the child that is put to sleep by these women's chants, Vannina's very young students are taught, through such exercises, the only roles that society asks them to fullfill. Women are mothers, grandmothers, or teachers, their voice is sweet, their songs are dear and, more importantly, their face resembles that of the Virgin Mary, the most idealized, disempowered, and disempowering image of woman to be ever concocted by the patriarchal regime.[10]

Upon her return to the classroom, which she only left for a few minutes, Vannina finds her students in an unexpected state:

> Quando sono tornata in classe ho trovato tutto per aria: i banchi erano stati spostati da una parte in modo da formare una specie di palcoscenico circolare. I bambini se ne stavano ammucchiati appollaiati sulle panche. Al centro dell'arena, sdraiata per terra c'era Maria Stella, e sopra di lei quattro ragazzini urlanti. Erano cosí presi dalla rappresentazione che non mi hanno sentita entrare. Sono rimasta un attimo sulla porta cercando di capire cosa stessero facendo. Poi improvvisamente ho capito: mimavano uno stupro. (255)
>
> [When I returned to my class I found everything upside down: the desks had been moved to one side so as to form a sort of circular stage. The children were all huddled together perched on the benches. In the middle of the arena, lying on the floor, was Maria Stella, and on top of her were four scrambling boys. They were so involved in the performance that they didn't hear me return, and I stood there by the door trying to understand what they were up to. Then all of a sudden it dawned on me: they were mimicking a rape. (268)]

The wild reenactment of a gang rape, at the center of a stage that has been carefully devised by the young children, clarifies the extent to which the socializing process into a phallocentric world begins at the earliest stage of a child's life. And it is this early that women learn not to defend one another, but to stand by their powerful men. Most of the other female students in the class, in fact, actually laugh at the tragic event that is being mimicked: "Le bambine erano tutte raggruppate da una parte e ridacchiavano divertite. Solo due fra le più piccole se ne stavano mute e sbalordite, la bocca aperta, gli occhi persi" (256) [All the girls had gathered to one side and were giggling with amusement. Only two of the smallest ones stood there in silence, dumbfounded, gaping with their mouths open and blank looks on their faces (269)]. What is even more astounding is the little victim's attitude towards the abuse. Conscious that she is just portraying human relationships—"Facevamo le scimmie dei grandi" (257)

[They were imitating the grown-ups (270)])—she actually appears to enjoy the attention derived from the victimizing act: "Maria Stella si agitava debolmente, la faccia nascosta dai pantaloni del compagno piú grande, senza respiro, mezza soffocata, ma anche sorridente e compiaciuta" (256) [Maria Stella tossed feebly about, her face hidden by her taller schoolmate's trousers, breathless, half choking, but also somewhat gleeful and satisfied (269)]. Already resigned to the passive role of the victim, the little girl abides by laws that she is unable to question: "- No, che c'entra, la femmina fa la donna e sta sotto, il maschio fa l'omo e sta sopra e la fotte" (257) ["No, of course not, the girl does the woman and stays underneath, and the boy does the man and stays on top and fucks her" (270)]. It is at this point that Vannina finally wages war against society: for the first time in her life. She decides to be true to the mission of the real educator, and thus begins to instruct her students on the fundamental aspects of sexual politics:

> Li sentivo in qualche modo contagiati dalla mia indignazione. Parlavo dello stupro, dei ruoli sessuali, con fervore e rabbia, come non mi era mai successo in tanti anni di scuola. (258)

> [I felt that they had been somehow infected by my indignation. I was talking to them about rape, about sex roles, with passion and anger, in a way that had never occurred before in so many years of teaching. (271)]

One last contribution to Vannina's final awakening derives from a dream that she has on the aftermath of Suna's death. In this dream, she sees herself flying and then falling on the ground: her legs hurt, she is summoned to walk by Suna who lends her a pair of crutches, those crutches on which she so valiantly tried to threaten a male universe. In a symbolic act of empowerment, Vannina drinks sweet milk from Suna's vagina: "Ho accostato le labbra; ho bevuto di quel latte che sapeva di alghe marine e bevendo sentivo che mi riempivo di forza, di coraggio" (266) [I brought my lips close to it: I drank some of that milk which tasted of seaweed, and as I drank it I felt it was filling me up with strength, with courage (280)], and, rejuvenated, she steps up, ready to follow her new path: "Poi ho puntato le grucce contro le ascelle; mi sono alzata. Le mie spalle gracili erano diventate robuste, sicure. E camminavo, senza gambe, andavo avanti leggera, per niente affaticata" (267) [Then I thrust the crutches under my armpits: I stood up. My frail shoulders had become sturdy and I found myself walking, without my legs, walking along lightly without any strain (280)].

No obstacle, now, separates Vannina from her own emancipation, even though it will cost the life of a child she never desired to have. On the surgeon's bed, she feels as if the fetus embodied an entire world of suffering, the suffering of so many victims of domestic abuse (267). With its following entry, the novel concludes: Vannina is now free, and alone. As she walks up the steps of the house where she has taken refuge from her husband, she realizes that, in some respects, her fight has just begun, and so has her life: "Ora sono sola e ho tutto da ricominciare" (269) [Now I am alone and I must start everything again from the beginning (282)]. Like Monique in "La femme rompue," the protagonist of *Donna in guerra* takes stock of her new status but, differently from her, she is alone, and not lonely. Alone she stands, because it is only by herself, as Maraini already stated in *Donne mie*, that the woman of the Seventies can engage in the war which will finally set her free:

> Woman can only reach freedom by herself, with her own head / and her own hands, learning to know her diversity, / her historical slumber, her true desires, her / self-deceits. But by herself, only by herself, through pain and war. (1994, 19)

And by standing alone, the woman of the seventies will indeed manage to win many a war. The history of the civil rights movement all over the Western world amply testifies to the great success women ultimately achieved. A decade of struggle and victories, so powerfully and symbolically portrayed by Maraini in her diary novel, ushered women into a period of relative security. During most of the eighties, and particularly in Italy, women reaped the fruit of their previous battles, enjoying unprecedented tranquillity. It did not take long, however, before it became clear that women had not won the war, but merely a series of battles. Just as Ronald Reagan and Margaret Thatcher came to power in the United States and the United Kingdom, a sudden reemergence of conservative politics brought about the *backlash* that so severely affected women all over the Western world. The diary fiction authored by Doris Lessing and Margaret Atwood analyzed in the following chapter indeed present a nuanced portrayal of the eighties, a decade ripe with dramatic contradictions.

4

Fall From Grace: Lessing, Atwood, and the Years of the Backlash

> Male fantasies, male fantasies, is everything run by male fantasies? Up on a pedestal or down on your knees, it's all a male fantasy: that you're strong enough to take what they dish out, or else too weak to do anything about it. Even pretending you aren't catering to male fantasies is a male fantasy: pretending you're unseen, pretending you have a life of your own, that you can wash your feet and comb your hair unconscious of the ever-present watcher peering through the keyhole, peering through the keyhole in your own head, if nowhere else. You are a woman with a man inside watching a woman. You are your own voyeur. (Atwood 1993, 388)

With these haunting words Margaret Atwood describes, in *The Robber Bride* (1993), the extent to which every woman, even the one who feels most "liberated," actually remains victim of the male panoptical gaze. The voyeuristic gaze of the "man peering through the keyhole" is safely installed in the mind of each woman, directing and controlling all her actions, all her thoughts: can a woman ever be free?

During the sixties, Lessing had already shown the price paid in order to achieve a female freedom which was, however, never complete and satisfying; in the seventies, Maraini had abandoned her Vannina, at the end of *Donna in guerra*, as she was ready to wage war against that patriarchal society which refused to set her free. As the eighties approach, things seem to have changed, but only at the level of appearances: while the preceding decade had witnessed strenuous battles and utopic dreams of radical change in society, the new decade purports to have brought about a new status for women. Yet, under a surface which proclaims full equality between the sexes, demonstrated by the presence of women in high-paid and well-respected jobs, the situation has actually changed very little. What appears to have subsided is the stormy "war of the sexes"; patriarchal society has conveniently made room for women in token positions, however such a move has only been motivated by the desire to calm the raging spirits of the "women-warriors." By bringing them in and by falsely acknowledging their equal rights, men have actually managed to put their female counterparts under a new, and more subtle form of subjugation. Opening on such an apparent settling of the waters, the eighties come to an end, however, on a much bleaker note, witnessing what Susan Faludi aptly calls "the backlash." As the threatening possibility of female empowerment suddenly becomes closer to actualization, a phallocratic establishment makes its presence felt once again through a subtle campaign for "family values" which is essentially meant to send women back to the *foyer*. Right-wing politicians preach their reactionary sermons all over Europe and America as women come to face, with enormous pain, the extent to which the course of their revolution has drastically been reversed.

In many respects, Doris Lessing's *The Diaries of Jane Somers* and Margaret Atwood's *The Handmaid's Tale* offer a clear depiction of this period: while Lessing's work contains the controversial portrayal of a self-made woman of the early eighties, Atwood's science fiction novel presents a dystopic transposition of the American society in a hypothetical twenty-first century dominated by those reactionary values which have made their reappearance at the end of the decade. Certainly, these two novels seem to have very little in common. Lessing's social realism is counterbalanced by Atwood's allegory; two different styles are juxtaposed: the hermetic nature of Atwood's poetic writing stems from the necessity to hide political overtones from sight, while Lessing's plain and clear language reveals the self-assured nature of its speaker, a woman who has no reason to question the permanence of her high status. Yet, as my analysis will show, these two books together offer a vivid and impassioned illustration of what Gayle Green calls "the dismembering and disremembering of the decade"(1991, 201).

The Diaries of Jane Somers by Doris Lessing

> I did the recipes, summer food, I did Young Fashion, went off with the photographers to Kenwood for a session, came back and worked by myself in the office, no one else there, until nine. I love being by myself, no telephones, nothing, only the watchman. (124)

A woman is alone at her desk, happy to be surrounded by an enormous amount of work that she feels confident she will manage; no one is around her but a watchman, a man whose main job is to make her feel safe. This woman is Jane Somers, protagonist of Doris Lessing's *Diaries of Jane Somers* (1984) and editor of *Lilith*, a fashion magazine that she has single-handedly shaped in the past thirty years. Jane Somers is a successful woman, yet she is also lonely and tormented. In stark contrast with the passage which opened my analysis of *Donna in guerra*, this excerpt from Lessing's novel depicts its protagonist's accomplishment of a series of tasks which are meant to symbolize her enormous achievement. Presented as a career woman who adores her profession, whereas Maraini's Vannina was initially portrayed as a discouraged teacher, Jane describes her work with the same detachment that had been so evident in Vannina's list of household chores; in both cases, a note of alienation somehow seeps through the words of the diarists but, while Vannina's frustration stems from her disempowered condition, Jane's extreme coldness is the factor that keeps her in control of her life: her solitude is necessitated by her extreme ambition . . . as an old saying recites, "It's lonely at the top. . . ."

The distant presence of a watchman is similar, yet different, to another presence which I analyzed in the first chapter, that of the guard who was patrolling the threshold of the tobacconist where Valeria bought her black notebook in *Quaderno proibito*. Similar, I say, because it is the panoptical presence of a man in uniform whose task is *watching*, yet different because an opposite equilibrium of powers is established in the fictional universe depicted by Lessing. While the Italian *carabiniere* was there to remind Valeria of the obstacles she had to overcome in order to write, the watchman in this novel acts as a reassuring figure, one who guarantees the safety of a working environment that Jane, anyway, fully masters. The fear experienced by Valeria is here replaced by Jane's condescending attitude towards an inferior, a man that, in some respects, she actually manages to patronize: "He's nice, George, I encouraged him to talk about his problems, won't go into that, but we can help, he needs a loan" (125). Financial security and a higher status are the elements which empower Jane, who reasserts her superiority by adopting the *royal we* when referring to her ability to provide help for this man. As she has previously stated, what allows her to speak for the magazine is her conviction that she could indeed personify *Lilith* (42). The astrological synonym for the "black moon," Lilith is a transgressive figure *par excellence*. Legendary first wife of Adam, "banished from Eden after it was impossible for them to live in harmony" (Lass 1987, 151), Lilith is said to have given birth to demons. Hers is the name of the devil's temptress, hers is the curse placed on women at childbirth: could she possibly represent a more threatening and empowering female role? Comparing herself to such a haunting character, childless Jane thus immediately establishes her position of power: she is a success story, she is the woman who has "made it big" in a male world that feels, somehow, threatened by her presence. Differently from her female colleagues Joyce and Phyllis, who have left their prestigious role at the magazine because of the responsibility they had towards their children, Jane has repeatedly shunned emotional attachments, preferring her work to her personal life. While not actually incarnating the negative connotations attached to the figure of Lilith, Jane has however remained true to a transgressive role in a society that wants her "married with children." When a long departed Joyce inquires, on the phone, about the state of the magazine in terms which fully depict the symbolic role represented by the legendary figure from which it takes its name, "'Well . . . and how fares the old bitch *Lilith?*" (331) Jane again identifies herself with the magazine responding to her friend as if she had asked her about Jane's own welfare: "'This old bitch . . . is very pleased to hear your voice" (332). Yet, as the reader soon discovers, Jane's real personality is quite different from that which she officially assumes when talking about her work. Behind such a "bigger-than-life" façade lies a much more vulnerable woman, the guilt-ridden Jane Somers who confronts the many skeletons in her closet in the pages of her long journal.

Published in 1984 under the name of *The Diaries of Jane Somers*, Lessing's work actually consists of two separate novels, *The Diary of a Good Neighbour* and *If the Old Could . . .*, which originally appeared in 1983 and 1984 under the pseudonym of Jane Somers. In what will always be remembered as one of the most successful literary hoaxes of the century, Lessing managed to submit for publication two works of fiction without revealing the true identity of their writer. Initially identified as the pen name of a famous London woman journalist, Jane Somers was later declared to be the fictional creation of Doris Lessing's genius. As only a few of its publishers had actually recognized the real identity of their writer, Lessing's two novels were indeed subjected to the harsh criticism which is usually encountered by the works of novelists who have just started their career. Much has been said about the reasons that led the author to such an extreme move. Lessing herself offered an explanation in the preface to the volume that contained both novels, now baptized as *The Diaries of Jane Somers*. Apparently, her intention was to show young writers that the submission of a book-manuscript is a process ruled by chance and that the outcomes "have nothing to do with them personally, or with their kind or degree of talent" (vii).[1] At the same time, she seemed to offer a slightly more convincing motivation when she admitted that, in a way, she aimed at challenging those critics who, throughout the years, had tried to pigeonhole her work in constricting cages. And those critics miserably failed Lessing's test, proving unable to acknowledge her authorship of the two fictional journals (vii). Unconsciously drawn into a game of hide and seek, critics were actually faced with an enormous task: what are the elements that identify the style of a writer? Is it actually possible to uncover the exact quantity/quality which characterize a writer's work? Where does the Jamesian "figure in the carpet" really lie? While I would not wish to let my reading of Lessing's two novels turn into a quest for an "unknown quantity," I eventually intend to demonstrate how *The Diaries of Jane Somers* aptly plays with the polysemic nature of the word *style*, offering an original commentary on the female condition in the early eighties at the same time that it comments on the controversial nature of writing.

The Diary of a Good Neighbor opens on Jane Somers's portrayal of her past. A recent widow, she regrets not having taken care of her ailing husband who slowly died of cancer; a recent orphan, she regrets not having offered assistance to her old mother, who passed away because of the same disease. As she approaches middle age, Jane is confronted with the emptiness of her life, exclusively devoted to a very successful career; her loneliness suddenly comes to the fore at the same time that guilt creeps into her life. As an unconscious remedy for her increasing solitude, as an indirect form of atonement for her past sins, she feels inexplicably drawn to an old lady she encounters down the streets of London: poor old Maudie, a woman on whom she suddenly reverses her undivided attention. Little does she know that, in just a few months, Maudie will become another victim of the same illness that decimated her own family: no business engagements, however, will stand in the way of her caring for the dying woman. As she remains by the bedside of her moribund friend until she finally dies, Jane thus expiates for her past indifference and, as the novel reaches its end, she eventually comes into her own, letting herself experience those feelings from which she previously shunned.

Five years have gone by since Maudie's death and an aged Jane, now in her fifties, opens her new diary with another chance encounter. This time, however, no surrogate mother figure enters her life; this time, it is her dissatisfying relationship with her dead husband that will be revisited through her affair with Richard, a doctor she accidentally meets in the London subway. At the same time that a new man demands her attention, another person walks into her life, creating enormous turmoil, but of a drastically opposite nature. Her niece Kate, a difficult teenager still in search of her own identity, knocks at her door and expects her aunt to introduce her into a glamorous world. The parallel progression of her love story with Richard and of her problematic relationship with Kate characterize this novel, which eventually ends when Kate, after a suicide attempt, finally moves out of her aunt's apartment at the same time that Richard, lured back to family life, rejoins his wife in Canada. Frustrated at her inability to help her own niece, and shaken by the tumultuous feelings Richard has awoken in her, Jane is eventually left in a state of emotional and psychological exhaustion. As she retreats to the Woolfian "room of her own" in order to heal her bleeding wounds, Jane appears to perform an opposite gesture to that which concluded her previous diary. Lying in the dark, on her empty and immaculate bed, she looks outside her window, staring at the relentless action occurring down the streets of London from which, unexpectedly, she decides to withdraw.

Aging certainly constitutes a pivotal element in Lessing's two novels, as Kate Fullbrook argues in *Free Women:*

> *The Diaries* deal with reactions to old age, infirmity and death, and with the helplessness of the young from the point of view of flashy, sanctioned, worldly success. They are some of the most moving novels ever written about the decline into old age and death by ordinary women. (1990, 169)

In the first diary, two very different worlds are constantly juxtaposed: the glamorous and efficient universe of *Lilith* and the despairing and dysfunctional microcosm where Maudie and other old ladies confront their dereliction. As it becomes immediately clear, an extreme form of apartheid separates these two worlds; the glossy pages of the women's magazine never make room for issues that vaguely refer to aging (20). Aimed at portraying an escapist perspective on life, *Lilith* excludes from its spectrum of analysis a reality that is somehow too painful to be confronted. Age, as Jane soon realizes, is feared by contemporary society (20). Young, sexy and full of potential—this is what the woman depicted by a fashion magazine is supposed to be,

> The Images. (a) A girl of twelve or thirteen . . . Miss Promise. (b) A girl about seventeen, emphasizing independence and confidence . . . (c) Leading your own life. Mid-twenties . . . Needing Mr Right but able to do with-

> out. (d) Young married woman, with a child. Emphasizing the child. (e) Married woman with part-time job, two children, running home and husband. (21)

No possible self-projection is allowed to women who, somehow, do not fit such standards: the women who represent the ideal audience of *Lilith* are never meant to age. From their childhood, they are brought up feeling that they must fulfill a promise: they shall be beautiful and successful, yet their success shall revolve around the quest for the ideal companion, to whom they shall bear two children while holding a part-time job. When they do become old, these women shall disappear from sight, so as not to act as a *memento mori* to those who are still in their prime.

The imposed veil behind which old women are hidden is thus raised in Lessing's novel as its protagonist follows a path which leads her to the discovery of something she has long repressed. As Jane revisits the untimely death of her husband at the beginning of *The Diary of a Good Neighbour*, two different voices are inscribed in her narration. While a voice from the past declares the injustice of the ordeal suffered, "When Freddie began to be so ill my first idea was: this is unfair. Unfair to me" (5) the new voice of awareness betrays Jane's guilt at her past selfishness: "Until then I thought of myself as a nice person" (5). When her mother passes away, the most painful feeling stems from the thought that, someday, she will die too: "I thought: will it be my turn next? What I felt was, *it isn't fair*" (7). The time elapsed since the tragic events allows Jane, however, to realize the childish nature of her reactions; be it the fruit of a sincere awakening or the sudden outburst of mere guilt, Jane's reexamination of her past leads her to an appalling conclusion: she is, or better, she was a profoundly immature human being.

The woman who describes herself as a "Child-daughter, child-wife" (10) comes to face, through her encounter with old Maudie Fowler, a veritable return of the repressed:

> I saw an old witch. I was staring at this old creature and thought, a witch. It was because I had spent all day on a feature, Stereotypes of Women, Then and Now. *Then* not exactly specified, late Victorian, the gracious lady, the mother of many, the invalid maiden aunt, the New Woman, missionary wife, and so on. I had about forty photographs and sketches to choose from. Among them, a witch, but I had discarded her. But here she was, beside me, in the chemist's. A tiny bent-over woman, with a nose nearly meeting her chin, in black heavy dusty clothes, and something not far off a bonnet. She saw me looking at her and thrust at me a prescription and said, "What is this? You get it for me." (12)

How appropriate that the image of the witch, that which is so obviously most threatening and most alien to her sensibility, actually gets to be omitted from her study of female stereotypes. Yet it is exactly this figure which, shortly afterwards, comes back to haunt her and actually calls out to her, almost performing an Althusserian act of "interpellation."

In her Jungian analysis of fairy tales, Jole Cappiello McCurdy defines the figure of the witch as a supernatural, numinous element which can actually be read as a manifestation of the unconscious: "It is to the unconscious as matrix, as preexistent, timeless, and indefinite, unknown and never completely knowable, that the attributes of the divine and numinous belong. There belong the spirits, the gods, the witches, the magical power" (1991, 10). Under this new perspective, the protagonist's encounter with Maudie eventually assumes symbolic relevance as childish Jane, who has strenuously refused to grow up after the death of her dearest relatives, suddenly finds herself caught in an initiatory rite. Like the young and naïve protagonists of many fairy tales, she is led to new discoveries about herself as she overcomes the many obstacles that the phantomatic witch lays along her path. Friend and foil at the same time, Maudie lures Jane into her den, asking her to take care of her many needs, those same needs that Jane's own mother once voiced in vain.

The strong contrast between Jane and Maudie is immediately demonstrated by the opposite reasons that drive them to the chemists. While old Maudie is there for her prescriptions, stylish and impeccably dressed Jane has come to buy a series of voluptuary beauty products which are all meant to efface the passage of time. Little does Jane know, however, that the spectacle offered by Maudie's decaying body will soon lead her to confront her own mortality,

> There is nothing of her. A fragile rib cage under creased yellow skin, her shoulder bones like a skeleton's, and at the end of thin stick arms, strong working hands. Long thin breasts hanging down. (51)

The Jane Somers who constantly refers, in her diary, to the utmost pleasure experienced while bathing, faces the old woman's resistance to the same activity: indeed, Maudie feels ashamed of her own body, which is a powerful reminder of the imminence of death. While *nothingness* aptly describes what is left of Maudie's person, *solidity* is the term through which Jane defines her own figure: "I looked at my body. It is a solid firm white body. . . . It doesn't sag or droop yet . . ." (23). That *yet* which demarcates the threshold between middle and old age appears as a clear symptom of Jane's growing anxiety. Such anxiety is eventually revealed when, after bathing Maudie, Jane reveals that she has stopped considering her own baths as an occasion for pleasure (54). Like Maudie, she might soon experience the *nothingness* that precedes death; like Maudie, she prefers not to indulge in her bath so as not to confront the frightening possibility that her body might have started to lose that solidity which always so bluntly stated her own being-in-the-world.

Jane's relationship with Maudie is symbolically depicted as a *rite de passage*, ever since the protagonist steps into the old woman's house for the first time: "And I went in with her, my heart quite sick . . . It was a long dark passage we were in" (13). As she crosses the initiatory threshold, a new life opens before her very eyes: like the hero of a fairy tale, she is bestowed empowering gifts which enable her to attain a different understanding of life. What she receives is a new power of insight, different from that shallow and egotistical vision which had played such a role in her career at *Lilith*. A new world unfolds before her eyes, a veil has been lifted and the streets around her suddenly appear to be populated by the once invisible old people (21).

Maudie's house, personifying the dwelling of the unconscious, is a place where Jane is inevitably drawn; in a parallel fashion, its very exit appears as a foray into an outer world that, however, will never reacquire its former connotations. As Maudie's death approaches, Jane suddenly realizes that the essence of the old woman will never perish, nor will the awakening process that she started in her younger friend: "I cannot make myself believe that this furious bundle of energy which is Maudie is going to disappear altogether . . . so strongly does Maudie come over that I cannot believe she could dissolve like vapour when the air warms up. No" (234). What reveals to be Maudie's most striking inheritance is Jane's painful acknowledgement of her own mortality, of her own vulnerability. Maudie's testament, however, does not contain a mere *memento mori*. As Jane soon realizes, it is from the cognizance of her own frailty that a new joy of life stems: no precious moment should ever be taken for granted, and no occasion for compassion should ever be left untried. The immensity of such a new awareness becomes evident when, caught by an unexpected attack of lumbago, Jane discovers the precarious nature of her painfully achieved autonomy:

> I have only to break a bone the size of a chicken's rib, I have only to slip once on my bathroom floor . . . *what a privilege, what a marvellous, precious thing, that I don't need anyone to assist me through this day, I can do it all myself.* (167)

The new Jane, the woman who has suddenly discovered a profound *joie de vivre*, is the protagonist of the second diary, *If Old Could Tell. . . .* The imperative command to live life to its fullest leads her to an unexpected discovery: even in her middle age, she can still be the object of male desire. What appears most paradoxical is that such thing happens just as her body starts to show the passage of time.

Ever since its opening paragraph, a peculiar tone is set in the novel, a tone which remains persistent throughout Jane's second diary:

> My heel caught as I stepped off the train. My right foot went into the gap. I fell. I was on all fours on the platform, among the people waiting to push on the train. As I scrambled up, they were jostling all around me. I stood teetering, and saw a man stepping fast towards me, and was struck at once, even in that confused moment by his command, his competence, his quickness. He caught me as I was going down again, and as a result of our joint attempts I found myself lying in his arms, one of my hands, the one clutching I had held on through it all, at the back of his neck (259)

Witnessing her initial fall, the reader is immediately reminded of what Jane remarked in her previous journal. As Jane lands on the floor, she could actually compromise her own health: could her famous statement on the precariousness of one's independence turn into a self-fullfilling prophecy? The brief sentence which descibes the actual event, "I fell," proclaims, in its elliptical presentation, extremely dramatic overtones. Yet, as the reader immediately learns, a man soon comes to her rescue: she falls in his embrace and, as their eyes lock, passion already lights its first sparks. It becomes evident, at this point, that what the reader is witnessing is a most symbolic scene: ready to catch her as she *falls*, her mysterious rescuer is the same man with whom she is already *falling* in love, Richard.

If the scene vaguely sounds like a *topos* from a Harlequin novel, what immediately follows further reinforces such an impression. "'I am a romantic novelist'" (259) Jane says as she attempts to justify her own awkwardness. A few years have elapsed since Maudie's death, and Lessing's protagonist seems to identify herself, now, in a new fashion. Gone are the efficient days as editor of *Lilith*, for which she still works, but with a lesser sense of commitment; gone are the days in which her job was her only source of self-definition; gone are the days that witnessed her blind resistance to emotional attachment. The new Jane almost "rejoyces" in depicting herself as a middle-aged romantic writer who walks unsteadily around the streets of a city she once mastered. Reality, these days, does not seem to be her strongest suit. Interesting parallels can be drawn between Jane and two characters from *The Golden Notebook*. Like Anna Wulf, Jane appears to be dealing with a writer's block and, like her fictional counterpart, Ella, she is a successful romantic novelist.[2]

As she portrays Jane's feverish recollection of her encounters with Richard, Lessing clearly mocks the writing style of British popular and disreputable writers such as Barbara Cartland. Jane's vivid imagination filters through its rose-colored glasses each event that she witnesses. Under such perspective, Richard appears as a romantic hero, at times presented as a modern version of the knight in the shiny armor, at others depicted as a tormented man in dire need to be saved from mysterious troubles. What enhances his mystique is his initial refusal to reveal his own past. However, as he sheds his mysterious allure by telling Jane about his troubled marriage to another career woman, he suddenly turns just into a tired middle-aged man: Jane's rose-colored glasses have been suddenly removed.

Dramatic overtones are subtly inserted in Jane's writing as she describes the settings of her early encounters with Richard. It is in April that they first meet, an April described through its white and blue hues (260). The unforgettable opening lines of T. S. Eliot's *The Waste Land* (1922) here act as a powerful subtext, against which several passages of Lessing's novel find new meaning:

> April is the cruellest month, breeding
> Lilacs out of the dead land, mixing
> Memory and desire, stirring
> Dull roots with spring rain . . . (1–4)

Like Eliot's "dull roots" stirred by the "spring rain," Jane's emotions are suddenly shaken from a long torpor; meeting her true love right when her aging body is slowly coming to resemble the Eliotian "dead land," she experiences a reawakening which could be described as a second, painful blooming. Like the lilacs springing from a dead land, Jane's feelings resurface during a spring which, as a late second chance at love, is not to be missed. Richard seems to be reading her mind when, at a certain moment, he exclaims that he shall not miss another spring (266). The mixture of "memory and desire" that April brings about reappears in Lessing's text as Jane painfully confronts the ghost of her dead husband, who has suddenly returned to haunt her dreams (269). Freddie, the husband she never loved, the man she forgot for so many years, keeps a frightful vigil over her nights, reminding her of her own cruelty, and of the many barriers she once raised against him: "A dream of loss and emptiness. Freddie was on the other side of a deep and dangerous river, full of black twisting water, and he stood there looking at me" (272). Staring at his wife across the river that separates the living from the dead, Freddie makes no move to reach out to her; the distance that separates them will however be crossed by Richard in an uncanny actualization of Jane's eerie dream: "There was a time when we separated, he going off along one edge of the little lake, I on the other . . . watching him, only a few paces away from me by water. It was my dream, Freddie standing on the other side of impassable water, and his long grave look . . . [we] met again at the corner of the lake, linking hands tentatively, as if what had brought us together to link them at the beginning had gone forever" (277). When the temporary separation of the two lovers suddenly evokes the presence of a painfully repressed past, old insecurities resurface, as does the ghost of the mistreated husband with whose memory Jane, however, will make peace through Richard.

The presence of Wastelandian lilacs and dull roots is often summoned during the descriptions of the lovers' frequent pilgrimage through the many London parks. These parks come to represent areas of refuge and solace where the two hide away from civilization, as if attempting to arrest the passage of time by sojourning in a contemporary version of Shakespeare's Arden. Like the magic forest where Shakespearean characters retreated, these gardens evoke an arcadic dreamworld where Jane's idyll with Richard is free to unfold, away from the inquisitive presence of Kate and Kathleen, Jane's niece and Richard's daughter, who try to follow them everywhere just to remind them of the impossibility of their relationship. Representing a reality from which the middle-aged couple is trying to escape, the two young women also symbolize the encumbering presence of those family ties that eventually separate Jane and Richard. Both portrayed as brooding and tormented adolescent figures, Kate and Kathleen are representative members of that youth which, somehow, has yet to learn the many pleasure of life, a life that, as Jane has painfully witnessed, is much too transient to be wasted away:

> I was thinking of them all as possessors of some treasure, but they disregarded it: a marvellous inheritance, but they did not know it; though warnings enough reach them of the vast deserts, and nothing that I or anybody else can say will make the slightest difference. (491–92)

Unaware of the passage of time, which will lead them to that old age suggested, in this passage, by the Wastelandian "vast deserts" looming in the distance, these young characters refuse to acknowledge the beauty of their youth. The epigraph to this novel, so filled with nostalgia and regret, here acquires profound relevance,

> If the young knew . . .
> If the old could . . . (259)

The extreme dissatisfaction it bespeaks certainly applies to both generations; the same accusation addressed to Kate and Kathleen returns to haunt the protagonist of Lessing's novel, guilty of having sacrificed her youth to a dream of success. As *If the Old Could* draws to its conclusion, Jane comes to face the end of her affair, which terminates because of Richard's commitment to his family. Differently from the younger generation, full of unrealized potential, the older characters of this novel fall victim to their responsibilities: as the proverb implies, while youth is impaired by its blindness, old age is restrained by its inability to surmount the steep wall of social constraints.

And what is the role of a woman's magazine if not that of reasserting, in a mild and occultly persuasive way, the validity of those same social constraints? Marriage, the institution that lies at the roots of society, finds in *Lilith* its most strenuous supporter. As they pretend to speak for the "liberated woman," these glossy publications actually reinforce patriarchal concepts that have only apparently lost their effectiveness. Accomplice to the perpetration of a form of "brainwashing" which eventually comes back to haunt her, Jane takes pride in presenting herself as the mastermind that directs *Lilith.* It is quite evident that the woman who portrays herself as a successful business manager is quite different from the middle-aged lady who befriends Maudie and falls madly in love with Richard. While at work, Jane falls victim to an image that engulfs her, an image which, however, appears to have acted as an enormous source of satisfaction in her past life. It was in order to maintain such an image that Jane had to choose her work over her family; it is in order to reappraise the emotional damage derived by such image that Jane turns to diary writing. Representing its glamour in everyday life, around the streets of London, at the fashion conferences that take her to places like Amsterdam and Madrid, and at the dreaded lunches "for Eminent Women" which she unwillingly attends, Jane feels pressured to appear the personification of good style. Style is indeed a word that constantly appears in her two diaries: Jane imparts lessons on style to her younger colleagues, she comments on the lack of style of the rest of her family, she administers advice on the importance of changing one's style as society evolves. As a matter of fact, Jane's concern for style appears to have run not only her career, but also her entire life. The purchase of a single dress, which plays an important role in the construction of her glitzy image, comes to be defined as an instrument of resistance against chaos: "I have bought a whole new outfit, madly expensive, I feel it as a bulwark against chaos" (94–95). Through this interesting rephrasing of the motto "when depressed, go shopping" Jane actually affirms her dependence on a world of appearances; her own defenses, she openly claims, are located "outside in clothes, hair, etc" (94). Wearing it like an armor that protects her against feelings, Jane actually admits to having turned her own style into a uniform: ". . . that makes my style a uniform! But I knew that! I wear it all the time. Even, said Freddie, in bed" (124). In *All Consuming Images*, Stuart Ewen seems to comment on Jane's profound sense of alienation when he defines style as an effective instrument of self-protection: "As a kind of armour for city life, style taught people that they could gain comfort from self-estrangement, from erecting a visible line of defense for a subjectivity that often experienced a sense of jeopardy" (1988, 76). Defining its bearer as an exclusive member of an *élite* whose way of life ". . . is unattainable for most, nearly all people" (16), style fosters an equal amount of emulation and hostility. Accustomed to the former, but not to the latter, Jane comes to face antagonistic reactions as she treads along the poor neighborhood where Maudie lives: "[The grocer] sounds as if he is accusing me. He is accusing my style. I am out of place in this little corner shop" (107). As the armor stops sheltering her from reality, as she becomes aware that she cannot hide much longer behind the barricade she has carefully constructed, Jane finally starts noticing that her preoccupation with style has turned her into a consummate performer. Richard's remark about her perfect looks sounds more like an accusation than as a compliment "'What an accomplished lady you are. . . . Your clothes—never have I seen a hair out of place'" (308). Like her perfect house, impeccably arranged as a lifeless shrine, Jane's polished appearance eventually turns against her, bespeaking an essential lack of sincerity: "I . . . was thinking that if all of me is an artifact, put together from those earlier influences I have forgotten, then it might explain why Richard could stand there looking at my bedroom, and say, You are not in this room" (334). After all, style *is* nothing but a mere performance: by the end of her second diary, however, Jane has turned into an actress who is tired of playing roles. London, the stage which witnessed her escapades with Richard as well as her professional success,[3] eventually appears as a distant theater. *If the Old Could . . .* concludes, in fact, as Jane looks at "the theatrical London sky" (502) from a distance. Her room is dark, yet London is full of lights: this time, she has decided to be part of the audience: no more masks, no more performances . . . back into her empty bedroom, she turns into an impatient spectator: "A stage set! House lights down . . . the sudden hush . . . the curtain goes up . . ." (502).

As she abandons the stage, Jane actually rejects her past involvement with *Lilith* as well as her recent emotional awakening. Once burned, twice shy, Jane withdraws into her room after having so intensely proclaimed the importance of living one's life to its fullest degree. Her abandonment of a work environment which subtly betrays the spirit of women's emancipation while proclaiming liberationist intents certainly appears as a courageous move which would undoubtedly encounter the approval of many a feminist thinker, yet her more drastic disconnection from the world of the emotions ends the diaries on an extremely bleak note. One of her journal's last entries opens with a sentence which acquires, in the context of my work, extremely symbolic overtones: "The clocks went back today" (485). The same action that signifies the end of summer and the approach of the colder seasons, appears to refer to a different "going back": in the mid-fifties, Valeria Cossati abandoned her diary and her dreams, thirty years later, Jane Somers suddenly chooses to follow the same path . . . so many years have gone by, so many battles have been fought, yet history, as Vico said, once again appears to repeat itself . . .

As my analysis of Lessing's portrayal of the woman of the eighties concludes, one last issue remains to be addressed: style, I said earlier, is a polysemic term around which *The Diaries of Jane Somers* essentially revolves at several levels of interpretation. Commenting on her own style, Jane emphasizes the importance of its extreme understatement: "My style is that at first people don't notice, and then their eyes come back and they examine detail, detail, the stitching on a collar, a row of pearl buttons" (65). Unnoticeable at first, Jane's style contains however its own defining traits, those traits that symbolically constitute her own trademark, her own *griffe*, her own signature. What strikes me as most peculiar about this passage is the way it lends itself to a reading that identifies style as a literary quality. Style is indeed the one feature which supposedly differentiates each writer, yet its detection has constantly represented an enormous challenge for any critic who embarked on the quest for the Jamesian "figure in the carpet." I believe Jane's remark on her clothing style should be read as Lessing's definition of her own writing style; indeed, it is exactly in this passage that the author suddenly intervenes in Jane's tale, subtly referring to her own voluntarily hidden identity. It is through such minimal traits, little details that could easily be missed by unattentive readers and critics, that Lessing's authorship of the two fictional diaries should thus be identified. And by turning Jane the fashion expert into another novelist, Lessing actually inscribes a new twist in her complicate web of references connected to style:

> I sit here, one in the morning, writing it down. My mind is so clear and sharp, whirling with thoughts. I've just had a new thought, it is this: writ-

> ing is my trade, I write all the time, notes to myself, memos, articles, and everything is to *present* ideas, etc., if not to myself, then to others. I do not let thoughts fly away, I note them down, I *present them*, I postulate the outside eye. And that is what I am doing now. I see that as I write this diary, I have in mind that observing eye. Does that mean I really intend to publish this? (64)

As Jane's actual writing turns into a replica of the writing she performed on her own body through her attentive choice of clothes, style again shifts from the fashion world to the literary arena. Both meant to be submitted to an audience, the perfectly dressed woman and the perfectly written book thus become interchangeable. Lessing's richly interwoven narrative inscribes then, in its folds, the gaze of the critic's "observing eye," challenging it in ways that only postmodern literature could ever postulate.

The Handmaid's Tale by Margaret Atwood

> Young women take for granted the most important conquests, without thinking that rights can be lost with extreme facility, because history is not made of continuous progress, it can actually take a backward step, it can witness an involution. The path of history does not follow the trajectory of a straight arrow, but that of a line which is often curved, and equality between men and women is not final. (Gaglione 1995, 22, my translation)

History repeats itself, Dacia Maraini implied in a recent interview when she was asked to comment on the objectives to be pursued by the youngest generations of women in their political struggles. History repeats itself, she said, and women should not forget that all the ground gained in so many years of strenuous fights could be reconquered by their enemy with the blink of an eye.

In the last few entries of her diary, Jane Somers suddenly confronts the aggressiveness of one of her male collaborators. Two new secretaries need to be hired at *Lilith*, and sex discrimination unexpectedly becomes an issue as young Henry, frustrated by the minimal presence of men on the staff of the women's magazine, insists on filling both positions with two people of his own sex: "'I would like to remind you,' said he, 'of the Sex Discrimination Act'" (480). What appears most evident is that Henry has willingly forgotten that he is part of "one of the few industries women can work in" (480), an industry whose only target is also represented by women. Embodying the newest patriarchal factions, the young man is the object of a haunting portrayal:

> Henry from Production takes command. He is revolutionary. Stern and unsmiling. At least, with us, though I dare say with his comrades he allows himself a measured smile. His clothes evoke the military: his cropped hair, a black brush, is not high style . . . but is meant to make one think of prison and guerrillas; probably terrorists, I wouldn't be surprised. (480)

A guerrilla fighter, maybe a terrorist, Henry takes charge of the weekly meeting imposing his ideas and, most of all, imposing his military will on a group of women he wishes to reduce to obedience. It was just in the preceding entry that Jane had ominously reported "the clocks are going to set back today" (477), as if symbolically foreseeing the impending takeover of a reactionary force on a women's world. Henry has just won his battle when a defeated Jane again states in her diary, "the clocks went back today" (485). The twilight which starts falling on the streets of London an hour in advance becomes a metaphor for a different twilight, that of feminist struggle. All the advancement achieved by the women of the Western world at the beginning of the decade suddenly appears to cause enormous discomfort in many men. And even Richard, the knight in shiny armor who had come to Jane's rescue, eventually voices his anger against the feminist movement, responsible for bringing about male disempowerment: "Oh, don't take any notice, Janna. I suppose I'm not rational on some subjects. But in the States this women's movement thing—*is cruel*—do you know that? They have institutionalized cruelty" (472).

While *The Diaries of Jane Somers* closes on such an ominous note, betraying the slow dawn of a new era, that of the "backlash," Margaret Atwood's *The Handmaid's Tale* actually takes such a premise to its fullest completion. It depicts a universe that could be read as a striking fictionalization of what Maraini asserted in her interview:

> It's strange, now, to think about having a job . . . All those women having jobs: hard to imagine, now, but thousands of them had jobs, millions. It was considered the normal thing. (182)

Virginia Woolf's famous statement "A woman must have money and a room of her own if she is to write fiction" (1929, 6) looms ironically in the background of Atwood's bleak portrayal of women's future in her 1986 dystopia. In the Republic of Gilead, arisen at the very end of the twentieth century from the ashes of the United States of America, women can neither hold a job, nor can they hold any property. What is even more disturbing, however, is that they are strictly forbidden to hold a pen.

The disturbing narrative which constitutes the main body of Atwood's *The Handmaid's Tale* is the diary of Offred, a woman who has suffered an utter process of disempowerment at the hands of a totalitarian regime established by a Christian Fundamentalist sect named "Sons of Jacob." Having killed the President of the United States and machine-gunned the entire Congress on what would be symbolically remembered as the President's Day Massacre, this group of religious fanatics proceeds to bring about a veritable reshaping of the once liberal and liberated American society. A new establishment is thus created, and its laws are strictly informed by what is meant to appear as a literal interpretation of the moral precepts inscribed in the Holy Scriptures. Divorce decrees are annulled, and so are marriages contracted upon the dissolution of previous conjugal bonds. The dramatic fall of the Caucasian birth rate, mainly caused by environmentally induced sterility and by what was perceived as a decline in morals, calls for drastic measures, which are meant to insure the survival of the entire race. An important passage from the Genesis offers a solution to this problem: it is the passage in which Jacob's wife, Rachel, realizing she cannot have children, decides to recruit her maid Bilhah as a surrogate mother. The young woman will be asked to give birth to Jacob's offsprings, and in symbolic acknowledgement of Rachel's role in the impregnation, she will actually deliver between Rachel's very legs:

> And when Rachel saw that she bore Jacob no children, Rachel envied her sister; and said unto Jacob, Give me children, or else I die.
> And Jacob's anger was kindled against Rachel; and he said Am I in God's stead, who hath withheld from thee the fruit of the womb?
> And she said, Behold my maid Bilhah, go in unto her; and she shall bear upon my knees, that I may also have children by her. (Genesis, 30:1–3)

Chosen as epigraph to Atwood's novel, this excerpt from the Bible describes the events that led to the birth of the twelve sons of Jacob, who eventually became the founders of the twelve tribes of Israel. Over two thousand years later, however, the same passage suddenly acquires a different symbolism, becoming the justification for the institution of the Gileadan "Handmaids," fertile women recruited to act as surrogate mothers in the families of those new rulers whose wives have been declared sterile. A strict division in castes lies at the root of this "brave new world." The *Handmaids*, forced away from their original families in order to rescue the future of their country, go through a program of reeducation at the Rachel and Leah Center, where an army of older, sterile women, the *Aunts*, systematically brainwash them. Once they leave the center, the Handmaids eventually enter the houses of the Commanders, dominated by frustrated and angry *Wives*, who see these young women as a constant reminder of their own infertility. While the Handmaids' only task is to procreate, the daily maintenance of the Commanders' household is performed by the *Marthas*, old maids who have retained the right to interact with the dominant class, if only as its inferiors. The *Econowives*, instead, are those women who have been left on the fringes of the system, reduced to poverty and utter invisibility. Unlike them, still able to carry on with their miserable lives, the *Unwomen* are a group of older, sterile, and potentially dangerous women. Ex-feminists and lesbians rank among this group, who has been destined to clean the toxic wastes accumulated in the Colonies, ravaged and polluted areas of the country which have long been abandoned. A world where language, writing, and the knowledge that derives from them have been declared inaccessible to women, Gilead essentially relies on nonlinguistic signs. All women are requested to wear a uniform whose color defines their social ranking. Handmaids are dressed in red; Wives in blue; Marthas in green; Econowives in red, blue, and green stripes, since they play all three roles in their poor *foyer;* Aunts wear brown austere uniforms and Unwomen, instead, dress in grey. I will address the obvious symbolic overtones of such use of colors later in the chapter. What remains to be stressed, however, is the absolute state of subjugation in which this "New Order" leaves all women, even those who appear to be in better conditions, even those who have seemed to embrace it of their own will.

The tale of Offred, the young Handmaid who narrates her story in Atwood's novel, is a painful recording of the events that have marked her unhappy life. Past and present intermix as Offred keeps track of her daily sorrow, mainly fostered by the memory of the family from which she was torn away: a husband she had married after his divorce and a little child she had just had by him have now disappeared into thin air. Flashbacks from her previous life are thus interwoven in the narration of her current experience as Handmaid to Fred, a powerful Commander whose wife, Serena Joy, cannot bear children. Her daily interactions with the members of her household are faithfully inscribed in her narrative, which also recounts a series of ceremonies she is forced to attend. One private ceremony, in particular, comes to be described in extreme details: her copulation with the

Commander, an act that she performs, following the example set by the Bible, while lying between Serena Joy's legs. A mechanic enactment of a state-sanctioned form of rape, the "Ceremony" is endured by poor Offred thanks to her ability to detach herself mentally from the event;[4] things become more complicated, however, once the Commander demands to meet with her behind his wife's back. The situation gets even more entangled when Serena Joy, realizing that her husband might actually be the one who is sterile, forces Offred to have sex with Nick, the young chauffeur who had previously acted as intermediary in the liaison developed between the Commander and his Handmaid. Caught between a rock and a hard place, Offred finds herself forced to go against the regime's strict laws, which want her to engage in sexual activities exclusively during the monthly "Ceremony" and solely with the Commander to whom she belongs. As her arranged encounters with Nick unexpectedly turn into passionate nights of true lovemaking, Offred commits her final infringement: falling in love, in fact, does not belong to the realm of possibilities prefigured for a Handmaid. Her narrative ends on a note of ambiguity: her illegal tryst with the Commander finally revealed, she is escorted by Nick to a van which takes her away from the assigned household. In this final passage, Nick suddenly assumes two new and contradictory identities. He reveals himself to the Commander's family as the member of the secret service delegated to deport the guilty Handmaid, while, at the same time, he secretly declares to Offred his actual affiliation with the underground resistance to the regime. As Nick whisks her away into the black van, a confused Offred concludes her narrative by stating the unclear nature of her future: "Whether this is my end or a new beginning I have no way of knowing. . . . And so I step up, into the darkness within; or else the light" (307).

A peculiar *coda*, however, follows the end of Offred's tale: the final section of the novel, entitled "Historical Notes," throws the reader in the midst of an academic conference occurring almost two centuries later in the mysterious land of Nunavit. The notes from the "Twelfth Symposium of Gileadan Studies" begin with the opening remarks of a woman professor. It becomes evident that, two hundred years later, women have regained their previous status, and Gilead is so removed in time that it has actually become a historical period worthy of scholarly perusal. As the document continues with the transcription of a paper delivered by a male professor, though, a different reality comes to the fore. The essay written by Professor Pieixoto, meant to act as a commentary on the manuscript containing Offred's haunting tale, presents several chauvinistic jokes which make perfectly clear that Gilead might be dead, yet its inheritance still informs the discourse of its successors. Important issues are addressed by the scholar's paper, which remarks that Offred's narrative was actually oral: its manuscript version stems from the transcription of several cassettes mysteriously found in a house in Maine. While not much effort is made to uncover the actual identity of Offred, different hypotheses are made concerning the identities of her oppressors, Serena Joy and Fred. As the notes draw to their conclusion, further information is provided regarding the advent and the decline of Gilead, yet no judgment is passed on its cruelty. While part of the reader's curiosity is obviously satisfied, much more yet remains to be unveiled, and the concluding line of the novel, "Are there any questions?" (324) obviously states that the presence of such inquiries is fully justified.

Atwood's foray into science fiction has certainly taken the road of dystopia because such is the genre which best lends itself to the creation of a powerful commentary on the dangers of contemporary society through the allegoric portrayal of another, twice-removed universe. Written during the Reagan years, just as Lessing's novel is a product of the Thatcher era, *The Handmaid's Tale* is obviously inspired by the disquieting rise to fame of several TV preachers, those same figures whom Susan Faludi (1991) declares responsible for the advent of the "backlash."[5] Imagining the devastating effect on women's rights caused by the possible ascent to power of reactionary figures such as Pat Buchanan or Pat Robertson, Atwood resorts to the political power of writing in order to warn her readers:

> I've implied that the writer functions in his or her society as a kind of soothsayer, a truth teller; that writing is not mere self-expression but a view of society and the world at large and that the novel is a moral instrument. *Moral* implies political, and traditionally the novel has been used not only as a vehicle for social commentary but as a vehicle for political commentary. (1980, 353)

As every good writer aware of the political quality of her work, Atwood thus embarks on her visionary portrayal of a "different" world that still bears, however, striking similarities to the world in which we all live. Like her creator, Offred goes to extreme lengths in order to tell her story, and it is through haunting tales like hers that, hopefully, readers all over the world shall gain new wisdom. Giving her version of the story, for her, is not just a cathartic means to overcome immense suffering, but it is a duty. It is the same shared by all compelling storytellers. In an essay entitled "An End to Audience?" (1980) Atwood remarks:

> Story-telling at its most drastic is the story of the disaster which is the world; it is done by Job's messengers, whom God saved alive because someone had to tell the story. *I only am escaped alone to tell thee:* When a story, "true" or not, begins like this, we must listen. (350)

As Offred's tale begins, the reader is immediately drawn into a narrative which essentially relies on a depiction of a universe which, while retaining its connection with its past, has still encountered dramatic changes. "We slept in what once had been the gymnasium," Offred says as she remembers her first days at the Rachel and Leah Center,

> A balcony ran around the room, for the spectators, and I thought I could smell, faintly like an afterimage, the pungent scent of sweat, shot through with the sweet taint of chewing gum and perfume from the watching girls, felt-skirted as I knew from pictures, later in mini-skirts, then pants, then in one earring, spiky green-streaked hair. (13)

As memories of a past life flood in, the old and the new worlds come to be brutally juxtaposed. The place where these young women are now deprived of their will, of their history, of their independence, the place where the involution of women's achievements is most dramatically evident actually witnessed, once, its contrary process. From felt skirt to mini-skirt, from pants to punk hairdo, the evolution of women's self-presentation and their growing independence from men unfolded, in that very gym, through their progressive disentanglement from timeless reliance on stereotypical conceptions of feminine beauty. Yet, the reader soon learns, the old gymnasium where the Harvard basketball team once played its games[6] is now a place where women undergo profound changes, a place where they enter still dressed in their diverse styles, a place whence they leave dressed in a red uniform.[7] Red as the crimson tank top Harvard's players once wore, the Handmaids' uniform defines, through its shape, the confinement under which these women are forced to leave. Covering the entire body from head to toe in a thick, red cloth, the Handmaids' uniform is also provided with a pair of white wings which are meant to obstruct these women's vision, while shielding their faces, at the same time, from the unwelcome gaze of the outside world: "Modesty is invisibility, said Aunt Lydia. Never forget it" (39). Blinded and reduced to invisibility, Handmaids are thus physically and mentally constrained: "In front of us, to the right, is the store where we order dresses. Some people call them *habits,* a good word for them. Habits are hard to break" (34–35). The redness of their habit frames them as much as their wings do: while effacing their individuality, the bright red uniform actually portrays them, to the bystander's eye, as the hunter's prey which is about to encounter its slaughter: "Everything except the wings around my face is red: the colour of blood, which defines us" (18). Red as if covered with blood symbolically shed at a sacrificial rite, the Handmaids find in another kind of bleeding, that related to menstruation, the sign of their own failure. Re-socialized in a community that expects them to act as bearers of countless children, the Handmaids are taught to consider menstruation as a personal defeat. Women's time has been arrested along with women's freedom: their independence gone, the Handmaids are left in the sole possession of their own body, a body which they possess yet they do not own, a body for which they are indeed considered a national resource. And it is exactly for this reason, thanks to their fertile body, that the Handmaids remain alive.[8] Condemned to measure the passage of time through their menstrual cycles, all the Handmaids fantasize, though, about a final escape which should eventually relieve them from a life of suffering. Men possess time, women are only supposed to endure it. Men set the pace of women's lives, establishing rituals they must follow, relegating them to endless waiting and forcing them into that boredom that was connoted as sensual ever since it was first depicted in those tales from the Far East where females were segregated in exotic harem. A boredom that, as Offred comes to believe, is only attractive when bespeaking female objectification "But maybe boredom is erotic, when women do it, for men" (79). In the house where Offred lives, "there's a grandfather clock in the hallway, which doles out time" (18). Patriarchal in its presence, it is described as painfully administering the slow passage of time. The real measure of time, however, is the bell, and its intrusive presence, peremptory in its conferral of order, only further reinforces the constrained nature of Offred's status.

The room in which she spends most of her time is another reminder of her confinement:

> . . . this could be a college guest room, for the less distinguished visitors; or a room in a rooming house, of former times, for ladies in reduced circumstances. This is what we are now. The circumstances have been reduced; for those of us who still have circumstances. (18)

The reduced circumstances in which this woman lies are thus aptly represented by the empty space that she inhabits. Of the furnishings that surround her, a hard pillow that bears the crocheted word "Faith," encased in a wreath of lilies, assumes extreme symbolic relevance (67). Hard as the condition in which she is placed, the cushion once again enforces, through its inscription, the religious diktat that informs Gilead's ruling ideology. Quite appropriately, faith's two complementary elements are missing: hope and charity. "There is no balm in Gilead" recites a famous psalm: what Atwood seems to be telling her reader, however, is that in this Gilead there is neither hope nor charity, and when faith is unaccompanied by them, the deadening effects of religious zealotry inevitably follow. The wreath made of lilies, flowers which connote the purity and innocence that should govern a good Handmaid's life, should remind the reader of another wreath whose haunting presence puzzles Offred since she first steps into her room.

> A chair, a table, a lamp. Above, on the white ceiling, a relief ornament in the shape of a wreath, and in the centre of it a blank space, plastered over, like the place in a face where the eye has been taken out. There must have been a chandelier once. They've removed anything you could tie a rope to. (17)

Installed at the center of the ceiling, the ornamental wreath has been deprived of the object that it once adorned: the chandelier has been removed because another Handmaid hanged herself from it. No inscription lies at the center of this wreath, no "faith" in the possibility of a terminal escape is allowed to Offred. The blankness which stares back at her from the core of the white garland reminds her of a "face where the eye has been taken out." In this room, where no mirror has been left to provide Offred with her mirror image, it is the empty wreath that reflects back her dispossessed image. The missing "eye" is indeed a missing "I": in all respects Offred is a missing person (113). Gone is her real name, replaced by a patronymic that stresses her dependence on the Commander: she is the Handmaid of Fred, Offred.[9] Gone is her family, from whom she was separated and with whom she will not be reunited. Her only mirroring stems from the encounter with women who are in her same condition, women who, like her, have been divested of their identity. And with Ofglen, her chosen companion, Offred runs a restricted number of errands, "Doubled, I walk the street" (33). In Ofglen's company, she marches along sidewalks that are red as her uniform, as if walking over her own dignity, as if stamping over her bereaved image.

Mirror of her dispossession, the plastered wreath also functions as vehicle of the sorrowful repossession of her past and of her lost identity when it suddenly turns into the ideal frame of a movie screen, inside which images from past events are suddenly projected (138). Memories of her family life, in fact, constantly reemerge as Offred tries to make sense out of her present condition. And contrary to what could be imagined, they are often unwelcome, attempting, as they usually do, to undermine the mental sanity that Offred feels the need to maintain so as not to lose herself (119). The need for self-composure becomes imperative because, otherwise, life would be unbearable: by recomposing herself, Offred creates a protective shield which allows her to perform duties she cannot understand and declare beliefs she cannot share: "I wait. I compose myself. My self is a thing I must now compose, as one composes a speech. What I must present is a made thing, not something born" (76). A good Handmaid is essentially "handmade," product of extremely subtle manipulation, an artifice. Brainwashed by a dominant discourse that is, in its turn, artificial, since it derives from a willful and tendentious misreading of the Holy Scriptures, Offred recomposes her self in the same complex fashion that characterizes her postmodern narrative.

Offred's tale, like Coleridge's *Rhyme of the Ancient Mariner* (1798), stems from the transcription of an oral narrative, oral because like most other women in Gilead (only the powerful Aunts can still read and write) Atwood's protagonist cannot hold a pen. The postmodern quality of such production essentially derives from its self-reflexive nature, expressed by the several instances in which Offred meditates on the actual process of spinning a tale, and on the obstacles encountered while doing it.[10] As Offred tells her own story, she often fantasizes on her role as "story-teller," a role that could lend her actual mastery over the events. A mastery that would turn her passive role, prescribed by the atrocious "narrative" spun by the dominant ideology of the regime, into the active role of heroine. By bearing witness to her own tragedy, she refuses to be a victim:

> I would like to believe this is a story I'm telling. I need to believe it. I must believe it. Those who can believe that such stories are only stories have a better chance. If it's a story I'm telling, then I have control over the ending. Then there will be an ending, to the story, and real life will come after it. I can pick up where I left off. It isn't a story I'm telling. It's also a story I'm telling, in my head as I go along. Tell, rather than write, because I have nothing to write with and writing is in any case forbidden. (49)

If she were just telling a story, Offred seems to imply here, then her nightmare would soon be over, because a story is just a story, it is fiction. Fantasies of actual empowerment are intriguingly juxtaposed to mere fantasies of escape: Offred alternates between the impulse to oppose active resistance to her ordeal with the temptation to withdraw into a passive fantasy world informed by denial. If telling her own story would actually keep her mind alert and alive, believing that what just happened to her is just a mere story would inevitably throw her, instead, into the dangerous depths of oblivion.

Exiled from the written *word*, the women of Gilead are left to rely on their male counterpart's monopolistic production of the oral *logos*. The Bible prescribes mandatory behaviors for them and the words of St. Paul, in particular, proclaim the necessity of their enslavement to that "modest apparel" which, in the shape of a uniform, constricts them like tamed animals in a cage. All this knowledge, however, is communicated to these women only through the voice of their Commanders. The treacherous power of reading and writing, the poisonous effect of the Derridean *pharmakon* is denied to the female species. When it was once conferred as a gift to them, they abused it by turning it into venom directed against their benefactors: "Our big mistake was teaching them to read. We won't do that again" (320). Traitors against their own gender, the Aunts support such stand-point by affirming that women's bigger mistake was to take advantage of a power they had undeservedly received: when a brainwashed Offred reflects on her current dispossession, the teachings imparted by the ruthless Aunts loom in the back of her thoughts. It is women's own fault, it is because of their past daring carelessness, she implies in the following passage, that the right of speech has been wrenched away from their own hands: "The Commander . . . has something we don't have, he has the word. How we squandered it, once" (99).

Hungry for autonomous knowledge, the women in the Commander's household now depend on his word, which he administers slowly, only to further emphasize their utter disempowerment. Wordless, these women are left in the dark, that darkness which is symbolically evoked in the "Night" that gives the title to seven out of the sixteen sections that compose Atwood's novel. Drawn to the Commander's voice like iron to a magnet, they observe him extract the actual Bible from a locked drawer that again symbolizes its off-limit status. And the Bible is locked essentially because the words proffered by Commanders and Aunts, those words that inform every aspect of life in Gilead, are often fruit of a partial interpretation that most aptly serves the purposes of the ruling class: "*From each,* says the slogan, *according to her ability; to each according to his needs.* We recited that, three times, after dessert. It was from the Bible, or so they said. St. Paul again, in Acts" (127). This slogan, that most powerfully decrees women's inferiority and subservience to men, is not an excerpt from the Bible: while it should be regarded as a prayer, it actually resonates more as a haunting spell under which all Handmaids are cast; its triple repetition, in fact, actually makes it sound like the key to a magic ritual akin to those performed by enchanters. Its content, which at first sight appears to be rooted in the leftist ideology of common sharing, eventually reveals its tricky, sexist nature: women are the sole givers, man are the only takers. St. Paul, whose epistles certainly deserve to be considered as founding texts of phallogocentrism, gets credited for the creation of the slogan. Wrongly supposed to stem from his Acts, this slogan is meant to inform the acts of those who followed in his patriarchal footsteps, the rulers of Gilead: his words, his Acts will be seen in action as they determine the fall of one too many women.

In a world that outlaws women's access to language, what could be possibly considered more subversive and sinful than their indulgence in the forbidden pleasures of wordplay? It is in such context that Offred's repeated dwelling on the strange connections established between terms that, only on the surface level, belong to different semantic fields, assumes the form of a peculiar addiction. Her "self-composure" thus comes to be uncannily related to the "composition" of her narrative, and the "handmade" nature of such composure comes to assume indirect reference to her status of "Handmaid." And it is as a form of passive resistance to the intruding power of societal brainwashing that, in order to maintain that same composure, Offred draws an endless chain of associations related to the word "chair" (120). As she evokes a seat, a leading figure, a form of capital punishment, a religious virtue, human flesh, she produces words that are only apparently disconnected and unrelated to one another. Indeed, they all unambiguously refer to the world she inhabits. Forced to await her own destiny in the passivity and in the solitude evoked by the chair on which she seats for hours on end, Offred is threatened to remain virtuous, and not indulge in the temptations of the flesh, by the dogmas established and enforced by male leaders. Furthermore, no forgiveness is bestowed upon those who challenge the rules of the game: death by hanging awaits any Handmaid who dares to go astray.

Within this same context, it is only fitting that, when the Commander suddenly decides to take Offred as his "illegal" lover, he draws her into his trap by offering her the pleasure of the forbidden. Alone in his room, in a place which should be strictly off-limits for her, Offred is challenged to a game of Scrabble. Once considered an innocent pastime for old people and teenagers, Scrabble assumes new connotation in a world where language has turned into a precious object of desire: "It's as if he's offered me drugs" (149). Free to share her dangerous addiction to wordplay with the Commander, Offred thus embarks on lengthy nights spent around a board game which allows her to release, indirectly, her repressed yearning to remaster language. Mastering language, in fact, is what Scrabble is all about and for once, by engaging in such game, Offred is actually offered the possibility to interact with her oppressor on an equal footing. Embodying the phallogocentric system that originally denied her access to language, the Commander awards her temporary reinstatement of her lost rights, but only to further his twisted seduction:

> *Larynx*, I spell. *Valance. Quince. Zygote.* I hold the glossy counters with their smooth edges, finger the letters. The feeling is voluptuous. This is freedom, an eyeblink of it. *Limp*, I spell. *Gorge.* What a luxury. The counters are like candies, made of peppermint, cool like that. Humbugs, those were called. I would like to put them into my mouth. They would taste also of lime. The letter C. Crispy, slightly acid on the tongue, delicious. (149)

All these words laid on the board strangely compose a sexual scenario, further connoted by the feelings experienced by Offred during the game. Two references to the human throat, *Larynx* and *Gorge*, are juxtaposed to the image of the forbidden fruit, the apple, the *Quince.* The term *Valance*, described in the Webster dictionary as both the drapery hanging from the edge of a bed and as the window drapery which usually conceals the presence of a curtain rod, can be thus associated both to the physical place where sexual activity occurs, the bed, and to the male sexual organ, of which "rod" is one of the many slang names. *Limp*, of course, is a term which is often adopted to describe a nonerect penis, while a *Zygote* is the end product of sexual intercourse, the fertilized egg. While evoking the presence of such words, Offred is said to experience a growing desire to taste in her mouth the letters that compose them. As she holds them, she feels their innate sensuality, they remind her of candies that were once called "humbug," a word which also signifies trickery. A game of scrabble thus turns to be described as a virtual act of oral sex, into which Offred is somehow tricked, like a child naïvely tricked into a sexual act by the offering of a candy. The same scenario is depicted again when, later in the text, Offred imagines what would happen if her clandestine game were to be suddenly discovered: "Kick in the door, and what did I tell you? Caught in the act, sinfully Scrabbling. Quick, eat those words" (191). What is most peculiar about such portrayals is certainly the association of the word and the penis: language is here a metaphor for the Lacanian phallus that, in the Gileadan society, men have finally seemed to gain back. And that self-assuredness in their reacquired potency is such that they actually enjoy boasting it in front of those from whom they originally snatched it away. Quintessential bearers of the phallus, women have been forced to surrender it through their final submission to male authority. Returning the phallus along with language, the penis along with the pen, Gileadan women are forever doomed to silence and disempowerment. Their final exclusion from the symbolic realm is breached by Offred: Scrabble, after all, is just a minimal sin compared to her major act of revolt expressed by the composition of her own story.

The compulsion to narrate her own tragedy, with whatever available means she may have, is symbolically transmitted to Offred by her predecessor, the other suicidal Offred whose final demise is constantly recalled to the novel's protagonist by the plastered wreath on the ceiling. Inscribed in the deepest recess of her cupboard, lies a message that Offred casually finds as she embarks on a careful perusal of her new premises:

> *Nolite te bastardes carborundorum.* I didn't know what it meant, or even what language it was in. I thought it might be Latin, but I didn't know any Latin. Still, it was a message, and it was in writing, forbidden by that very fact, and it hadn't yet been discovered. Except by me, for whom it was intended. It was intended for whoever came next. (62)

A sentence in a foreign language, presumably in Latin, the language of the founders of patriarchy, awaits Offred in the dark secluded corner of the cupboard. It is an encoded message, a riddle whose subversive nature stems from the fact that it is *written* and that its cryptical nature essentially derives from the usage of an instrument that is doubly forbidden. Not only is it expressed in writing, but it is also expressed in the language that, symbolically, should be most alien and inaccessible to women. Discovered while the narrator was kneeling down, the mysterious message soon turns into a subversive prayer that Offred repeats to herself in those moments when her resistance to the iniquitous system becomes most necessary, during those ceremonies for which empty and oppressive rituals have been established by the regime (101). Adopted as a source of obstruction against the Commander's orders, this enigmatic line comes to be finally interpreted by the Commander himself, during one of the sinful Scrabble sessions. Emboldened by the power obtained through the new illegal role she now plays in Fred's life, Offred ventures to ask the solution to the riddle, pretending that it is just a strange sentence that has emerged from the sea of memories of her past life. When the Commander requests that she writes the sentence on a piece of paper, Offred feels suddenly overwhelmed by the emotions unleashed by the fact that, for the first time in years, she is actually allowed to hold a pen:

> The pen between my fingers is sensuous, alive almost, I can feel its power, the power of the words it contains. Pen is Envy, Aunt Lydia would say, quoting another Centre motto, warning us away from such objects. And they were right, it is envy. Just holding it is envy. I envy the Commander his pen. It's one more thing I would like to steal. (196)

Exactly when she is about to learn the content of the subversive message, Offred reexperiences the power of writing, the power of the pen. Once again, the association between power, pen and penis is drawn: the slogan of the re-educational center, "Pen is Envy" is an obvious rewriting of the term through which Freud and his successors justified the women's supposed inferiority to men, Penis Envy. By envying the Commander's pen, Offred thus states her socially induced inferiority complex while actually reassessing, at the same time, her desire to oppose resistance, to rebalance the *status quo* which demands her own subjugation. By envying the Commander's pen, Offred indeed states her own desire to steal back the phallus from those who have turned it into the symbolic stick with which the women of Gilead are daily beaten into submission. And it is the voluptuous feeling experienced while holding the pen that further strengthens, in many respects, Offred's desire to keep telling her story: oral as it may be, her narration still contains immense transgressive power of resistance. A new universe of signification discloses under Offred's very eyes, as the Commander unravels the mysterious meaning of the sentence, *Don't let the bastards bring you down* (196). Another language, not real Latin, is the actual linguistic encoder of the message: it is indeed Pig-Latin. The language invented by students frustrated with the study of the mother-tongue of the founders of Rome, Pig-Latin appears as a quintessential instrument of resistance to the established power. Yet, in the pages of the old Latin textbook owned by the Commander, this particular code assumes strong chauvinistic connotations, due to its usage for mockery of images of women in captivity. The same ink which inscribed the revolutionary message, "don't let the bastards bring you down" is actually responsible for disfiguring a picture of the Venus of Milo, a statue which already portrays an image of female beauty which is essentially amputated. The old work of art, in fact, is famous for depicting a woman who has neither hands nor legs. Another masterpiece of antiquity appears on the next page, and while it has not been the object of vandalization at the hand of the student who owned the book, it still evokes one of the earliest episodes of misogyny ever witnessed in the Western World: the Roman abduction of the Sabine women. Not unlike the young women who have been forced to act as Handmaids in the Gileadan regime, the women from Sabinia, an area close to Rome, had been massively kidnapped in order to serve as mates to the Roman warriors. At the margin of the photo, however, a verb is conjugated again in Pig-Latin, "*pim pis pit, pimus pistis pants*" (196) a verb which has no real meaning, but which ends its conjugation with the word *pants*, a term which metonimically reinscribes male supremacy over women.

The adoption of Pig-Latin for the inscription in the cupboard acquires further relevance when juxtaposed to a passage in the text where a bored Offred describes herself as a prize pig: "I wait, washed, brushed, fed, like a prize pig" (79). Constricted in seclusion like the pig, Offred feels that her function in Gileadan society is essentially that of being a sacred possession destined to be sacrificed for the greater good of her owners. And the same understanding of such predicament seems to have been reached by the woman who preceded her: hence the usage of a language that, somehow, they were both meant to share because of their tragic condition. What the message says, "don't let the bastards bring you down," however states these women's desire to reverse their lot. It is a narrative in itself, summarizing in a few words a host of feelings and frustration: it is actually the empowering force that eventually leads Offred to recount her own story. Like the inscription in the cupboard, like another virtual message in a bottle, Offred's tale is left to be unearthed only after her death. And like a testimony from the "everywoman," the "everyvictim" of her time, it is meant to alert new generations to the possibility of the reoccurrence of similar events.

It is through the novel's "Historical Notes" that the reader should thus expect to encounter proof of the effects produced by the reception of Offred's message. However, the document which should bear witness to the end of a misogynist regime, actually bespeaks, through its lines, the subtle persistence of phallocentric attitudes which, like Offred's habits, are too hard to break. Professor Pieixoto's remarks about the title of the narrative, based on a chauvinistic pun that elicits the audience's laughter, indirectly reinforces the tone of utter discouragement which deeply underlies the Atwood's entire book (313). Reduced to a tall tale, the story of Offred's tragic life thus comes to be exposed to the ridicule at the hands of a group of men, who eventually appear to have performed one last patronizing gesture when they imposed a title, "The Handmaid's Tale" to Offred's testimony. And the original namelessness of her testimony was indeed supposed to reinstate the universality of the events it recounted. What is most striking is that such a bleak portrayal of backward mentality is actually reserved for that part of society which should show most extreme open mindedness: the academia. Things might change for the best, Atwood seems to imply, yet prejudice against women will never fully disappear.

As a dystopic, futuristic tale, Atwood's novel however is supposed to speak to a different audience from that imagined by Offred: its immediate readers, in fact, belong to generations which are closer in age and experience to that of her mother. And for this same reason, it is Offred's mother that offers the reader some of the most powerful occasions for reflection over the backlash era. A feminist activist, a progressive thinker, and a distant parent, Offred's mother is often portrayed as an extremely angry woman. Her involvement with the Women's Lib is initially seen by her daughter as the element that caused most frictions in their relationship. While her mother, in fact, has never ceased to exhort women to stand up for their rights, Offred openly acknowledges her own past uninvolvement in politics: "As for you, she'd say to me, you're just a backlash. Flash in the pan. History will absolve me" (131). And it is quite remarkable that the very term *backlash* came to define the way Offred's mother once saw her own daughter's disinterest in politics. In the lights of the events that would later occur, Offred's mother appears to have obtained absolution not only from History, but from that same daughter who once used to question her political beliefs. Aware of the mistakes committed in the past, those mistakes that forbade her to think that, one day, she might find herself victim of her own political ignorance, Offred eventually understands and accepts her mother's legacy:

> She expected too much from me, I felt. She expected me to vindicate her life for her, and the choices she'd made. I didn't want to live my life on her terms. . . . I am not your justification for existence, I said to her once. I want her back. I want everything back, the way it was. But there is no point to it, this wanting. (132)

By the end of her tale, Offred learns of her mother's tragic end: like many other undesirable women, she has been sent to the Colonies, where certain death awaits her. And it is, in some respects, as a testimony to her sacrifice, as well as to that of the other Offred, the other woman to whom she is linked by a different form of female genealogy, that Offred recounts her story. Uncertain of Offred's final escape from Gilead, the reader is thus asked to meditate on a very bleak future that, after all, is fruit of an allegorical portrayal of the backlash society. *Nolite te bastardes carborundorum* is the message that should remain, however, in the mind of readers all over the world: as the rights of women dangerously come to be threatened more and more every day, as conservative factions engage in battles destined to challenge women's achievements, Offred's haunting tale strongly reasserts the necessity of women's refusal to identify as merely helpless victims.

Three different narratives that are clearly linked by a common thread, Lessing's two diaries and Atwood's dystopic tale come together at the intersection of the Thatcher/Reagan era. Once they are juxtaposed, they present readers with a very bleak view of the world, one that would eventually be shared by women writers in other Western countries. It was only in the very last decade of the century, as the conclusions to this book will amply prove, that Italy came to experience the conservative wave that was so powerfully spreading all over the Western world. And the voice of the last female diarist I choose to analyze (the narrator of Susanna Tamaro's *Va' dove ti porta il cuore*) does indeed share many of these conservative values, values that will mark the passage from the feminist to the post-feminist era.

Conclusion: A Grandmother's Legacy

> L'infelicità abitualmente segue la linea femminile. Come certe anomalie genetiche, passa di madre in figlia. Passando, invece di smorzarsi, diviene via via più intensa, più inestirpabile e profonda. Per gli uomini quella volta era molto diverso, avevano la professione, la politica, la guerra; la loro energia poteva andare fuori, espandersi. Noi no. Noi per generazioni e generazioni, abbiamo frequentato soltanto la stanza da letto, la cucina, il bagno; abbiamo compiuto migliaia e migliaia di passi, di gesti, portandoci dietro lo stesso rancore, la stessa insoddisfazione. Sono diventata femminista? No, non temere, cerco soltanto di guardare con lucidità ciò che sta dietro. (39)

> [Unhappiness is generally transmitted through the female line, passing from mother to daughter the way some genetic abnormalities do. And instead of diminishing as it passes, it steadily grows more intense, more ineradicable and profound. That era was very different for men; they had their professions, their politics, their wars, they had outlets for their energy. Not us. For countless generations we've been confined to the bedroom, the kitchen, and the bathroom; we've taken millions of steps, made millions of gestures, each one encumbered by the same rancor and the same dissatisfaction. Have I become a feminist? No, don't worry, I'm just trying to see clearly what's behind all this.] (50–51)

At the end of 1992, an old Italian woman named Olga writes a series of long letters to her granddaughter, who is now living in America. When, after sharing a house for a number of years, the two women separated, they reached an agreement, according to which no attempt would be made to contact one another. Willing to hold to her promise, Olga vows not to mail this bundle of letters: she keeps writing, though, turning the unsent epistles into a journal of the last few weeks of her life, a diary that her granddaughter will discover upon her return to a house that, by then, will be empty. Aware of the approach of death, Olga finally feels that she can unburden her soul on paper: a lifetime of secrets is thus revealed, a lifetime of silent suffering is voiced. Three generations of women, a mother, a lost daughter and a distant granddaughter become, then, the protagonists of another sorrowful tale, the one created by Susanna Tamaro in the pages of her acclaimed best-seller *Va' dove ti porta il cuore* (1994), a novel which has managed to sell, in four years, over two million copies all over the world.

In the passage just quoted, the old diarist tightly relates unhappiness to a female lineage. Women, she says, are destined to suffer because, unlike men, they cannot find solace in the public sphere; the private space, represented by the house in which they are willingly held captive, is their only realm of action. Time and the progress it brings should have somehow changed such a predicament yet, Olga maintains, women's suffering has only increased, and so has their perennial dissatisfaction. Frustrated and angry, old Olga asserts that, however, such an awareness has not made her more sympathetic with the feminist cause. And deeply anti-feminist is the message that pervades her letters, a message that she subtly tries to hide under her apparent interest in the well-being of her young relative. Letters addressed by an old matriarch to the little bird who fled the suffocating nest, leaving her to die in absolute solitude, the epistles that compose *Va' dove ti porta il cuore* are not just the testament of love and wisdom that they purport to be. Behind the thick veil of commonplace statements through which the narrator declares her support for her granddaughter's strife for independence, lies the not so subtle intention to induce a profound sense of guilt into the heart of the young woman. The heart, invoked by the narrator as the mover of all things, and placed by the author in the title of the novel, is the ideal addressee of this bundle of letters. It is through her heart that Olga's granddaughter should eventually learn, upon her grandmother's death, the extent of the hurt provoked by her abandonment. It should be that same heart, Olga maintains at the end of her last letter, that should lead her granddaughter towards her future decisions: "Stai ferma, in silenzio, e ascolta il tuo cuore. Quando poi ti parla, alzati e va' dove lui ti porta" (165) [Stay still, be quiet, and listen to your heart. Then, when it speaks, get up and go where it takes you (204)]. Set in motion by her heart, by the instinctive transport it evokes, Olga's granddaughter is thus indirectly told not to follow her brain. Silent and still, she should forget her own rationality, dismiss the subversive power of her voice, and let her emotions take over her life.

Ever since *Va' dove ti porta il cuore* first appeared, Italian reviewers embraced Olga's appeal to the heart, and read Tamaro's novel as an uncomplicated testament to motherly love.[1] No attention was thus paid to Olga's ulterior motives, no emphasis was placed on the dangerous implications deriving from her advocation of the superiority of the heart over the brain. Taken at face value, the letters from *Va' dove ti porta il cuore* were then praised for their emotional portrayal of a female character who would soon be turned into the very personification of altruistic love. Olga's conservative values were thus indirectly justified and supported by a crowd of readers who avidly consumed her letters, letters that spoke to the heart, letters that indirectly reaffirmed the very same reactionary beliefs which had suddenly reemerged in the rhetoric of the dominant class of Italian right-wing politicians of the Nineties.

In my study of contemporary diary fiction written by women, I have followed the evolution and the involution of the feminist struggle. Different countries have witnessed different levels of political achievements. Disempowered all through the Western World during the fifties, women begun to improve their condition in the sixties, mostly in more advanced countries such as France, England, and the United States. Italy appeared to follow suit in the following decade, which testified to strenuous battles that eventually led to considerable achievements. While the eighties marked the threshold of a new dark age in those same countries that had initially set the stage for women's social advancement, Italy again followed suit only ten years later. But, while Reagan's and Thatcher's politics were blatantly eroding those civil rights which had been the public bone of contention for many a decade, the Italian Right Wing dealt its blows in a much subtler fashion, slowly but effectively capitalizing on the public discontentment deriving from the institutional crisis occurred at the beginning of the nineties. When in 1993 the First Republic was officially declared dead, killed by its own internal corruption, an arrogant class of new politicians, whose refined communication skills aptly underplayed its reactionary beliefs, suddenly came to the fore. At the same time that *Va' dove ti porta il cuore* made its first appearance in Italian bookshops, new elections proclaimed these politicians as absolute winners. Who voted for them? Who was to be held responsible for Italy's sudden reawakening of Conservativism? The same generations of voters who were to identify in a most unproblematic fashion with Tamaro's novel, teenagers and older people,[2] young Italians casting their first vote, convinced that a radical change would be beneficial to the nation's politics, and old reactionaries, nostalgic for past regimes, and disgusted by the "loosening" of morals indirectly supported by the liberalism of recent rulers. The same indirection which awarded these politicians access to power, informs the discourse of the narrator of Tamaro's novel, whose conservative overtones gained it the *imprimatur* of the highest representative of patriarchal authority, the Roman Catholic Church. Praised by a leading Catholic newspaper, *L'Avvenire*, as "One of the best novels of the

'90s,"[3] *Va' dove ti porta il cuore* was the only book that appeared simultaneously in the national best-seller list and in the equivalent ranking produced by Catholic booksellers all over the country. Furthermore, in a survey conducted among Church-going teenagers by the Catholic magazine *Famiglia Cristiana*, Tamaro was ranked the seventh most popular person in Italy, after names such as Pope John Paul II and Antonio Di Pietro, the judge responsible for indicting the corrupt politicians of the First Republic.

Tamaro's novel, I repeat, is not as simplistic as some of its critics and readers seem to have portrayed it. Often ripe with literary, religious, and mythic overtones, Olga's long letters lend themselves to a close reading that discloses their ambiguous nature, and betrays the hidden presence of a powerful textual commentary on the incomprehension that often arises among women belonging to different generations. The portrayal of a dysfunctional family, *Va' dove ti porta il cuore* opens on Olga's decision to reveal to her granddaughter the events that led to the premature death of Ilaria, daughter of the narrator, and mother of the letters' addressee. In order to confer proper perspective to such a dramatic moment of her life, Olga needs to revisit, however, other painful memories, those related to her childhood and youth and those that led to the departure of her granddaughter. Raised in a cold, aristocratic family, she was educated in a strict Catholic school, and then married Augusto, a much older man whom she never loved. During a sojourn at a health spa, she met Ernesto, a married man with whom she suddenly fell in love. Offspring of her secret adulterous relationship, Ilaria was born amidst a web of poorly hidden deceptions. Ernesto's tragic death in a car accident marked the beginning of the difficult relationship between mother and daughter: unconsciously seen as a painful reminder of a lost love, Ilaria became a nuisance to her own mother, who suddenly grew distant and aloof. Finally recovered from the death of her lover, Olga witnessed another demise, that of her husband, who admitted to his knowledge of Ilaria's real paternity on his deathbed. Grown up in such a tense environment, Ilaria moved to another city, where she started, and never completed, her graduate studies. Emotionally unstable, she returned from a trip to Turkey bearing a child in her womb, another fatherless daughter. After the young girl was born, Ilaria's precarious mental health further declined; her insecurities grew deeper and her resentment towards her mother increased. After repeated encounters with an alleged psychoanalyst, Ilaria started to blame, for her present condition, the man she thought was her father. Unable to address her anger to a man who was, by then, dead, she turned to her mother, searching for answers that would motivate the unhappiness of her own childhood. When a frustrated Olga eventually revealed the secret identity of her real father, a shocked Ilaria stormed out of her house and was killed, like Ernesto, in a car accident. Such a tragic event thus originated Olga's custody of her granddaughter, with whom she had a perfect relationship until the young woman became curious about her own parents. Who was her father? And why did her grandmother always refuse to speak of her own daughter? Again, secrets, lies, and misconstructions drew these two women apart, to the extent that, after the granddaughter's departure for the United States, no further communication was ever reestablished between them.

On the surface level, Olga's long letters seem to claim the old woman's decision to acknowledge her own responsibility in the immense suffering of those who surrounded her. Her past inability to handle the relationship with her own daughter seriously appears to inform her desire to do right by Ilaria's offspring: for this reason, it seems, she has chosen to abide by her granddaughter's yearning for freedom. Her epistles should thus be meant to signify a final act of release, a virtual blessing that she imparts from a distance: "Scrivile una lettera, un piccolo diario dei tuoi giorni che continui a tenerle compagnia. . . . Un testamento? Non proprio, piuttosto qualcosa che ti segua negli anni, qualcosa che potrai leggere ogni volta che sentirai il bisogno di avermi vicina" (15) [Write her a letter, a little record of your days for her to keep after you're gone. . . . Writing my testament? Not exactly; I'd rather think of it as something that will stay with you through the years, something you can read whenever you feel you need my close to you (20–21)]. The voice that directs Olga to this last adventure is that of a rose, a flower that her granddaughter planted in the garden many years before. In the same way that Olga had claimed ownership of her daughter's child, through the care of whom she was trying to make up for the mistakes committed with Ilaria, the young girl had once desired to have, in her grandmother's garden, a rose of her own, a flower whose growth would be her sole responsibility: "Davanti alla mia obiezione che ne avevamo già tante hai risposto: 'Ne voglio una che sia mia soltanto, voglio curarla, farla diventare grande'" (9) [When I objected that we already had lots of roses, you said, "I want one that's all mine, I want to take care of it and make it grow tall" (12)]. Years have gone by and both the rose and its owner have bloomed, and turned into arrogant creatures: "Questa mattina, in giardino, mi sono fermata a lungo davanti alla tua rosa. Nonostante sia autunno intoltrato, spicca con il suo color porpora, solitaria e arrogante, sul resto della vegetazione ormai spenta" (9) [This morning, in the garden, I stood in front of your rose for a long time. Even though we were well into fall, it's still bright red, standing out solitary and arrogant while the other plants are brown and dead (11)]. "I ricordi che ci sono intorno a me sono i ricordi di te bambina, cucciolo vulnerabile e smarrito. E' a lei che scrivo, non alla persona difesa e arrogante degli ultimi tempi" (11) [The memories that surround me are memories of you as a child, a vulnerable and confused puppy. It's her I'm writing to, to that child, not to the arrogant, defensive person of later years (14, my modified translation)]. To the arrogance springing from the young woman's daring claim for independence, Olga juxtaposes the vulnerability her young relative possessed when she was still a child. And if her letters are addressed to that vulnerable child, it is because only that *persona* of her granddaughter could be pictured as the willing recipient of the advice the old woman is about to administer. When examined more attentively, in fact, Olga's epistles essentially read as a last attempt to manipulate her granddaughter into becoming a replica of her own grandmother. If the narrator prefers to remember her daughter as a vulnerable puppy, it is because puppies are animals that are eventually bound to resemble their owners. Aware that by openly admitting such malleability in dogs, she would risk betraying her hidden intent, Olga voices this belief while actually dismissing it as a mere commonplace: "E' un luogo comune che i cani dopo una lunga convivenza con il padrone finiscano piano piano per assomigliargli" (104) [It's a commonplace that a dog and his master, if they live together for a long time, will gradually begin to look like each other (130)]. Olga's indirection never ceases to inform her writing: it underlies each reference to her own physical decline, bespeaking her subtle attempt to place eternal guilt in the heart of the ungrateful youth who abandoned her: "Più volte sono arrivata fino al telefono e l'ho sollevato con l'intenzione di mandarti un telegramma. Ogni volta però, appena rispondeva il centralino, decidevo di non farlo. La sera, seduta in poltrona—davanti a me il vuoto e intorno il silenzio—mi interrogavo su cosa fosse meglio. Su cosa fosse meglio per te, naturalmente, non per me. Per me certo sarebbe molto più bello andarmene con te accanto. Sono sicura che se ti avessi avvisato della mia malattia, tu avresti interrotto il tuo soggiorno in America e ti saresti precipitata qui. E poi?" (14) [Several times I've gone so far as to pick up the telephone to send you a telegram, but every time the operator came on the line I changed my mind. In the evening, sitting in my armchair—with the void in front of me and silence all around—I would ask myself what would be the best thing to do. Best for you, naturally, not for me. For me, of course it would be much nicer to have you beside me when I go. If I had told you about my illness, I'm sure you would have interrupted your stay in America and rushed home. And then? (18)]. The perlocutory force of such statements effectively reveals the double nature of Olga's writing. The description of her loneliness, of her repressed desire to cry for help, is presented in such powerful manner that it indeed reaches the heart of the reader: one can only imagine the devastating effect that these lines will have on the granddaughter upon her return home after Olga's death.

Remorse and guilt constitute the undischargeable lot that many a Catholic inevitably bears for life: while Olga strenuously affirms her emancipation from the strains imposed by religious discourse, she effectively reimposes them on the person she loves most. An overbearing sense of guilt is the sole inheritance that Olga eventually passes on to her granddaughter, the same sense of guilt that she had forcefully encountered, and tried to resist, during her formative years in a Catholic school. The old woman's apparent resentment against those guilt-inducing practices that lie at the core of Catholicism springs forth in the pages dedicated to the description of her experiences in grade school.

> Forse non te l'ho mai detto, ma i primi cinque anni di scuola li ho fatti dalle suore, all'istituto del Sacro Cuore. Questo, credimi, non è stato un danno da poco per la mia mente già così ballerina. Nell'ingresso del collegio le suore tenevano allestito per tutta la durata dell'anno un grande presepio. C'era Gesù nella sua capanna con il padre, la madre, il bue e l'asinello e tutto intorno monti e dirupi di cartapesta popolati soltanto da un gregge di pecorelle. (56)

> [Maybe I never mentioned it, but I had my first five years of school with the sisters at the Sacred Heart Academy. Believe me when I tell you that this did more than slight damage to my little brain, which was already in something of a spin. The sisters kept a huge crèche set up all year long in the entryway to the school. There was Baby Jesus in his manger, his father, his mother, the ox, and the ass, and all around the stable were papier-mâché mountains and precipices populated only by a flock of little sheep. (69–70)]

Not just the mere *locus* of public worship, the nativity placed at the entrance of Olga's catholic school is indeed a powerful instrument of societal monitoring:

> Ogni pecorella era una allieva e, a seconda del suo comportamento durante il giorno, veniva allontanata o avvicinata alla capanna di Gesù. Tutte le mattine prima di andare in classe passavamo lì davanti e passando eravamo costrette a guardare la nostra posizione. Dal lato opposto alla capanna c'era un burrone profondissimo ed era lì che stavano le più cattive,

> con due zampette già sospese nel vuoto. Dai sei ai dieci anni ho vissuto condizionata dai passi che faceva il mio agnellino. Ed è inutile che ti dica che non si è quasi mai mosso dal ciglio del dirupo. (56)
>
> [Each sheep stood for a pupil, and it got moved closer or farther from Jesus' stall according to how we behaved during the day. We passed the crèche every morning on our way to our classrooms, and so we were forced to look at our positions. On the side opposite the stable there was a deep, deep chasm, and all the worst sheep stood on its edge with two little hooves already dangling over the void. Between the ages of six and ten the steps my lamb took determined the conditions of my life. And I don't have to tell you she hardly ever moved away from the rim of the precipice. (70)]

Terrorized by devious nuns who enforced the internalization of a doctrine informed by fear and punishment, Olga admits to having been profoundly damaged at a fundamental stage of her life. The awareness of the perilous influence of religion does not deter her, however, from adopting the subtleties of that same religious discourse in order to replicate the same framing inducement of remorse at the expenses of her departed granddaughter. In the last few pages of her letter/diary, Olga reports the unearthing of an old nativity that she kept in the attic. Memories of happier days suddenly spring to her mind: she remembers when her little granddaughter used to misplace the little sheep so as to engage her grandmother in a peculiar game of "hide and seek." Impersonating the misplaced sheep, the child would start bleating and Olga would be then prompted to embark on her quest, "Allora iniziavo la ricerca, lasciavo ciò che stavo facendo e con te dietro che ridevi e belavi giravo per la casa dicendo: 'Dove sei pecorella smarrita? Fatti trovare che ti porto in salvo" (164) [And then the search would begin, I'd stop whatever I was doing and go through the house saying, "Where are you, little lost sheep? Help me find you, I'll take care of you, you'll be safe" (202)]. Turned into the "lost sheep," the image that most identifies, within Catholic iconography, the distraction embodied in sinful activity, the young granddaughter is already prefigured as a lost soul whose redemption shall only be achieved through her grandmother's intercession. The line that immediately follows, "E adesso, pecorella, dove sei? Sei laggiù adesso mentre scrivo, tra i coyote e i cactus" (164) ["And now, little sheep, where are you? You're over there among the coyotes and the cactus as I write . . ." (203)] further amplifies the range of this comparison: her lost granddaughter is alone in the land of perdition, in an America that comes to resemble, through the use of *laggiù*, "down there," the abyss in which Olga's childhood sheep was constantly about to fall. Surrounded by wild animals and arid vegetation, she is thus portrayed as a wandering soul who, once again, is in search of guidance, that guidance that only her grandmother can possibly provide.

It is through her last gift to her granddaughter, that which will accompany the bundle of letters, that Olga most clearly betrays her desire to act as the spiritual guardian meant to bring about the young woman's unnecessary redemption. In the dusty attic, Olga indeed finds an object that she feels drawn to leave with her young relative: it is an old baking mold, which has been in the family for several generations:

> Questo stampo apparteneva a mia nonna cioè alla tua trisavola ed è l'unico oggetto rimasto di tutta la storia femminile della nostra famiglia. . . . Pensa quante volte nella sua esistenza è entrato e uscito dal forno . . . quante mani diverse eppure simili l'hanno riempito con l'impasto. L'ho portato giù per farlo vivere ancora, perché tu lo usi e magari, a tua volta, lo lasci in uso alle tue figlie, perché nella sua storia di oggetto umile riassuma e ricordi la storia delle nostre generazioni. (159)

> [This pan belonged to my grandmother—your great-grandmother—and it's the only object we have left to show for all the female side of our family history. . . . Think how many times in its existence it's gone in and out of the oven, how many different (yet similar) hands have filled it with batter. I've brought it down so that it can live again, so you can use it and maybe leave it to your own daughters when the time comes, because the history of this humble object sums up and reflects the history of our family's generations. (198–99)]

Unique reminder of a female lineage, the baking pan is a mold which symbolizes the life of restraint and captivity destined to those women who had willingly embraced their subjection to patriarchy. The Italian word for baking mold, *stampo*, aptly evokes interesting connotations related to the sort of "imprinting" performed by the culinary object. Virtually shaped, "imprinted" by a paternalist discourse which demanded their confinement to the *oikos*, these women were thus destined to subject themselves to the same act of framing superimposed by the baking mold onto the shapeless dough. Olga's decision to leave the old *stampo da torta* with her granddaughter thus signifies her desire to perpetuate the same disempowerment to which she once fell victim. Remembering how she had once taught her grandchild to bake a cake, she places a strong emphasis on the young woman's resistance to wear an apron: "Così siamo andate in cucina e abbiamo iniziato una lunga battaglia. Prima di tutto non volevi infilarti il grembiule, dicevi: 'Se me lo metto poi dovrò mettere anche i bigodini e le ciabatte, che orrore!'" (160) [So we went into the kitchen and commenced a long battle. First of all, you didn't want to put on an apron. You said, "If I put that on I'll have to wear curlers and slippers, too. *Heinous*" (199–200)] It is exactly such a minimal gesture that betrays her granddaughter's defiant attitude towards societal expectations: refusing to wear an apron, she is actually resisting stereotypes that would eventually frame her into impotency. Those slippers that she so strenuously fears to wear are the same ones in which her grandmother has been walking for so many years, they are the slippers that Olga hopes that the young woman will choose to wear after reading her diary: "Chissà se infilerai le mie pantofole dopo aver letto questa storia? Spero di sì, spero che ciabatterai a lungo da una stanza all'altra . . . " (142) [Maybe you'll put on my slippers after you read my story? I hope so, and I hope that you'll spend a long time shuffling from room to room, . . . (176)] Like the baking form and the apron, the slippers will be there, in the empty house, to await the return of the lost sheep; like those other objects, they should be embraced out of guilt, out of a remorse that would spring from that heart that she has been asked so peremptorily to follow.

Through Olga's letters, the granddaughter should become part of that female lineage so shaken by constant pain and unhappiness: the long epistles, unveiling so many secrets, have indeed provided the young woman with her real history, with the strong roots that bind her to her female ancestors. According to Olga's last words, it is thanks to these firm roots that her young relative will be able to withstand the pain and the uncertainties that her future will certainly bring:

> Ogni volta che ti sentirai smarrita, confusa, pensa agli alberi, ricordati del loro modo di crescere. Ricordati che un albero con molta chioma e poche radici viene sradicato al primo colpo di vento, mentre in un albero con molte radici e poca chioma la linfa scorre a stento. (165)
>
> [Every time you feel lost, confused, think about trees, remember how they grow. Remember that a tree with lots of branches and few roots will get toppled by the first strong wind, while the sap hardly moves in a tree with many roots and few branches. (204)]

Olga's ideal tree has strong roots and branches, and like that tree, her granddaughter should stay firmly grounded in her own roots, in her own history while, at the same time, branching out into the world, but never in an extreme fashion. Her development, in fact, should always be harmonious, and that harmony should essentially stem from the constant awareness that her future must always be intimately linked to her past, a past she must not forget, a past she must not outgrow. Olga's final call to the past aptly contains a textual reference to a different lineage, to a literary lineage strictly linked to the birth of patriarchal society and phallogocentrism, the epic tradition. In the *Aeneid*, the epic tale which narrates the founding of Rome, the heart of the country in which Tamaro's novel takes place, Virgil likens its hero, Aeneas, to a tree shaken by the winds of temptation, here represented by Dido's last desperate plea. Demanding that he postpones his mission in order to lie longer in her embrace, Dido attempts to convince Aeneas not to leave, but the hero remains firm in his purpose:

> . . . Sed nullis ille mouetur
> fletibus, aut uoces ullas tractabilis audit;
> fata obstant placidasque uiri deus obstruit auris.
> Ac uelut annoso ualidam cum robore quercum
> Alpini Boreae nunc hinc nunc flatibus illinc
> eruere inter se certant; it stridor, et altae
> consternunt terram concusso stipite frondes;
> ipsa haeret scopulis et quantum uertice ad auras
> aetherias, tantum radice in Tartara tendit:
> haud secus adsiduis hinc atque hinc uocibus heros
> tunditur, et magno persentit pectore curas;
> mens immota manet, lacrimae uoluontur inanes. (4:438–49)

> But by no weeping is he stirred, and no words that he hears may bend him. Fate withstands, and lays divine bars on unmoved mortal ears. Even as when the eddying blasts of northern Alpine winds are emulous to uproot the secular strength of a mighty oak, it wails on, and the trunk quivers and the high foliage strews the ground; the tree clings fast on the rocks, and high as her top soars into the aëry sky, so deep strike her roots to hell; even thus is the hero buffeted with changeful perpetual accents, and distress thrills his mighty breast, while his purpose stays unstirred, and her tears are shed in vain. (1950, 74)

Carrying echoes from a literary past which strongly informed patriarchal ideology, Olga's last words thus further strenghten her subtle attempt to frame the young addressee of her letters. Had *Va' dove ti porta il cuore* been a real epistolary novel, it would have contained the presence of two voices: the voice of the young woman would have thus been inscribed in the narrative, providing a response to Olga's deeply charged letters. Tamaro's novel, however, only presents the reader with one voice, one rendition of the facts, one ideologically informed series of utterances. No answer to these letters is provided in the text, it is up to reader to respond to Olga's queries: and Italian readers and reviewers have obviously fallen into her guilt trap, into her guilt trip. By reading her letters in an unproblematic fashion, they have symbolically taken over the role of their diegetic addressee in the way that would have most satisfied the old grandmother. The rage and the frustration that the granddaughter might have felt, when faced with her relative's ultimate attempt to break her wings, have thus been erased and rendered impossible by a reading of the text which sorely missed its most crucial ambiguities.

Tamaro's grandmother indeed ends her letter/diary by performing a gesture opposite the one enacted by the protagonist of *Quaderno proibito*. While Valeria decided to retreat into darkness by setting her daughter free, Olga effectively sets out to draw her fugitive granddaughter back into the stuffy rooms of her suffocating house. Valeria's dark notebook is destroyed by the fire that symbolizes her martyrdom, Olga's letters, instead, firmly remain on her kichen table, destined to effect not her own martyrdom but her granddaughter's. It is not for the reader to know whether the young woman will fall into that trap or dismiss Olga's final words. Fifty-two years after De Céspedes wrote the story of Valeria's thwarted awakening, a story which ended, however, on a symbolic recomposition of a dramatic generation gap, Tamaro portrays a different story, one which emphasizes the irreconcilable differences existing between two women socialized, in different periods, through opposite ideological discourses. Sign of the times in which it was written, Tamaro's work perfectly bespeaks the contradictory nature of an advanced society where conservativism and progress still rub shoulders, a society in which some women can still act as their own worst enemies.

The same times that witnessed the unprecedented success, in Italy, of Susanna Tamaro's novel also testified to another unexpected success, that of Helen Fielding's *Bridget Jones's Diary* (1996) and of its sequel, *Bridget Jones: The Edge of Reason* (1999). *Va' dove ti porta il cuore* was soon translated in several languages, yet abroad it did not fare as impressively as it did in Italy. The two fictional diaries penned by Helen Fielding, instead, became instant successes everywhere they were published, and eventually inspired countless imitations, mostly in the United Kingdom. Written in brisk and colloquial style, Fielding's two novels cover two years in the life of Bridget Jones, a thirty-something Londoner in perennial search of happiness. As witnessed by the very first pages of her first diary, happiness for Bridget Jones mainly resides in finding a boyfriend, losing weight, fighting addictions (cigarettes and alcohol), and "happening" on a decent job. The new *everywoman* of the late nineties, Bridget Jones has long moved past feminism: her novels will indeed not be analyzed in depth in this book because they do belong to the post-feminist era, and therefore inaugurate what could be termed "post-feminist diary fiction." In stark contrast with Tamaro's novel, which falls within feminist diary fiction mainly because of its direct engagement with a feminist ideology that it subtly undermines, Fielding's two fictional journals steer clear of political engagement. Bridget's voice is often hysterically funny, it is the voice of women who have learned to see the world through self-help books that have taught them that Men and Women, while being born in opposite planets, are fatally meant to come together in perennial harmony. It is a voice that, in judging the importance of marriage, openly returns back to values expounded by Jane Austen in *Emma* (1816), *Sense and Sensibility* (1811) and, most evidently, in *Pride and Prejudice* (1813). And *Pride and Prejudice* is indeed the narrative that constitutes the very backbone of both diaries, as clearly witnessed by the fact that Bridget Jones's object desire is indeed Mark *Darcy.* Driven by her romantic quest for happiness, Bridget forfeits her own independence in order to marry a new Mr. Darcy, giving up that very same room in which mirrors and windows had once allowed her predecessors to write the fictional history of the feminist struggle.

Notes

Introduction

1. Based on the primacy of men, and on their indisputable paternalistic control over women, phallocentrism inform most patriarchal societies. In *On Deconstruction*, Jonathan Culler identifies phallogocentrism, previously coined by Hélène Cixous, as a term which most clearly defines such a symbolic order: ". . . the hierarchical opposition of *man* and *woman*. Some writers have claimed that this is the primordial opposition on which all others are based and that, as Hélène Cixous puts it, the aim of logocentrism, though it could not admit it, has always been to found phallogocentrism, to assure a rationale for a masculine order ('Sorties,' pp. 116–19)" (165).

2. In *Diary Fiction*, H. Porter Abbott considers such a setting to be particularly typical for male diarists: ". . . where is the diarist? In the male version (the version most frequently imitated) he is seated at a desk. On the desk there is ink, pen, and a paper. The desk is in a room. The room contains at least two things: a window with a view and a mirror" (15).

3. The mirror and the window are also present in the room of Tennyson's "Lady of Shalott" (1832); the prison bars that hold the woman diarist in captivity, however, are replaced, in Tennyson's poem, by a curse that forbids the woman from looking out of the window. Constantly sitting by her loom, the Lady of Shalott is only allowed to perceive the world outside from its reflection in a mirror, the mirror from which she draws the images then reproduced in her weaving. Her deadly contact with reality, occasioned by the sudden desire to disobey the rules which have enforced her seclusion, results in the cracking of the mirror, and in her subsequent demise. The ultimate image of dispossession of the female artist, Tennyson's character actually anticipates and carries to a tragic extreme a literary *topos* peculiar to feminist diary fiction.

Chapter 1: Time Given, Time Taken, Time Lost

All parenthetical references in the text are from *Quaderno proibito* by Alba de Céspedes, its English translation by Isabel Quigly, *The Secret;* and Jacques Derrida's "Titre (à préciser)," *Feu la cendre*, and *Donner le temps*, with their translations, *Cinders* (by Ned Lukacher) and *Given Time* (by Peggy Kamuf).

1. ". . . questi pacchetti . . . contengono regali utilitari—un paio di guanti per Michele, calzini per Riccardo, una scatola di cipria per Mirella" (33) [. . . they were all useful presents: gloves for Michele, socks for Riccardo, some powder for Mirella (26)].

2. In *Donner le temps*, Derrida states that time is the most perfect gift because it never returns, and it is most unique because it is "... le don qui donne non pas un donné mais la condition d'un donné en général, qui donne donc l'élément du donné en général" (76) [the gift that gives not a given but the *condition* of a present given in general, that gives therefore the element of the given in general (54)].

3. It could be argued that, being the desk drawer located in an office, a place where business precedes aesthetic concerns, the lack of a mirror has its own *raison d'être*. It should also be remarked that, while every good Italian secretary is essentially valued for her efficiency and self-effacement, she is often asked to provide, in addition to her skills, *una bella presenza*. The good looks of a secretary thus become an asset of the firm itself, a *gift* that the woman volunteers with the awareness that there will be no countergift, because she comes to play a role that a chauvinistic society expects of her. Hence the real reason for the absence of the mirror, which is, by definition, a narcissistic medium, a tool that would induce a dangerous sort of self-gratification. After all, it only takes a comb and some powder to keep up those good looks which are only meant to make the boss happier. Self-effacement definitely becomes Valeria's lot, both at home and at work.

4. "Nello scrivere la data di oggi improvvisamente mi avvedo che siamo alla vigilia della primavera. Stamani, in ufficio, avevo lasciato la finestra aperta e udivo salire dal giardino, nel silenzio della mattina ancora aspra, le timide voci degli uccellini" (144) [When I wrote today's date I suddenly noticed that tomorrow spring will be here. Today in the office I left the window open and, in the silence of the still, fresh morning, I heard the chirpings of the birds coming up from the garden (136)].

5. *Donner le temps* contains the discussion of the etymology of the word *gift*, borrowed from Marcel Mauss's work on the gift itself: "l'étymologie de *gift*, traduction du latin *dosis*, lui-même transcription du grec *dosis*, dose, dose de poison" (Derrida 1991, 53 n 1) [the etymology of *gift*, a translation of the Greek *dosis*, itself a transcription of the Greek *dosis*, dose, dose of poison (36n1)]. Every gift, then, seems to incorporate a poisonous potential: "... si donner est spontanément évalué comme 'bon'... il reste que ce "bon" peut aisément se renverser . . . en tant que bon, il peut aussi être mauvais, empoisonnant *(Gift, gift)*, et cela dès le moment où le don endette l'autre . . ." (25) [. . . if giving is spontaneously evaluated as *good* . . . it remains that this 'good' can easily be reversed . . . as good, it can also be bad, poisonous (*Gift, gift*), and this from the moment the gift puts the other in debt . . ." (12)].

6. "'A casa' egli continuava 'il sabato c'è piú movimento del solito, i ragazzi invitano sempre i loro amici, fanno chiasso. Io dico che ho un appuntamento in ufficio, ed esco.' ha concluso con un sorriso furbo" (87) ["At home on Saturdays," he went on, "there's always more going on than usual. The children ask their friends in and they make a racket. I say I have an appointment at the office and go out," he ended, with a knowing smile (79)].

7. ". . . il quaderno. Se avessi già saputo che Guido mi amava non lo avrei mai comprato, ma forse, se non l'avessi comprato, non mi sarei mai fatto caso [sic] a Guido come non facevo caso a me stessa" (250) [. . . the notebook. If I'd already known that Guido loved me I'd never have bought it; but perhaps, if I'd never bought it, I'd have never noticed Guido, just as I never noticed myself (242)].

8. Derrida's discussion stems from the different connotations that could derive from the juxtaposition of the homophonic sentences "Il y a la cendre," and "il y a là cendre."

9. "She is missing from G. Spagnoletti's *Romanzieri italiani del nostro secolo* (1967), where in the tenth chapter women writers are, as we might say, 'ghetticized'

under the heading 'Aleramo, Banti, Terni Cialente, Manzini'. De Céspedes is nowhere to be seen in the ten thousand pages of Grana's *Novecento . . .*" (Bruce Merry, *Women in Italian Literature: Four Studies Based on the Work of Grazia Deledda, Alba de Céspedes, Natalia Ginzburg and Dacia Maraini* [James Cook: University of North Queensland Press, 1990], 40)

10. "Un titre n'a lieu que sur le bord de l'oeuvre: s'il se laissait incorporer au corpus qu'il intitule, s'il en faisait simplement partie, comme un des éléments internes, un de ses pièces, il cesserait de jouer le rôle et d'avoir la valeur d'un titre. S'il était totalement extérieur au corpus et détaché de lui, éloigné de lui par une distance supérieure a celle que prévoient la loi, le droit, le code, il ne serait plus un titre" (11) [A title takes place on the work's border: if it lets itself be incorporated by the corpus it entitles, if it were just part of it, like one of its internal elements, one of its components, it would stop playing the role and having the value of a title. If it were totally exterior to the corpus and detached from it, distanced from it by a superior distance to that requested by the law, by the codes, it would no longer be a title (my translation)].

11. "Le titre de 'La fausse monnaie' déjà se divise, se trahit, se déplace. Il a deux référents: 1. ce qu'on appelle la fausse monnaie et 2. ce texte-ci, cette histoire de fausse monnaie. Il a deux référents qui tous deux le titrent—comme on titre de la monnaie et comme on la garantit: l'un est la fausse monnaie elle-meme, l'autre est le récit qui a pour référent ou pour contenu narré la fausse monnaie" (112–13) [The title "Counterfeit Money" is already divided, betrayed, displaced. It has two referents: (1) what is called counterfeit money and (2) this text *here*, this story of counterfeit money. It has two referents that both title it—or titrate it as one titrates money and guarantees it: one is counterfeit money itself, the other is the narrative that has counterfeit money as its referent or narrated content (85)].

12. Through a complex process of *mise-en-abîme*, the counterfeiter who is present in the prose poem, then, becomes an *alter ego* of the counterfeiter Baudelaire. "Cette histoire (ce contenu narré) raconte donc, du meme coup, mais par figure et obliquement, en tant qu'histoire de fausse monnaie, de fiction ou de simulacre, et le récit (narrant) et la narration (narrée). L'histoire fait partie d'elle-même, elle est partie, une partie d'elle-même, elle incorpore ou intériorise cela même dont elle est une partie, le texte intitulé 'La fausse monnaie'. Encadré, enchassé, bordé, débordé, le plus petit devient, métonymiquement, plus grand que le plus grand—qui le borde et le cadre" (123) [This story (this narrated content) tells, then, at the same blow, but by way of a figure and obliquely, as a story of counterfeit money, of fiction or of simulacrum, *both* the (narrating) narration *and* the (narrated) narration. The story makes up a part of itself, it is part, a part of itself, it incorporates or interiorizes the very thing of which it is a part, the text entitled 'Counterfeit Money.' Framed, embedded, bordered, debordered, overrun, the smaller becomes, metonymically, larger than the larger—that borders and frames it (94)].

Chapter 2: Neurotic Cassandras

All parenthetical references in the text are from *The Golden Notebook* by Doris Lessing; *A memoria* by Dacia Maraini; "La femme rompue" by Simone de Beauvoir, with its translation, "The Woman Destroyed" (by Patrick O'Brian); and *Black Sun*, Leon Rudiez's English translation of *Soleil noir* by Julia Kristeva.

1. In *The Other Side of the Story: Structures and Strategies of Contemporary Feminist Narrative* (Ithaca: Cornell University Press, 1989), Molly Hite argues

against previous readings of "Free Women" which identified it as Anna's novel, a text which should thus stand out as the fictional product in which the material reported in notebooks acts as primary, "true" source. Hite believes that such a move would establish a process of prioritization within the two narratives which would eventually lead to fatal misreadings: "The two narratives are thus not only irreconcilable; neither can be construed as taking precedence over the other" (99).

2. "'Write down: The two women were alone in the London flat" (639).

3. "The two women were alone in the London flat. 'The point is,' said Anna, as her friend came back from the telephone . . ." (3).

4. In her deconstructive reading of Lessing's book, Linda S. Kauffman associates the Derridean notion of *pli* to the idea, corroborated by Lessing in her interview with Florence Howe, that "Free Women" was supposed to be interpreted as an envelope to the text: "Like the Derridean notion of a fold, a *pli* in the text, Lessing calls "Free Women" an envelope for the rest of the novel." Linda S. Kauffman, *Special Delivery: Epistolary Modes in Modern Fiction* (Chicago: University of Chicago Press, 1992), 172.

5. Lessing felt somewhat betrayed by the early critics of her novel, who seemed to focus uniquely on the feminist or the racial theme, while disregarding the most central theme, that of breakdown: "But nobody so much as noticed this central theme, because the book was instantly belittled, by friendly reviewers as well as by hostile ones, as being about the sex war, or was claimed by women as a useful weapon in the sex war" (viii).

6. On a different note, it is extremely tempting to read all these marks as symbols of the issues raised in the black notebook. Hence, the doodlings would signify the difficulty of writing or writing as stemming from *ennui;* the shift between musical symbols and monetary signs would represent the politics of adaptation, seen as a commercialization of an artistic product, a "selling out" to the rules of capitalism; the eventual return to musical symbols would stand for Anna's final decision not to let her novel be adapted, and the interlocking circles would evidentiate the extent to which all the problems discussed in the notebook are intimately related to one another.

7. As a third-person subject pronoun, the word *Ella* perfectly fullfills its role as desired projection of her own creator: the function of the subject pronoun, in fact, is to substitute the name of the person it represents.

8. Critics have often contrasted the bleak ending of "Free Women," where both Anna and Molly part as they abandon their "free" state in order to buy into the conventions of a society they had previously boycotted, with the more hopeful ending of the notebooks, where Anna and Saul part as they finally return to writing. Hite says that "Neither version is definitive. If the conclusion of 'Free Women' emphasizes compromise and debilitating irony as effects of the closure imposed by traditional realism, the self-reflexive 'conclusion' of the Golden notebook resolves anxiety into art, in effect subsuming the fragmentation of the social order to the novelist's unifying vision and affirming that the way to redeem the time is to write about it" (1989, 99). Kauffman interestingly compares Lessing's novel to Barthes's *S/Z*, "'Free Women' is to *The Golden Notebook* as Balzac's 'Sarrasine' is to Barthes' *S/Z*" (1992, 173.) Sprague, instead, argues that "The final collision of Anna and Saul is climactic. Their separation ends the inner novel as the deceptive separation of Anna and Molly ends the outer "Free Women" novel. We might say that Anna/Saul represents the esoteric content of the novel and Anna/Molly its exoteric content, the content that satisfies the uninitiated" (1987, 68).

9. Hite draws a parallel between other characters and Tommy, whom she sees as "*becoming* a parody of the self-limiting human being, in a particularly grisly and

symbolic manner . . . Tommy's backward metamorphosis from a complex and deeply engaged young man to a single-minded and therefore coherent personality constitutes a fable pointing up how other characters are also self-maimed, self-blinded" (1989, 73).

10. Unless cited parenthetically, all translations of Dacia Maraini's texts are mine.

11. In his introduction to the first and only edition of Maraini's novel, Renato Barilli states "While Maria possesses an 'autistic' memory, that is a memory 'which does not respond to logic, temporal, or rational links . . . the memory of the unconscious where everything is the equivalent of itself' . . . she has completely lost the 'social' memory, that from which a rational and correct employment of our acts depends, acts which then fall within the framework of collective goal and values" (7).

12. *Preistoria* and *storia* respectively mean *prehistory* and *history.*

13. As already demonstrated in chapter 1, Jacques Derrida draws a direct connection between economics and the domestic sphere, evidenced by the fact that the Greek term *oikos* (*foyer*) is the etymological root of the word *economy.*

14. Toril Moi powerfully sustains a similar argument in *Feminist Theory and Simone de Beauvoir* (Oxford: Blackwell, 1990).

15. The word *chasm* adopted by Leon Roudiez in his English translation of *Soleil noir* refers to the French word *gouffre,* a term evoking the fearful abyss faced by all three diarists.

Chapter 3: The War Years

All parenthetical references in the text are from *Donna in guerra* by Dacia Maraini, with its translation, *Woman at War* (by Mara Benetti and Elspeth Spottiwood).

1. In this passage of the novel, as in many other occurrences of similar descriptions, Paola Blelloch identifies the presence of a repressed violence subtly hidden through the narrator's dry voice: "The daily banality hides an underground element of repressed violence, that we feel vibrating in the broken rhythm of sentences, in the lack of adjectives which qualify things and actions, in the expanding of details that, like in a spiral, evolve in always larger circles" (1987, 136, my translation).

2. "La casa che abbiamo affittato assomiglia a un girino, tutta testa e niente corpo: una stanza da letto con due finestre, una cucina buia, niente bagno. Il gabinetto è un buco sudicio: per lavarsi bisogna adoperare il lavello o il tubo per innaffiare" (4) [The house we've rented resembles a tadpole, all head and no body: a bedroom with two windows, a dark kitchen, no bathroom. The toilet is a filthy hole: to wash yourself, you have to use the kitchen sink or the garden hose (4)].

3. It is worth noting that Maraini's text here contradicts itself by including two entries marked "15 agosto": in the first one, which is chronologically placed between the 14th and the 16th of the same month, the narrator writes of her encounter with Suna, and then concludes by remarking that she went to see Tota and Giottina, yet nothing interesting happened: "Erano i soliti racconti sulle orge nelle ville di lusso" (65) [It was the usual stuff about the orgies inside of the luxury villas (65)]. The second entry which bears the same date is placed, instead, between August 17 and August 19, and it clearly states, at its beginning, that Vannina never saw Suna that day: "Oggi non ho visto Vittorio. E neanche Suna" (74) [Today I haven't seen either Vittorio or Suna (74)]. While all the evidence points to the fact that this last entry actually refers to August 18, and not to August 15, it becomes quite clear, however, that

this is not a mere typo which was accidentally overlooked by writer and publisher. The events narrated in this section of the novel, in fact, acquire stronger symbolic relevance once combined with the date under which they were registered.

4. “In the process of killing the animal, the hunter (re)establishes his secondary identity, that is, his masculine self. It is, in reality, the mental construct of masculinity that is fed by violence and death.” Marti Kheel, “License to Kill: An Ecofeminist Critique of Hunters” in *Animals and Women: Feminist Theoretical Explorations* ed. by Carol J. Adams and Josephine Donovan (Durham and London: Duke University Press, 1995), 108.

5. Another powerful contrast can be established between these two men and Hassan, Suna's father, that Vannina will meet in Naples. A true womanizer, he lets his body speak his own self-complacent aggressivity: “Rispondere voleva dire cedergli. L'ho guardato da capo a piedi. E lui ha inarcato il bel corpo snello sotto i miei occhi. Ha messo in evidenza le lunghe gambe tornite, i fianchi stretti, il pube” (165) [To answer him would have been equivalent to giving in to him. I looked him up and down. He arched his slim, graceful body in front of my eyes, showing off his narrow hips, his crotch, and his shapely legs (172)].

6. “- Sei cosí bella Suna!—Di sopra, come una cogliona di sirena. Qualche volta quando siamo nudi nel letto vedo che [Santino] mi guarda: il petto bello, lo so, il ventre bello sí, i fianchi belli hm hm, e poi improvvisamente le pupille fanno ghghghgh e si stringono infastidite, al posto delle gambe ho una coda rigida, schiumosa fredda, che ci fai con una sirena a letto?” (112) [“You are so beautiful, Suna.” “Yes, up here as far as down here, like a fucking mermaid. Sometimes when we are naked in bed I see him look at me: my beautiful breasts, I know all about that, my beautiful belly, yes, my beautiful hips, hmmmm hmmm, then all of a sudden his pupils go ghghghgh and shrink in disgust, instead of legs I have a stiff cold leathery tail. What can you do with a mermaid in bed?” (114)].

7. In his article on Maraini's novel, Anthony Tamburri argues that Suna's inability to tear herself away from Santino proves that she is not a good feminist: “Suna, the most enlightened of the female characters, does not incarnate the ideal feminist. Her strong feelings for Santino deprive her of the necessary courage to renounce their relationship, however precarious it may be” (1990, 148). Carol Lazzaro-Weis, instead, maintains that Suna's inconsistent behavior is justified by the fact that *Donna in guerra* is a modern romance, a genre which contemplates such events: “Suna's final characterization as the pathetic abandoned woman has disturbed critics hoping to find in her a new feminist and/or female figure. Romance weaves stories around stereotypes, however, and Suna is not the only character who reverts to traditional patterns” (1993, 76).

8. A mouthpiece for Maraini's strenous attack against phallocentric dismissal of older women, Suna speaks in terms akin to those adopted by the author in *Donne mie:* “It is easy to love someone who gives up life / for us, someone who has neither sex nor thoughts that / are predictable, earthly or virtuous. / And still, this is not enough. An old woman / knows, from the way she is looked at on a tram or at the market / how little she matters and how much disgust she inspires in others. / Her old age does not bring to mind wealth, / wisdom, honor or experience. / Her old age brings to mind only wrinkles, / a moulded belly, bad breath, / and teary eyes, and to whom has little imagination, she brings to mind / her white and wrinkled hairless pube. / . . . / An old woman is nothing, / she is worth less than a nickel. An old woman is just a body / dried up and late to die out of selfishness and malignity. / . . . / An old woman who still craves flesh / to kiss is considered a harpy, a / pervert who needs to be shut in a madhouse” (1974, 23–24).

9. "Siamo stati alla pizzeria. . . . Ha parlato sempre Vittorio, del movimento, del suo amore, del terrorismo, della guerra del Medio Oriente, degli americani, del suo cazzo, del papà, e di tante altre cose" (149) [We went to the pizzeria. . . . Vittorio talked all the time about the Movement, about his passion for Suna, about terrorism, about the war in the Middle East, about the Americans, about sex, his father, and many other things (156)].

10. Once again, Maraini had previously voiced the same concern for the repressive power of the school system in *Donne mie:* "The words of your mother, of your teacher, / of your schoolmates push you like / a light-skinned calf towards slaughter. / It is uncertain when begins this subtle / corruption of your human integrity, / . . . / . . . on the shiny desk of a kindergarten class, / while a near-sighted and patient teacher instructs you on / how to draw little houses with gardens and flowers with yellow" (7–8).

Chapter 4: Fall From Grace

All parenthetical references in the text are from *The Diaries of Jane Somers* by Doris Lessing and *The Handmaid's Tale* by Margaret Atwood.

1. In *Rereading Doris Lessing,* Claire Sprague openly questioned Lessing's motives: "Her altruism is suspect. Artistic deception is never that simple. The Jane Somers caper involved more profound personal and artistic needs" (1987, 111).

2. In *The Other Side of the Story,* Molly Hite argues that Jane, like other Lessing's characters, "might be the ironic products of Ella's musing" (1989, 102).

3. "I have spent hundreds of enjoyable hours by myself in and around London, my great bazaar, my lucky dip, my private theatre" (314).

4. In her book-length study on Atwood, J. Brooks Bouson states that, notwthstanding Offred's aloof description of the event, what is being portrayed still remains a rape scenario, which assumes even more dramatic connotations when considering that Commanders should also represent, in some twisted way, Father figures for the Handmaids. The religious world of Gilead thus appears to be rooted on the legalization of two extreme forms of abherration: rape and incest: "Despite the text's denial, this passage does dramatize a terrible kind of rape. Because the Handmaid takes on the role of the dutiful child-daughter in the father-commander's household, the Ceremony is presented as a thinly disguised incest drama" (1993, 145).

5. "If the contemporary backlash had a birthplace, it was here within the ranks of the New Right, where it first took shape as a movement with a clear ideological agenda. . . . The leaders of the New Right were rural fundamentalist ministers whose congregations were shrinking and electronic preachers whose audience was declining" (1991, 230).

6. It is evident, indeed, that the events narrated in *The Handmaid's Tale* take place in Cambridge, Massachusetts. What used to be the cradle of knowledge of the New World, Harvard University, now hosts within its tall walls the reactionary *intelligentsia* which directs Gilead.

7. Several Atwood scholars have analyzed *The Handmaid's Tale* as a particular rewriting of Perrault's "Little Red Riding Hood" and the Grimms' "Little Red Cap." Among them, it is worth remembering Sharon Rose Wilson's "Off the Path to Grandma's in *The Handmaid's Tale,*" in her book *Margaret Atwood's Fairy-Tale Sexual Politics* (1993, 270–94) and David Cowart's "Puritanism and Patriarchy: *The Handmaid's Tale,* taken from his *History and the Contemporary Novel* (1989, 105–19).

8. "In Gilead, woman's body becomes the territory to master; female sexuality is harnessed to the 'higher good' of the body politic; and viable ovaries become a 'national resource'" (Kauffman 1992, 229).

9. The name Offred has often intrigued Atwood critics, who have identified its diverse symbolic connotations: "But 'Offred' is also a typically Atwoodian double pun, on 'offered' and 'afraid'" (Papp Carrington 1987, 128). "Reflecting the bizarre custom—not confined to Gilead—of giving a woman the name who 'commands' her, Offred's name also suggests 'Off-red' as a secret rebel . . . and, especially, the 'red' figure who goes 'off' the path to immerse herself in nature" (Wilson 1993, 279).

10. For a more detailed analysis of Atwood's novel as a postmodern text, see the article by W. F. Garrett-Petts, "Reading, Writing and the Postmodern Condition: Interpreting Margaret Atwood's *The Handmaid's Tale*" (1988).

Conclusion

All parenthetical references in the text are from *Va' dove ti porta il cuore* by Susanna Tamaro, with its translation, *Follow Your Heart* (by John Cullen).

1. Silvia Fumarola called it "a sort of sentimental will, left to the young granddaughter" (1994, 29, my translation). For Silvia Sereni, Olga's letters merely constitute " the extreme attempt to make up for things which were never during one's existence" (1994, 96, my translation). And Oreste Del Buono, in an article by Denise Pardo, affirms that "'It is a beautiful novel which contains the strenuous effort to overcome the generation gap'" (1994, 109, my translation).

2. Asked to comment on the unexpected success of Tamaro's novel, Virna Lisi, the actress who was chosen to play Olga in its filmic adaptation affirmed that such public raving essentially sprang from the book's ability to speak to the younger and the older generations alike, "For me, this reading was extremely emotional because the book is very easy, yet, at the same time, very profound. It reaches eighteen-year-old women as well as eighty-year-old women" (Schelotto 1996, 54, my translation). Lisi's reaction further confirms that, because of its ability to speak directly to the heart, *Va' dove ti porta il cuore* can lend itself to an emotional reading, one that essentially relies on the reader's empathy with the protagonists. Like Olga's granddaughter, the reader suspends her rationality, and follows the call of the heart.

3. This comment is excerpted from the book jacket of the novel's English translation.

Bibliography

Abbott, H. Porter. *Diary Fiction: Writing as Action.* Ithaca: Cornell University Press, 1984.

Acutis, Cesare. "Un eroe della cultura." Introduction to *La Vita è sogno* by Pedro Caldéron de la Barca. Turin: Einaudi, 1980.

Adams, Carol J. "Woman-Battering and Harm to Animals." In *Animals and Women: FeministTheoretical Exploration*, edited by Carol J. Adams and Josephine Donovan. Durham and London: Duke University Press, 1995.

Adams, Carol J. and Josephine Donovan. "Introduction." In *Animals and Women: Feminist Theoretical Exploration.* edited by Carol J. Adams and Josephine Donovan. Durham and London: Duke University Press, 1995.

Alexander, Marguerite. *Flights from Realism: Themes and Strategies in Postmodernist British and American Fiction.* London: Edward Arnold, 1990.

Altman, Janet Gurkin. *Epistolary: Approaches to a Form.* Columbus: Ohio State University, 1982.

Anderlini, Serena. "Prolegomena for a Feminist Dramaturgy of the Feminine: An Interview with Dacia Maraini." *diacritics* 21, nos. 2–3 (Summer-Fall 1991).

Atwood, Margaret. "An End to Audience. (1980)" *Second Words.* Boston: Beacon Press, 1982.

———. *Bodily Harm.* Toronto: McClelland and Stewart, 1981.

———. *Cat's Eye.* Toronto: McClelland and Stewart, 1988.

———. *Surfacing.* Toronto: Mc Clelland and Stewart, 1972.

———. *The Edible Woman.* Toronto: McClelland and Stewart, 1969.

———. *The Handmaid's Tale.* London: Virago Press, 1986.

———. *The Robber Bride.* New York: Nan A. Talese, 1993.

Bachelard, Gaston. *La poétique de l'espace.* Paris: Presses Universitaires de France, 1957.

Barthes, Roland. *Sur Racine.* Paris: Seuil, 1963.

Baudelaire, Charles. "L'albatross." In *Les fleurs du mal.* Paris, 1861.

Beauvoir, Simone de. *La femme rompue.* Paris: Gallimard, 1967.

———. *La force de l'age.* Paris: Gallimard, 1960.

———. *La force des choses.* Paris: Gallimard, 1963.

———. *Mémoires d'une jeune fille rangée.* Paris: Gallimard, 1958.

———. *Tout compte fait.* Paris: Gallimard, 1972. English Translation, *All Said and Done*, by Patrick O'Brian, New York: Puttnam, 1974.

Bersani, Leo. *Arts of Impoverishment: Beckett, Rothko, Resnais.* Cambridge: Harvard University Press, 1993.

Blelloch, Paola. *Quel mondo dei guanti e delle stoffe.* Verona: Essedue, 1987.

Bouson J. Brooks. *Brutal Choreographies: Oppositonal Strategies and Narrative Designs in the Novels of Margaret Atwood.* Amherst: University of Massachusetts Press, 1993.

Brodzki, Bella, and Celeste Schenck, ed. *Life/Lines: Theorizing Women's Autobiography.* Ithaca: Cornell University Press, 1988.

Brookner, Anita. *Hotel du Lac.* London: Grafton, 1985.

Cardinal, Marie. *Le passé empiété.* Paris: Grasset et Frasquelle, 1983.

———. *Les mots pur le dire.* Paris: Grasset et Frasquelle, 1975.

Carroli, Piera. *Esperienza e narrazione nella scrittura di Alba de Céspedes.* Ravenna: Longo, 1993.

Carter, Angela. *The Passion of New Eve.* London: Gollancz, 1977.

Casorati, F. "Quaderno proibito." *Vita e pensiero* (March 1953): 145–49.

Cavarero, Adriana. *Nonostantc Platone: Figure femminili nella filosofia antica.* Rome: Editori Riuniti, 1990.

Céspedes, Alba de. "Lettera a Natalia Ginzburg." *Mercurio* 36–39 (1948): 105–10.

———. *Quaderno proibito.* Milan: Mondadori, 1952. English translation, *The Secret,* by Isabel Quigly. New York: Simon and Schuster, 1958.

———. *Il rimorso.* Milan: Mondadori, 1963.

Chesler, Phyllis. *Women and Madness.* Doubleday: New York, 1972.

Chodorow. Nancy. *The Reproduction of Mothering: Psycoanalysis and the Sociology of Gender.* Berkeley: University of California Press, 1978.

Cixous, Hélène, and Catherine Clément. *La jeune née.* Paris: Union Générale d'Editions, 1975.

Comninou, Maria. "Speech, Pornography, and Hunting." Ib *Animals and Women: Feminist Theoretical Exploration,* edited by Carol J. Adams and Josephine Donovan. Durham and London: Duke University Press, 1995.

Cowart, David. *History and the Contemporary Novel.* Carbondale and Edwardsville: Southern Illinois Press, 1989.

Culler, Jonathan. *On Deconstruction: Theory and Criticism after Structuralism.* Ithaca: Cornell University Press, 1982.

Derrida, Jacques. "Titre (à préciser)." *Nuova Corrente* 84 (1981): 7–32.

———. *Donner le temps* . Paris: Galilée, 1991.

———. *Feu la cendere.* Paris: Des Femmes, 1987.

Didier, Béatrice. *Le journal intime.* Paris: Presses Universitaires de France, 1976.

Diotima. *Il pensiero della differenza sessuale.* Milan: La tartaruga, 1987.

Drabble, Margaret. *The Middle Ground.* New York: Bantam, 1980.

———. *The Millstone.* Harmondsworth: Penguin, 1965.

———. *The Radiant Way.* London: Weidenfeld and Nicolson, 1987.

———. *The Waterfall.* Fawcett: New York, 1977.

Duras, Marguerite. *India Song.* Paris: Gallimard, 1974.

———. *L'amant.* Paris: Editions de Minuit, 1984.

———. *Le ravissement de Lol V. Stein.* Paris: Gallimard, 1964.

Eliot, T. S. *The Hollow Men.* London: Faber and Faber, 1925.

———. *The Waste Land.* London: Faber and Faber, 1922.

Ernaux, Annie. *La femme gelée.* Paris: Gallimard, 1981.

Ewen, Stuart. *All-Consuming Images: The Politics of Style in Contemporary Culture.* New York: Basic Books, 1988.

Fallaci, Oriana. *Lettera a un bambino mai nato.* Milan: Rizzoli, 1975.

Faludi, Susan. *Backlash: The Undeclared War Against American Women.* New York: Crown, 1991.

Field, Trevor. *Form and Function in the Diary Novel.* Totowa, New Jersey: Barnes and Noble, 1989.

Fielding, Helen. *Bridget Jones: The Edge of Reason.* London: Picador, 1999.

———. *Bridget Jones's Diary.* London: Picador, 1996.

Foucault, Michel. *Surveiller et punir.* Paris: Gallimard, 1975. English translation, *Discipline and Punish,* by Alan Sheridan. New York: Vintage, 1979.

Friday, Nancy. *My Mother/My Self.* Dell: New York, 1977.

Friedan, Betty. *The Second Stage.* New York: Summit, 1981.

Fulbrook, Kate. *Free Women: Ethics and Aesthetics in Twentieth-Century Women's Fiction.* Philadelphia: Temple University Press, 1990.

Fumarola, Silvia. "Le donne di Tamaro forti nei sentimenti." *La Repubblica* 6–25–1994.

Gaglione, Paola, ed. *Conversazione con Dacia Maraini: Il piacere di scrivere.* Rome: Omicron, 1995.

Gallop, Jane. *Feminism and Psychoanalysis: The Daughter's Seduction.* Ithaca: Cornell University Press, 1982.

Garrett-Petts, W. F. "Reading, Writing and the Postmodern Condition: Interpreting Margaret Atwood's *The Handmaid's Tale.*" *Open Letter* 7, no. 1 (Spring 1988): 74–92.

Ginzburg, Natalia. *Lessico famigliare.* Turin: Einaudi, 1963.

Goldstein, Ruth M., David Kiremidjian, and Abraham H. Lass. *The Dictionary of Classical, Biblical, and Literary Illusions.* New York: Fawcett, 1987.

Grazia, Victoria de. *How Fascism Ruled Women.* Berkeley: University of California Press, 1992.

Green, Gayle. *Changing the Story: Feminist Fiction and the Tradition.* Bloomington: Indiana University Press, 1991.

Greer, Germaine. *Sex and Destiny.* New York: Harper & Row, 1984.

———. *The Female Eunuch.* New York: McGraw Hill, 1971.

Guiducci, Amanda. *Donne e serva: Storia non sentimentale della degradazione femminile.* Milan: Rizzoli, 1983.

———. *Due donne da buttare.* Milan: Rizzoli, 1976.

Hassam, Andrew. *Writing and Reality: A Study of Modern British Diary Fiction.* London: Greenwood Press, 1993.

Hengen, Shannon. *Margaret Atwood's Power: Mirrors, Reflections and Images in Select Fiction and Poetry.* Toronto: Second Story Press, 1993.

Herrmann, Claudine *Les voleuses de langue.* Des femmes : Paris, 1976.

Hite, Molly. *The Other Side of the Story: Structures and Strategies of Contemporary Feminist Narrative.* Ithaca: Cornell University Press, 1989.

Irigaray, Luce. "And the One Doesn't Stir Without the Other." *Signs* 7, no. 1 (1981): 60–67, trans. H. V. Wenzel.

———. *Ce sexe qui n'est pas un.* Paris: Editions de Minuit, 1977.

———. *Speculum de l'autre femme.* Paris: Editions de Minuit, 1974.

Jardine, Alice. *Gynesis: Configurations of Women and Modernity.* London: Macmillan, 1985.

Kaplan, E. Ann. *Motherhood and Representation: The Mother in Popular Culture and Melodrama.* London: Routledge, 1992.

Kauffman, Linda S. *Special Delivery: Epistolary Modes in Modern Fiction.* Chicago: University of Chicago Press, 1992.

Keefe, Terry. *Simone de Beauvoir: A Study of Her Writings.* Totowa, New Jersey: Barnes and Nobles, 1983.

Kheel, Marti. "Licence to Kill: An Ecofeminist Critique of Hunters." *Animals and Women: Feminist Theoretical Exploraiton.* edited by Carol J. Adams and Josephine Donovan. Durham and London: Duke University Press, 1995.

Kristeva, Julia. *Pouvoirs de l'horreur.* Paris: Seuil, 1980.

———. *Soleil noir: Depression et mélancolie.* Paris: Gallimard, 1987.

Kuester, Martin. *Framing Truths: Parodic Structures in Contemporary English-Canadian Historical Novels.* Toronto: University of Toronto Press, 1992.

La Belle, Jenijoy. *Herself Beheld: The Literature of the Looking Glass.* Ithaca: Cornell University Press, 1988.

Lagorio, Gina. *Tosca dei gatti.* Milan: Garzanti, 1983.

Lazzaro-Weis, Carol. *From Margin to Mainstream: Feminism and Fictional Modes in Italian Women's Writing, 1968–1990.* Philadelphia: University of Pennsylvania Press, 1993.

Lessing, Doris. "To Room Nineteen." *Stories.* New York: Vintage, 1978.

———. *A Proper Marriage.* New York: Simon & Schuster, 1952.

———. *Briefing for a Descent into Hell.* New York: Knopf, 1971.

———. *Landlocked* New York: Simon & Schuster, 1958.

———. *Martha Quest.* New York: Simon & Schuster, 1952.

———. *Memoirs of a Survivor.* London: Octagon, 1974.

———. *The Diaries of Jane Somers.* New York: Vintage, 1984.

———. *The Fifth Child.* New York: Knopf, 1988.

———. *The Four-Gated City.* New York: Bantam, 1969.

———. *The Golden Notebook.* New York: Simon and Schuster, 1962; reprinted New York: Bantam Books, 1981.

———. *The Good Terrorist.* London: Grafton, 1985.

———. *The Summer Before the Dark.* London: Jonathan Cape, 1973.

———. *A Ripple from the Storm.* New York: Simon & Schuster, 1958.

Lonzi, Carla. *Sputiamo su Hegel.* Milan:Rivolta femminile, 1970.

Loy, Rosetta. *Le strade di polvere.* Turin: Einaudi, 1988.

Maraini, Dacia. *A Memoria.* Milan: Bompiani, 1967.

———. *Donna in guerra.* Turin: Einaudi, 1975. English translation, *Woman at War,* by Mara Benetti and Elspeth Spottiswood. New York: Italica Press, 1988.

———. *Donne mie.* Turin: Einaudi, 1974.

———. *L'età del malessere.* Turin: Einaudi, 1962.

———. *La bionda, la bruna, e l'asino.* Milan: Rizzoli, 1987.

———. *Memorie di una ladra.* Milan: Bompiani, 1972.

———. *La vacanza.* Milan: Lerici, 1962.

Marks, Elaine, ed. *Critical Essays on Simone de Beauvoir.* Boston: Hall, 1987.

Martens, Lorna. *The Diary Novel.* Cambridge: Cambridge University Press, 1985.

McCurdy, Jole Cappiello. "The Structural and Archetypal Analysis of Fairy Tales." In *Psyche's Stories: Modern Jungian Interpretations of Fairy Tales.* edited by Murray Stine and Lionel Corbett. Wilmette, Illinois: Chiron, 1991.

Merry, Bruce. *Women in Italian Literature: Four Studies Based on the Work of Grazia Deledda, Alba de Cespédes, Natalia Ginzburg and Dacia Maraini.* James Cook: University of North Queensland Press, 1990.

Millet, Kate. *Sexual Politics.* New York: Random House, 1969.

Mitchell, Juliet *Psychoanalysis and Feminism.* Pantheon: New York, 1974.

Moi, Toril. *Feminist Theory and Simone de Beauvoir.* Oxford: Basil Blackwell, 1990.

———. *Sexual/Textual Politics: Feminist Literary Theory.* London: Methuen, 1985.

Montini, Ileana. *Parlare con Dacia.* Verona: Bertani, 1977.

Morante, Elsa. *Il mondo salvato dai ragazzini.* Turin: Einaudi, 1968.

———. *La storia.* Turin: Einaudi, 1974.

Morgan, Robin, ed. *Sisterhood is Powerful.* New York: Vintage, 1970.

Morrison, Toni *The Bluest Eye.* New York: Pocket Books, 1970.

Morrison, Toni. *Song of Solomon.* New York: New American Library, 1977.

Morrison, Toni. *Sula.* New York: New American Library, 1973.

Muraro, Luisa. *L'ordine simbolico della madre.* Rome: Editori Riuniti, 1991.

Nicholson, Colin, ed. *Margaret Atwood: Writing and Subjectivity.* New York: St. Martin's Press, 1994.

Onofri, Sandro. "Libri, ecco la top ten formato tonaca." *L'Unità.*

Paglia Camille. *Sexual Personae.* New York: Vintage, 1990.

———. *Sex, Art, and American Culture.* New York: Vintage, 1992.

———. *Vamps and Tramps.* New York: Vintage, 1994.

Papp Carrington, Ildikó de. "A Swiftian Sermon." *Essays on Canadian Writing* 34 (Spring, 1987): 127–32.

Pardo, Denise. "Susanna dei miracoli." *L'espresso* 5–6-1994

Parsani, M. Assunta, and Neria di Giovanni. *Femminile a confronto: Tre realtà della narrativa contemporanea: Alba de Céspedes, Fausta Cialente, Gianna Manzini.* Bari: Lacaita, 1984.

Perkins Gilman, Charlotte. "The Yellow Wallpaper." In *The Yellow Wallpaper and Other Writings.* New York: Bantam, 1989.

Plath, Sylvia. *The Bell Jar.* New York: Bantam, 1963.

Raoul, Valerie. *Distinctly Narcissistic: Diary Fiction in Quebec.* Toronto: University of Toronto Press, 1993.

———. *The French Fictional Journal: Fictional Narcissism / Narcissistic Fiction.* Toronto: University of Toronto Press, 1980.

Rhys, Jean. *Wide Sargasso Sea.* New York: Norton, 1966.

Rich, Adrienne. *Of Woman Born.* Norton: New York, 1976.

Sanvitale, Francesca. *Madre e figlia.* Turin: Einaudi, 1980.

Schelotto, Gianna. "Virna Lisi: Ma certo che c'è un segreto." *Sette: Corriere della sera* 3 (1996): 53–56.

Sereni, Silvia. "Cara nipote, ti scrivo . . ." *Epoca* 6–7-1994.

Smith, Sidonie. *A Poetics of Women's Autobiography: Marginality and the Fictions of Self-Representation.* Indianapolis: Indiana University Press, 1987.

Sprague, Claire. *Rereading Doris Lessing: Narrative Patterns of Doubling and Repetition.* Chapel Hill: University of North Carolina Press, 1987.

Stanton, Domna C., ed. *The Female Autograph: Theory and Practice of Autobiography from the Tenth to the Twentieth Century.* Chicago: University of Chicago Press, 1984.

Tamaro, Susanna. *Va' dove ti porta il cuore.* Milan: Baldini & Castoldi, 1994. English translation, *Follow Your Heart*, by John Cullen. New York: Doubleday, 1995.

Tamburri, Anthony J. "Dacia Maraini's *Donna in guerra:* Victory of Defeat?" In *Contemporary Women Writers in Italy: A Modern Renaissance*, edited by Santo L. Aricò. Amherst: University of Masschusetts Press, 1990.

Van Spanckeren, Kathryn, and Jan Garden Castro, eds. *Margaret Atwood: Vision and Forms.* Carbondale and Edwardsville: Southern Illinois University Press, 1988.

Virgil. *Aeneid.* English translation by J. W. Mackail. New York: Random House, 1950.

Walker, Alice. *Meridian.* New York: Washington Square Press, 1976.

———. *The Color Purple.* New York: Washington Square Press, 1982.

Wilson, Elizabeth. "Yesterday's Heroines: On Rereading Lessing and de Beauvoir." *Notebooks Memoirs Archives: Reading and Rereading Doris Lessing.* edited by Jenny Taylor. Boston: Routledge and Kegan Paul, 1982.

Wilson, Sharon Rose. *Margaret Atwood's Fairy-Tale Sexual Politics.* Jackson: University of Mississippi Press, 1993.

Wittig, Monique. *Les guerrilléres.* Paris: Editions de Minuit, 1969.

Woolf, Virginia. *A Room of One's Own.* London: Hogarth, 1929; reprinted by Grafton, 1977.

Index